More Praise For
Heralds of the Second Coming

Stephen Walford's book, *Heralds of the Second Coming*, will be a beacon of light to many, exhorting all to watch and pray that those who will go through the "great tribulation" may persevere with courage in the "Faith of our Fathers living still through dungeon, fire, and sword" until Christ's final victory over Satan—thanks to Mary, His Immaculate Mother and ours as well.

> CARDINAL IVAN DIAS, *Prefect Emeritus of the Congregation for the Evangelization of Peoples; Cardinal Member, Congregation for the Doctrine of the Faith*

A masterful job of weaving the thread of the prophetic messages given by the Blessed Virgin in recent times as contained in papal statements. *Heralds of the Second Coming* could serve as a wakeup call to a world that has forgotten God and continues down a slippery slope of materialism, hedonism, and secularism.

> BISHOP JOSEPH FABER MACDONALD, *Bishop Emeritus of Saint John, New Brunswick*

We should not underestimate the value that comes from approaching Church teaching on the "last things" (novissimi) by way of the insights offered by recent popes as they reflect on the sometimes terrible messages coming to us from private revelations. Stephen Walford has done much more than the service of collating and thematizing the writings of the popes in the light of these often terrifying messages about persecution, martyrdom, and the end times. He is to be complimented—it is a work of faith and scholarship.

> ARCHBISHOP THOMAS E. GULLICKSON, *Apostolic Nuncio to Ukraine*

Stephen Walford's *Heralds of the Second Coming* offers a look at some fascinating persons, events, and pronouncements, chiefly Our Blessed Lord, Our Blessed Mother, His Second Coming, her appearances, and the doctrines of the Church as enunciated by the most recent Vicars of Christ. In an age in which so much is said—and left unsaid—about the future, this volume undertakes an important study of what the popes have taught regarding the end times, all against the backdrop of Our Lady's maternal reassurances that those who believe in, love, and serve her Divine Son are well prepared for the years to come.

What may we glean from Mr. Walford's helpful text? The Successors of St. Peter would have us know that our hearts are to be fixed on our Creator and His wise, benevolent plan for us. Indeed, instead of succumbing to fear, have trust. Rather than wallowing in sin, live virtuously. In a word, as St. Paul exhorted the Romans (13:14), and as the popes have repeated, "put on the Lord Jesus Christ, and make no provision for the flesh, to gratify its desires."

The Mother of God—our Mother—wants the very same for us.

MONSIGNOR CHARLES M. MANGAN, *Director, Office of the Marian Apostolate, Diocese of Sioux Falls, SD*

HERALDS OF THE SECOND COMING

Stephen Walford

HERALDS OF
THE SECOND COMING

Our Lady, the Divine Mercy, and the Popes of the Marian Era

From Blessed Pius IX to Benedict XVI

Foreword
by
His Eminence
Cardinal Ivan Dias

 Angelico Press

First published in the USA
by Angelico Press
© Stephen Walford 2013
Foreword © Cardinal Ivan Dias 2013

For information, address:
Angelico Press, 4619 Slayden Rd. NE
Tacoma, WA 98422
www.angelicopress.com

ISBN 978-1-62138-015-3 (pbk: alk. paper)
ISBN 978-1-62138-017-7 (cloth: alk. paper)

NIHIL OBSTAT: Rev. William Wilson
CENSOR LIBRORUM
IMPRIMATUR: † Rt Revd Philip Egan
Bishop of Portsmouth, 25 December 2012
(*The Nihil Obstat and Imprimatur are the Church's
declarations that a work is free from error in matters
of faith and morals. It in no way implies that the
Church endorses the contents of the work.*)

Cover image credit: detail of the
Polyptych of the Last Judgment
("the Beaune Altarpiece")
by Rogier van der Weyden, c. 1445–1450

Cover design: Michael Schrauzer

CONTENTS

Foreword [i]
Acknowledgements [v]
Introduction [1]

PART I
Watchman, How Much Longer the Night?

1. The Present Situation [7]
2. The Final Battle Dawns [16]
3. The Popes of the Marian Era [29]
4. The Second Vatican Council:
The Vision of Eschatological Hope [60]

PART II
Blessed John Paul II: Herald of the Second Advent

5. The Church Experiences the New Advent [95]
6. The Pope of Fatima [111]
7. The Spark from Poland? [122]
8. The Youth, Watchmen of the Morning [138]
9. A Great Springtime for Christianity:
The Second Coming and the Eternal
Kingdom of Christ [151]

PART III
Epilogue

Pope Benedict XVI—*Excita, Domine
potentiam tuam, et veni* [179]
Appendix I: St. Hildegard of Bingen—Doctor of the Church
The Five Ferocious Epochs [209]
*Appendix II: Urbi et Orbi Easter Allocution
of Pope Pius XII, 1957* [218]
Select Bibliography [221]
Index [223]

DEDICATION

⊕

I dedicate this book to the Most Blessed Virgin Mary, my Queen and Mother; truly the Co-redemptrix,[1] Mediatrix, and Advocate, in heartfelt gratitude for bringing forth the Divine Redeemer in His first coming, and for preparing the Church and the World for His second coming.

The world will not exist for much longer and God still wants to give graces to people before the end, so that no one will be able to say during the judgment that he did not know about the goodness of God and did not hear about His Mercy.

The words of St. Faustina Kowalska
on her deathbed to her spiritual director,
Blessed Michael Sopocko.[2]

The world is in flames, the battle between Christ and the Antichrist has broken into the open. If you decide for Christ, it could cost you your life. . . . Give us the grace to speak the bride's words with a pure heart: Come! Come, Lord Jesus. Come soon!

Exhortations of St. Teresa Benedicta of the Cross:
The Elevation of the Cross, September 14, 1939 and
The Marriage of the Lamb, September 14, 1940.[3]

1. The prefix "co" comes from the Latin term "cum" which means "with" and not "equal to." Co-redemptrix therefore refers to Mary's unique participation in the saving event of Redemption, carried out through the perfect sacrifice of her divine son Jesus Christ.
2. From the unpublished Diary of Blessed Michael Sopocko, courtesy of the Congregation of the Sisters of Merciful Jesus, founded by Blessed Michael Sopocko.
3. Teresa Benedicta of the Cross, *Edith Stein: Essential Writings* (Maryknoll, NY: Orbis Books, 2002), 132, 141.

[We], members of the Church, must be watchful and ready. We must also do everything possible to prepare the world for Christ's final Coming-for Judgment.

Pope John Paul II, "Homily at Mass,"
Blantyre, Malawi, May 5, 1989.[4]

NOTE

All biblical translations that I have used in my own original text are taken from the *New American Bible*, revised edition, copyright, Confraternity of Christian Doctrine, Washington D.C. All Scriptural passages contained within quotes are kept in their original form.

4. Http:// www.vatican.va/.

Foreword

THE CATHOLIC CHURCH, at the dawn of the third millennium after Christ, finds itself in the midst of a fierce battle between the forces of good and evil, between God and Satan, resulting from the fall of our first parents Adam and Eve in the Garden of Eden. This ferocious combat has wound its way through history and will continue until the end of time. The intensity of this conflict has increased most notably in the past two centuries, as the forces of evil have misled a large segment of humanity to bow before the pseudo-gods of rationalism, secularism, and relativism: their aim is to create a world where God is irrelevant, and is replaced with the idols of hedonism and materialism, while banishing the natural law and conscience to history.

The popes of the past century have recognized this assault and spoken of it in prophetic terms encouraging the Church to read the signs of the times in the light of its eschatological journey towards the new heaven and new earth.

A decisive moment in the spiritual combat was when the Blessed Virgin entered into the battle fray in the nineteenth century with her apparitions at Rue du Bac in Paris, and thereafter at La Salette and Lourdes in France, and in many other places all around the world, some of which still await the approval of the Holy See.

These supernatural events could, in a sense, open the pages of the Book of Revelation with more clarity, as in chapter twelve, narrating the confrontation between the "Woman clothed with the sun, with the moon under her feet, and on her head a crown of twelve stars" (12:1), and a "great red dragon" (12:1–17). It is the same Woman mentioned in Genesis when God cursed the serpent saying: "I shall put enmities between you and the Woman, between your seed and her seed: she shall crush your head" (3:15).

Mary is, indeed, the Woman of Genesis and the Woman of the Apocalypse. The Marian era that is reaching its climax now is

i

shrouded in the mystery of Divine providence. It is preparing the Church for the final showdown between God and Satan, involving the persecution of Christians by the Antichrist and the inevitable martyrdom that will follow, as the last part of the third secret of Fatima would seem to foretell. The Holy Spirit has guided the recent popes to understand the importance of these challenging times and to fulfill certain wishes from heaven in preparation for the final clash: for instance, the Consecration to the Immaculate Heart of Mary, the Divine Mercy devotion and dedicating the second Sunday of Easter to it, and the recitation of the Holy Rosary. In their ordinary magisterium, they have drawn our attention to the crisis unfolding; we may recall the warnings of modernism and apostasy of St. Pius X, the mystical intuition of Pius XII and the "smoke of Satan" seen by Paul VI.

On the other hand, the past century, in particular, has abounded in signs pointing towards "a new heaven and a new earth." Pope John XXIII prayed for a New Pentecost and convoked the Second Vatican Ecumenical Council which, besides strengthening the inner cohesion and sanctity of the faithful, opened avenues of dialogue with other Christian communities, with non-Christians, and even with non-believers. His successors toiled unceasingly to promote "a civilization of love." Blessed John Paul II gave a sharper focus to the eschatological dimension of the Church as he proclaimed a "new advent." Pope Benedict XVI stated recently: "Indeed, it was a concern of John Paul II to make clear that we are looking ahead to the coming of Christ: that consequently the One who has come is also, even more so, the One who is to come and that, from this perspective, we should live out our faith toward the future" (*Light of the World*, 63). For the great Polish Pontiff, a joyful watchfulness for the second advent of Jesus was to be an ever-present theme of his— even calling the youth of the Church "sentinels who keep watch, preparing for the glorious return of the risen Lord." Pope Benedict XVI has also spoken prophetically in similar fashion in recent years declaring: "One day, not far off, everything will find its fulfillment in the Kingdom of God, a Kingdom of justice and peace" (First Vespers of Advent, 2009). He has also prayed for the hastening of the Triumph of the Immaculate Heart of Mary at the Shrine of Fatima, and in union with his great predecessor urged vigilance from all the faithful in the face of the gathering dark clouds. For our present Holy Father, truly a theologian pope, the Catholic Church must awaken from its interior sinfulness and be purified, as it awaits what the Lord will allow for its passion and resurrection—for only in this way will the Lord find faith on earth when He returns (cf. Lk. 18:8).

What the popes of the Marian era have given us is a prophetic stream running alongside that of private revelations from visionaries and mystics. They confirm, through the authority of their office, the knowledge that we live in days leading towards the greatest triumph of God and the installation of His eternal Kingdom. They speak of hope and joy for the complete renewal of the Universe, and in doing so invite us to live like the saints immersed in the love of God and neighbor. There are many signs taking place on earth and in the heavens that point towards the dawning of a new day. In spite of the pain and suffering endured by so many throughout the world we can live our faith, safe in the knowledge that the final victory of good over evil is already assured and that God is preparing the fulfillment of the great prophecy found in the Book of Revelation: "And God shall wipe away all tears from their eyes; and there shall be no more death, neither sorrow, nor crying, neither shall there be any more pain: for the former things have passed away" (Rev. 21:4).

The Blessed Virgin Mary has an important role to play in Christ Our Lord's second advent. St. Louis-Marie Grignion de Monfort begins his renowned *Treatise on the True Devotion to the Blessed Virgin Mary* with these words: "It was through the Blessed Virgin Mary that Jesus came into the world, and it is also through her that He must reign in the world." It is indeed amazing to see how Mary has been involved in the well-being of the children she received at the foot of Jesus' cross on Calvary. Who can forget her many apparitions from Akita in Japan to Kibeho in Rwanda; from Walsingham and Aylesford in Great Britain to Lavang in Vietnam; from Knock in Ireland to Medjugorje in Bosnia-Herzegovina; from Paris, La Salette, and Lourdes in France to Vellankanni in India; from Saragozza and Garabandal in Spain to Guadalupe in Mexico; from Fatima in Portugal to Naju in Korea; from Cuapa in Nicaragua to Altötting in Germany; from San Nicholas in Argentina and Czestechowa in

Poland to Aparecida in Brazil; from Amsterdam in the Netherlands to Zeitoun in Egypt; from Beauraing and Banneux in Belgium to Betania in Venezuela; and—in Italy—from Pompei, Siracusa, and Civitavecchia to Saint Mary Major, Sant'Andrea delle Fratte, and Tre Fontane in Rome. The Blessed Virgin is weaving an enormous network, building up a large army of her devoted children in order to launch a frontal and final assault against Satan, and thus paving the way for the glorious victory of Jesus Christ, her beloved Son. Truly: "Who is she who comes forth as the morning rising, fair as the moon, bright as the sun, terrible as an army set in battle array?" (Song 6:10).

The exact day and hour of Christ Our Lord's second coming is a closely guarded secret in the bosom of God our heavenly Father. It remains for us to heed Jesus' exhortation: "Be prepared, because it will come upon you like a thief in the night."

Stephen Walford's book, *Heralds of the Second Coming: Our Lady, the Divine Mercy and the Popes of the Marian Era from Blessed Pius IX to Benedict XVI*, will be a beacon of light to many, exhorting all to watch and pray that those who will go through the "great tribulation" may persevere with courage in the "Faith of our Fathers living still through dungeon, fire, and sword" until Christ's final victory over Satan, thanks to Mary, His Immaculate Mother and ours as well.

CARDINAL IVAN DIAS

Prefect Emeritus of the Congregation for the Evangelization of Peoples; Member, Congregation for the Doctrine of the Faith

FEAST OF BLESSED PIUS IX, February 7, 2012

Acknowledgements

I OWE a debt of gratitude to many people for their considerable contribution in bringing this book to fruition. I would like to thank His Eminence Cardinal Ivan Dias for offering me his wisdom, knowledge, and prayers; To His Excellency, Archbishop Thomas E. Gullickson, the late Bishop Joseph Faber MacDonald, Rev. Professor Thomas J. Norris, Monsignor Charles M. Mangan, Fr. Donald Calloway MIC, Dr. Ralph Martin, His Eminence Cardinal Karl Josef Becker, His Eminence Cardinal Prospero Grech, Rev. Professor Anthony Kelly, Professor Tracey Rowland and Fr. Aidan Nichols, OP, for their expertise and very useful suggestions.

I would also like to thank Fr. Michael Maher, SM, for providing me with certain texts of Blessed John Paul II and for his encouragement while researching this book. I am grateful to Deacon Eric Stoltz for help in locating speeches of Blessed John XXIII, Jeanette Salerno for her help in locating information concerning Fr. Joseph Pius Martin, and the staff of the Catholic National Library for their help in locating many archive speeches. To Heraldo, Sarah, and Timothy Biasi, Monsignor Charles M. Mangan and Colin Crawley, I would like to express my great appreciation for their help in translating Italian and German texts. For editorial help I thank my brother Peter for his considerable expertise. To all those who have prayed for the success of this endeavor, I ask the Lord and His Blessed Mother to reward them for their generosity.

Finally, I express my great gratitude to John Riess for sharing my vision to bring this important subject to as wide an audience as possible, to my wife Paula for her patience and help in improving the text, and to my beautiful children, Daniel, David, Sophie, Joseph, and Anna for their continued encouragement.

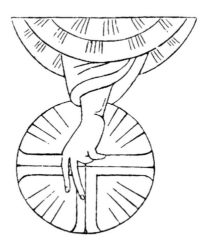

Introduction

THE TRUTH of the Second Coming of Jesus at the end of time has proved to be difficult for many Catholics to relate to. It is an area of theology that many find irrelevant to their everyday lives; something perhaps best left to the placard-wielding doom merchants. However, the clarity of this teaching is to be found throughout the pages of Sacred Scripture, through the Tradition of the Church Fathers, notably St. Augustine and St. Irenaeus, and in the Magisterium of the popes. A possible reason for this attitude of incredulity is the obvious horror at the prospect of the end of the world. In envisioning this end, the focus of many consists of an image of universal conflagration where the only peace is the peace of death, not only for man but the physical world also. But is that scenario one that is true to the plans of Divine Providence as revealed by Jesus? In truth it is not. It is a partial account of the wondrous work that the Lord will complete on the last day. The destiny of humanity and all creation at the end of time will consist of the complete renewal of the world and the universe, in which the Kingdom of God will come. Earth will become Heaven and the Holy Trinity will dwell with the community of the redeemed in an endless day illuminated by the light that is God—the Father, the Son and the Holy Spirit.

I suspect that the ignorance of many stems from the lack of clear teaching coming from the clergy. There is no real reason for confusion in this area as the Second Vatican Council document, *Lumen Gentium*, and the *Catholic Catechism* make the authentic teaching very clear. With the knowledge that the end will give way to a new beginning, the Christian should be filled with hope, not fear, expectation, not apprehension.

It is important to stress at this point that it is not my intention to speculate as to specific times and dates, as that knowledge belongs to God the Father himself; rather the intention is to offer the teachings and guidance of the recent popes in this matter, and to show

1

that they are warning of the approaching Second Coming of the Lord. Pope Pius XII stated in his Easter Message of 1957: "Come, Lord Jesus. *There are numerous signs that Thy return is not far off.*" St. Peter warns us that "everything will soon come to an end" (1 Pet. 4:7), while at the same time exercising caution: "But there is one thing, my friends, that you must never forget: that with the Lord, a "day" can mean a thousand years, and a thousand years is like a day" (2 Pet. 3:8). So let us leave the time scale open, that way controversy can be avoided and the words of the popes will speak for themselves.

The origins of this book go back many years, all the way back to my formative years, in fact. One of my earliest memories was being told the stories of St. Pio's legendary battles with Satan, as well as similar accounts involving Blessed Alexandrina Maria da Costa. This left me with a tremendous sense of the spiritual war being waged for our souls—even if it seemed to me, as a young child, that these great mystics were fighting on our behalf. On other occasions the great apparitions of the Blessed Virgin at Fatima were discussed, and I distinctly recall praying the Rosary for the many imprisoned priests and faithful under Communist tyranny at the beginning of the reign of Pope John Paul II. Add to that the assassination attempt on the Polish Pontiff on May 13, 1981, the exact anniversary of Mary's first apparition at Fatima, and in my mind it began to appear that our generation was perhaps living the final battle as foretold in Sacred Scripture. From here I developed an interest in eschatology, that area of theology that is concerned with the last things. The powerful apocalyptic messages of several Church approved apparitions, notably La Salette and Fatima, also served to arouse within me a special interest in the Catholic teaching on what is commonly known as the End Times.

I have several reasons for writing this book. The first is to complement the many books written about apparitions, prophecies, and mystics concerning the end times. One of the main unifying threads of authentic visionaries is always obedience to the pope and his teaching authority. This support for the pontiff is a great characteristic of Marian movements, which sadly seems to be lacking at times in some other groups within the Catholic Church. Hopefully, for those of us who take seriously these warnings from heaven, this book will help shed more light on why the Blessed Virgin is pleading with humanity to be converted. Any doubts concerning the eschatological nature of messages emanating from these apparitions can be set aside after reading the following pages.

Secondly, I would like to address those Catholics who don't accept private revelations. Of course the Church teaches that nobody has to accept any private revelations, even those approved by Rome, like Fatima or Lourdes. Many will say that accepting the teachings of the Magisterium and obedience to the Holy Father is enough to please the Most Holy Trinity. This is certainly true. Peter is the Rock on which the enemies of Christ are destined to stumble. He alone is at the helm, steering the Church ever closer to its eternal destiny in the New Jerusalem. Pope St. Pius X spoke these words about the importance of the papacy: "When we speak of the Vicar of Christ, we must not quibble, we must obey ... the one hope, the one remedy, is the Pope." Yet the Supreme Pastor of the Church also has a prophetic role in calling the people of God to prepare daily for that great moment when evil will be destroyed forever and Jesus returns on the clouds to reign as King in the civilization of love. The uniqueness of this book, I hope, lies in the uncovering of the vast teachings of the recent pontiffs concerning the last days: "spectacularly present, yet strangely overlooked" in the words of Fr. Aidan Nichols, OP. It is not only the theology, but *more* importantly at this critical juncture of history, the prophetic statements that form its central nucleus. The papal encyclicals, *ad Limina* addresses, and speeches from the last century and a half clearly portray a world in turmoil, of a creation groaning under the sins of mankind. But they also speak of hope, hope of the redemption of our bodies and of the entire universe. This latter theme rises like a great crescendo the closer we come to the end. It is noticeable that with the coming of the pontificate of Blessed John XXIII and the Second Vatican Council, this hope begins to take prominence in the writings of the popes. Surely this is a sign from the Holy Spirit that the dawn of an everlasting day is nearing.

It is my hope that this book will fill a much needed gap in literature related to the "*novissimis*," as there is a need to correct, with the authentic teachings of the papal magisterium, certain "private" interpretations of apparition messages; especially those relating to the coming of the Kingdom of God on earth. This will allow us to grasp a greater understanding of the hour of history in which we belong.

Although not primarily about private revelations, there are references to several approved ones, especially Fatima, the Divine Mercy writings of St. Faustina Kowalska, and the mystical works of St. Hildegard of Bingen, as they are essential to our understanding of the papacies of Blessed John Paul II and Benedict XVI.

It is also my hope that in uncovering some of the archive speeches of the earlier popes, it might help increase our knowledge and love of them, and urge us to ask for their intercession in this grave era for the Church. An era, however, that is, providentially, also intrinsically Marian.

PART I

Watchman,
How Much Longer the Night?

❧ 1 ❧

The Present Situation

For as it was in the days of Noah, so it will be at the coming of the Son of Man. In those days before the flood, they were eating and drinking, marrying and giving in marriage, up to the day that Noah entered the ark. They did not know until the flood came and carried them all away. So will it be also at the coming of the Son of Man.

(Matt. 24:37–40)

ON OCTOBER 16, 1978, the pontificate of Pope John Paul II began with a resounding message to the Church and the World: "Be Not Afraid." This message was a timely reminder of the words of Our Lord given to St. John on the island of Patmos: "Do not be afraid. I am the First and the Last, the one who lives" (Rev. 1:17). Many years later the Holy Father would explain further the importance of those few words chosen at the dawn of his reign:

> When on October 22, 1978, I said the words "Be not afraid!" in St. Peter's Square, I could not fully know how far they would take me and the entire church. Their meaning came more from the Holy Spirit, the consoler, promised by the Lord Jesus to his disciples, than from the man who spoke them. Nevertheless, with the passing of the years, I have recalled these words on many occasions. . . . Why should we have no fear? Because man has been redeemed by God. The power of Christ's Cross and Resurrection is greater than any evil which man could or should fear.[1]

This message, an inspiration from the Holy Spirit given to all humanity, came towards the end of a most brutal century which was permeated by many evils and which affected every society and race

---

1. John Paul II, *Crossing the Threshold of Hope* (London: Random House, 1994), 218.

on earth. The many global, regional, and civil wars killed or maimed millions. In fact, according to Zbignew Brzezinski, national security advisor to the Carter administration, about eighty seven million people died in the wars of the twentieth century alone.[2] How could we ever forget the two World Wars, the terrible ethnic cleansing of the Balkans and Rwanda and the various regional civil wars, which continue to this day? The words of Jesus recorded in St. Matthew's Gospel have certainly come to fruition in the past one hundred years:

> Nation will rise against nation, and kingdom against kingdom; there will be famines and earthquakes from place to place. All these are the beginning of the labor pains.... Immediately after the tribulation of those days, the sun will be darkened, and the moon will not give its light, and the stars will fall from the sky, and the powers of the heavens will be shaken. (Matt. 24:7–8, 29)

False prophets have also appeared under many guises to tempt the faithful to apostasy, most notably the two great messianic political movements of Communism and Nazism. Both believed that they could create and establish a kingdom of peace and justice on earth through social and political means. Their vision of power, however, was to deny God's sovereignty over all people and even to destroy the remembrance of Him in the life of those subject to their domination. Religious freedom and human rights were trampled upon as countless numbers of people were murdered or imprisoned.

Other, more subtle false prophets have arisen in recent decades, including a variety of cults and sects, causing great harm in certain areas of the world, especially in North and South America. In April 1991, at the Fourth Extraordinary Consistory, Cardinal Obando of Nicaragua told the other cardinals that a "Protestant explosion" had seen the number of non-Catholics in Latin America grow from four million in 1967 to thirty million in 1985. By 1991 that figure had grown to forty million. Obviously there is no suggestion that all these people have converted to sects, but it cannot be denied that in

2. Ralph Martin, *The Catholic Church at the End of an Age* (San Francisco: Ignatius Press, 1994), 18.

recent years the threat they pose to the Church has increased dramatically. Latin America is not the only region to be affected by this problem. In the *Instrumentum Laboris* for the Second Special Assembly for Africa held in the Vatican in 2009 we read:

> Christians grow weak, because they do not have a sound grasp of their faith which enables them to live and "make a defence to anyone who calls you to account for the hope that is in you" (1 Pet. 3:15). Sacred Scripture, which ought to be an assistance, has not yet become a part of their lives as a source of understanding their journey with God in the midst of the world and through history. Sometimes, they have recourse to witchcraft and the lamentable practices . . . or allow themselves to be influenced by political ideologies and Christian sects which attack the Catholic Church. Moreover, the Church suffers from priests and women and men religious who sometimes give bad example in looking to occult practices—which can even occur at times of praying for healing and deliverance—and vying for social positions, instead of devoting themselves to serving the least of the brethren.[3]

The popes have constantly appealed to the bishops of the Universal Church to be aware of the subtle snares being laid for the faithful. Even the clergy themselves have been targeted, a notable case being that of the Zambian Archbishop Emmanuel Miligno, who found himself leaving the source of truth and life for the sect of Sun Myung Moon. Of course, an attack on one member of the Church is an attack on the entire Mystical Body of Christ itself, affecting every soul and contributing to the gradual persecution that the Church is currently experiencing.

The Vatican has also addressed the problem of the New Age Movement,[4] perhaps the fastest growing spiritual phenomenon in the whole world; the spiritual thirst of many, especially young people, being quenched by a terribly deceptive doctrine, surely formulated by Satan himself in order to attract as many souls as possible

---

3. "The Church in Africa in Service to Justice, Reconciliation, and Peace," *Instrumentum Laboris,* Vatican City, 2009, http:// www.vatican.va/.

4. "Jesus Christ the Bearer of the Water of Life, A Christian reflection on the 'New Age,'" *The Pontifical Council for Culture & The Pontifical Council for Interreligious Dialogue,* February 3, 2003, http:// www.vatican.va/.

away from the true faith. Before his election to the See of St. Peter, Pope Benedict XVI once remarked: "Where man leaves faith behind, the horrors of pagandom return with reinforced potentialities."[5]

Our recent times have also witnessed a widespread decline in morals, which has coincided with a massive falling away from church attendance in all denominations. The late Cardinal Winning of Glasgow stated that, "with the exception of Malta and Ireland, Sunday mass attendance seldom rises above 25% ... they [lapsed Catholics] cut themselves off from the sacraments, which are a source of grace. They deprive their children of their birth right, their culture and their identity."[6] And so without the truth of the Holy Spirit to guide them, many have created a law for themselves which is totally in opposition to God's law of love. The gift of sexuality has been abused, giving rise to a large number of sexually transmitted diseases. Corruption of the consciences of young and old alike has led to a situation where homosexuality is openly welcomed and encouraged in certain parts of the world, while sexual relationships prior to marriage are now normal for most couples. On the African continent many people are dying daily due to the abuses of their body, affecting also many innocent children who find themselves infected from the time of conception.

The prophetic encyclical *Humanae Vitae* issued by Pope Paul VI in 1968 suggested that with the acceptance of artificial contraception, a culture of immorality and death would be the result. There can be no argument that his warning has not come to pass. The figures on abortion speak for themselves: millions of unborn have perished and the advent of partial birth abortion in America was to be considered as depraved as anything committed by Joseph Mengele and the Nazi regime. Blessed John Paul II stated in 1993, that the culture of death has taken on apocalyptic proportions:

This struggle parallels the apocalyptic combat described in the First Reading of this Mass. Death battles against Life: a "culture of death"

---

5. Joseph Cardinal Ratzinger, *Salt of the Earth* (San Francisco: Ignatius Press, 1997), 220.

6. Thomas Cardinal Winning, *Good News* (Allen Hall, London: National Service Committee, September/October, 2001), 3.

seeks to impose itself on our desire to live, and live to the full. There are those who reject the light of life, preferring "the fruitless works of darkness" (Eph. 5:11). Their harvest is injustice, discrimination, exploitation, deceit, violence. In every age, a measure of their apparent success is the death of the Innocents. *In our own century, as at no other time in history, the "culture of death" has assumed a social and institutional form of legality to justify the most horrible crimes against humanity*: genocide, "final solutions," "ethnic cleansings," and the massive "taking of lives of human beings even before they are born, or before they reach the natural point of death" (*Dominum et vivificantem*, 57). The absolute nature of their (the hostile forces') attack is symbolized in the object of their evil intention: the Child, the symbol of new life. The "dragon" (Rev. 12:3), the "ruler of this world" (Jn. 12:31) and the "father of lies" (Jn. 8:44), relentlessly tries to eradicate from human hearts the sense of gratitude and respect for the original, extraordinary and fundamental gift of God: human life itself. *Today that struggle has become increasingly direct.*[7]

In more recent years, Pope Benedict XVI has taken to heart the problems facing families throughout the world in the struggle to remain faithful to the Gospel of life:

Dear parents, commit yourselves always to teach your children to pray, and pray with them; draw them close to the Sacraments, especially to the Eucharist . . . and introduce them to the life of the Church; in the intimacy of the home do not be afraid to read the sacred Scriptures, illuminating family life with the light of faith and praising God as Father. Be like a little Upper Room, like that of Mary and the disciples, in which to live unity, communion and prayer![8]

Pope Pius XII had declared in the middle of the twentieth century that, "the sin of the century is the loss of the sense of sin."[9] John Paul II spoke at length on this subject in his 1986 encyclical *Dominum et*

---

7. John Paul, "Homily for World Youth Day," August 15, 1993, Cherry Creek State Park, Denver, http:// www.vatican.va/.

8. Benedict XVI, "Homily on the Occasion of the National Day of Croatian Catholic Families," June 5, 2011, Zagreb, http:// www.vatican.va/.

9. John Paul II, Encyclical Letter *Dominum et Vivificantem* (Boston, St. Paul Books and Media, 1986), 80, no. 47.

Vivificantem concerning the Holy Spirit in the life of the Church. He stated, "The Church constantly implores from God the grace that integrity of human consciences will not be lost, that their healthy sensitivity with regard to good and evil will not be blunted."[10] Sadly it *is* this blunting of consciences that has led to the present antichristian climate in which we find ourselves. In our era of relativism, the word "conscience" signifies that for moral and religious questions, it is the subjective dimension, the individual that freely decides on what course of action to take; as Pope John Paul II stated in *Veritatis Splendor*:

> The individual conscience is accorded the status of a supreme tribunal of moral judgment which hands down categorical and infallible decisions about good and evil . . . in this way the inescapable claims of truth disappear, yielding their place to a criterion of sincerity, authenticity and "being at peace with oneself."[11]

In the search for obedience to God's law, the Church calls us to seek the truth as a sure and certain means of reaching salvation; essentially, we are made holy by "obedience to the truth" (1 Pet. 1:22). In terms of the abandonment of the faith and rejection of moral teaching, we can trace the neglect of the sacrament of Confirmation (at least the understanding of its importance) and the lack of prayer to the Holy Spirit as reasons why truth does not rule the conscience as God desires. Therefore, as a consequence of this, a cancer has developed throughout the world, and even within the Church, which raises aloft the flag of "freedom."

At the time of Pope John Paul's visit for World Youth Day held in Denver in 1993, polls were carried out to discover the thoughts and beliefs of American Catholics. The results showed that 49% of Catholics disagreed with the Church's teaching on homosexuality, and 87% disagreed with the official teaching on family planning,[12] while another poll from the early 1990s suggested that only 30% of Catholics in America believed in the true presence of Jesus in the Blessed

---

10. Ibid.

11. John Paul II, Encyclical Letter *Veritatis Splendor*, August 6, 1993, no. 32, http:// www.vatican.va/.

12. "How U.S. Catholics view their Church," *USA Today*, August 10, 1993, 6A.

Sacrament.[13] The 2003 publication of the post-synodal exhortation *Ecclesia in Europa* showed Pope John Paul's view that Europe is also living what he called a "silent apostasy." Significantly, the document took as its central theme the Book of Revelation; no doubt the pope's intention being to impress upon the Church the relevance of its prophetic content for us here and now:

> In proclaiming to Europe the Gospel of hope, I will take as a guide the Book of Revelation, a "prophetic revelation" which discloses to the community of believers the deep and hidden meaning of what is taking place. . . . The entire Church in Europe ought to feel that the Lord's command and call is addressed to her: *examine yourself, be converted, "awake, and strengthen what remains and is on the point of death"* (Rev. 3:2).[14]

In tandem with this falling away of belief in the central tenets of Catholic doctrine, the Church has been plagued by a continuous stream of dissenting voices and organizations in the past few decades. The *We are Church* movement espouses women priests, artificial contraception, and married priests, while the *Leadership Conference of Women Religious* in the United States has continually peddled an anti-magisterial agenda, advocating among other things a homosexual lifestyle and new age fads, while neglecting the authentic development of charisms associated with its Orders. Obedience to legitimate authority within the Church has been questioned ever more frequently in recent years and the teachings of the Church no longer adhered to even by many priests. The liturgical abuses that the vast majority of Catholics have been subject to in the western world stem from this culture of autonomy from Rome, and the turmoil caused by this wave of evil in the Holy Temple of God caused Sr. Lucia of Fatima to recount the Blessed Virgin's warnings from 1917:

> Our Lady requested and recommended that the Rosary be prayed every day, having repeated this in all the Apparitions as if fore-

---

13. Gianni Cardinale, "Clinton and Us," 30 *Days*, no.12 (1992): 32.
14. John Paul II, Apostolic Exhortation, *Ecclesia in Europa*, June 2003, nos. 5, 26, 28, http:// www.vatican.va/.

warning us that in these times of diabolical disorientation, we must not let ourselves be deceived by false doctrines that diminish the elevation of our soul to God by means of prayer.[15]

The sexual abuse scandals of recent times confirm a demonic infiltration in the heart of the Church in what could be seen as a strategic attempt by the Devil to destroy the reputation of the priesthood. By targeting innocence and purity among the little ones (cf. Matt. 18:6), the revering of the priest as an *alter Christus* (another Christ) is turned on its head; the absolute antithesis of Jesus Christ the High Priest.

There is a spiritual battle being waged for souls. There will be only one outcome—the final defeat of Satan and the coming of the Eternal kingdom of Christ. This is the reason why the Polish pope called us to cross the threshold of hope with no fear of the future, whatever it may hold. Scripture assures us that the victory has already been won through the suffering and death of Jesus, and the second Passover has been accomplished. Now we await that final Passover when the Church will be crucified only to rise again glorious, in imitation of its Savior.

The following chapters will aim to show how the recent popes, especially John Paul II, have prepared the Church and the world to live the conclusion of the end times—the purification and great tribulation—through their magisterial teachings.

On the Jubilee of the Disabled on December 3, 2000 at the Basilica of St. Paul-Outside-the-Walls, Pope John Paul encouraged the faithful with these words:

> Look up and raise your heads, because your redemption is drawing near" (Lk. 21:28). In the Gospel text offered for our meditation on this First Sunday of Advent, St. Luke highlights the fear that terrifies human beings before the final upheaval. In contrast however, the Evangelist presents with far greater emphasis the joyful prospect of Christian expectation: "Then," he says, "they will see

---

15. Uma vida ao serviço de Fátima, "Pequeno tratado, da vidente, sobre a natureza e recitação do Terço," Chapter VI, "Escola tipografica das missões cucujães, Cucujães." Imprimatur by Dom João Venâncio, Bishop of Leiria, May 13, 1971. English translation available at http:// www.fatima.org/.

the Son of man coming in a cloud with power and great glory" (Lk. 21:27). This is the message which gives hope to the believer's heart: the Lord will come "with power and great glory." This is why the disciples are asked not to be afraid, but to look up and raise their heads, "because your redemption is drawing near" (Lk. 21:28).[16]

The popes call the Universal Church to stay awake and watch, waiting for the completion of the "fullness of time" (Gal.4:4) which will be revealed at the second coming of the Lord. The exhortation "Be not afraid" (Jos. 1:9) is also accompanied by a similar message "Give thanks to the Lord, for he is good; for his mercy endures for ever!" (Ps. 117:1). If the civilization of love is to be built in our era, then these words will need to resound in the heart of every believer, encouraging us all in the task of the New Evangelization.

---

16. John Paul II, "Homily for the Jubilee of the Disabled," December 3, 2000, St. Peter's, Rome, http:// www.vatican.va/.

2

The Final Battle Dawns

I saw a scroll in the right hand of the one who sat on the throne. It had writing on both sides and was sealed with seven seals. Then I saw a mighty angel who proclaimed in a loud voice, "Who is worthy to open the scroll and break its seals?" But no one in heaven or on earth or under the earth was able to open the scroll or to examine it. I shed many tears because no one was found worthy to open the scroll or to examine it. One of the elders said to me, "Do not weep. The lion of the tribe of Judah, the root of David, has triumphed, enabling him to open the scroll with its seven seals." (Rev. 5:1–5)

IN ORDER to understand the gravity of the situation facing the Church and humanity at the dawn of the third millennium, it is important to trace the development of the final battle that is being waged in the spiritual realm. This epic struggle, which traces its roots all the way back to the rebellion of Lucifer and his expulsion from God's presence, has in the second Christian millennium produced many warning signs. They point to a particular era in salvation history in which the forces of good and evil will finally converge to fight one last time before the Lord of history commands time to end as we know it, leaving only the eternity of peace or torment.

Many signs of this approaching storm appeared throughout the second millennium, from the 1054 schism between the Catholic and Orthodox Churches, to the still more explosive Protestant Reformation of the Middle Ages. The work of the devil is evident in the disunity and scandal caused by these ruptures: a total contradiction to the divine will of Jesus when he prayed his great petition to God the Father: "Father . . . that they also may be in us" (Jn. 17:21). Philosophers began to question the mystical aspects of the Church, giving rise to the exclusive value of science and reason. These errors eventually led to the Protestant doctrine that the bread and wine are only symbols of the body and blood of Christ, reducing, in their understanding, the Holy Sacrifice of the Mass to be nothing more than a meal, rather than the renewal of Christ's Sacrifice on the Cross. Tradition was rejected, leaving Sacred Scripture as the sole source of divine Revelation; the fact that the teaching magisterium was also rejected meant that anyone was free to interpret Scripture as they wished. Faith in the word of God was gradually eroded through the latter centuries of the millennium, bringing forth a far more subtle and suffocating persecution of the Church.

The counter-Reformation years saw the gradual response of the Church to the troubles caused by the Protestant breakaway. The Council of Trent (1546–1563), which once again clearly defined the main doctrines and dogmas of Catholicism, was the first contribution to the defense of the faith. This Council restated that:

> There are Divine traditions not contained in Holy Scripture, revelations made to the apostles either orally by Jesus Christ or by the inspiration of the Holy Ghost and transmitted by the Apostles to the Church.[1]

Thus the teaching on Tradition as a source of public revelation along with Sacred Scripture was reaffirmed. The Council also defined as dogma the belief in the existence of Purgatory, a teaching that the Church had taught from its infancy. As well as the Magisterium, there were saintly men and women whom God raised up at this time; St. Margaret Mary gave the beautiful teachings on the love emanating from the Sacred Heart of Jesus, while St. Theresa of Avila and St. John of the Cross were the great mystics of the age. Examples of compassion for the poor and the sick came from St. Vincent de Paul and St. Aloysius Gonzaga; the Lord also sent great miracle workers to combat the supplanting of faith by reason, notably St. Joseph of Cupertino and St. Martin de Porres.

---

1. Desmond Birch, *Trial, Tribulation and Triumph Before, During and After Antichrist* (Santa Barbara: Queenship Publishing, 1996), 9.

One aspect of the Church's history during this era, which sheds some light on the divine providence of God through time, was the startling expansion of its missionaries throughout the world. At a time when the Old World was at war and dismantling its faith, the Lord was opening up a new missionary era in the New World—the Americas. This apostolate, bringing the Gospel to all nations, was under the leadership of Our Lady, who converted approximately nine million people in just a few years after her apparitions to St. Juan Diego in Mexico in 1531. In the words of Dr. Ibarra, a well-known Mexican preacher of the nineteenth century:

> It is true that immediately after the conquest, some apostolic men, some zealous missionaries, mild, gentle conquerors who were disposed to shed no blood but their own, ardently devoted themselves to the conversion of the Indians. However, these valiant men, because of their fewness, because of the difficulty of learning new languages, and of the vast extent of our territory, obtained, in spite of their heroic efforts, but few and limited results.
>
> But scarcely had the Most Holy Virgin of Guadalupe appeared and taken possession of this her inheritance, when the Catholic Faith spread with the rapidity of light from the rising sun, through the wide extent and beyond the bounds of the ancient empire of Mexico. Innumerable multitudes from every tribe, every district, every race, in this immense country . . . unable to resist such sweet and tender invitations, came in crowds to cast their grateful hearts at the feet of so loving a Mother, and to mingle their tears of emotion with the regenerating waters of Baptism. Our Lady of Guadalupe it was, who worked numberless prodigies of conversion to the Faith, with the irresistible attractions of her graciousness and the ingenious invention of her kind charity.[2]

The cult of Our Lady of Guadalupe has grown through the recent centuries, leading Pope St. Pius X to proclaim on August 24, 1910, Our Lady of Guadalupe as Patroness of Latin America. This intervention of the Lord in the Americas, led to the proliferation of missionary activity in ever expanding territories, contributing to the

---

2. Francis Johnston, *The Wonder of Guadalupe* (Devon: Augustine Publishing Company, 1981), 57.

command of Jesus to preach the Gospel to all the nations until the end of time. A quite remarkable aspect of this endeavor was the speed in which Christianity took root—evidence that the Lord is capable of hauling in a miraculous catch at any time, even in our own dark days of tribulation. It was not only the Americas who were being introduced to the message of salvation; in the East the great missionary apostle St. Francis Xavier was taking the Gospel to India, Goa, and Japan. The sufferings endured by the native peoples, made, in his words, "a permanent bruise on my soul."[3]

In the seventeenth century, the heresy of Jansenism—a theological system deriving from the book *Augustinus*, by Cornelius Jansen, Bishop of Ypres (d. 1638)—was beginning to subvert the faithful back in Europe. Jansenism questioned the reality of free will while at the same time denying that Christ had died for all men without exception. It was harsh and pessimistic in its substance, doubting the infinite mercy of God; Holy Communion was looked upon as a reward, rather than the medicine for our spiritual and bodily ills. It was at this time that Divine Providence decreed that two great Marian saints should emerge to combat this grave heresy, to spread devotion to Mary and to lay the foundations for the Marian era. They are: St. Alphonsus Maria de Liguori, (1696–1787), and St. Louis Marie Grignion de Montfort (1673–1716).[4]

St. Alphonsus, an Italian bishop and founder of the Congregation of the Most Holy Redeemer [Redemptorists] wrote many books on moral theology, devotion to the Holy Eucharist, and prayer. One of

3. Donald Attwater and Catherine Rachel John, *Dictionary of Saints* (London: Penguin, 1995), 145.
4. Interestingly, a few years later, the Society of Mary [Marists] was founded by Fr. Jean Claude Colin in France. In the summer of 1813, he met with fellow seminarian Jean-Claude Courveille, who told of a vision of Mary he had experienced in the Cathedral Shrine at Le Puy. He stated that Mary had talked about a Society to be founded in the battle for the Faith at these end times. Fr. Colin, inspired by this episode, began to form a group of seminarians with a missionary zeal to bring to fruition the victory of Mary. It was Fr. Colin's belief that the end of the world was nearing and the Marists would play an important role in the preparation for it. *See* http://www.acertainway.info/origins/something-new-for-our-times/the-end-times/.

his most famous works, however, is *The Glories of Mary*, which integrates the Mariology of the Church Fathers, notably St. Augustine and St. Ambrose, whilst defending it against the prevalent anticlericalism and rationalism of the Enlightenment. The book reveals the necessity of placing Mary at the heart of our spiritual life, and of her central role in salvation history:

> No one denies that Jesus Christ is our only mediator of justice, and that he by his merits has obtained our reconciliation with God. But, on the other hand, it is impious to assert that God is not pleased to grant graces at the intercession of his saints, and more especially of Mary his Mother, whom Jesus desires so much to see loved and honored by all. Who can pretend that the honor bestowed on a mother does not redound to the honor of the son? . . . St. Bernard says, "Let us not imagine that we obscure the glory of the Son by the great praise we lavish on the mother; for the more she is honored, the greater is the glory of the Son." "There can be no doubt," says the saint, "that whatever we say in praise of the Mother is equally in praise of the Son" (Non est dubium, quidquid in laudibus Matris proferimus, ad Filium pertinere—De Laud. V. M. hom. 4).[5]

The power of the Blessed Virgin's intercession as mediatrix of mercy for all her children, especially those furthest away from the Kingdom of God, is one aspect emphasized by St. Alphonsus:

> How great, then, should be our confidence in this Queen, knowing her great power with God, and that she is so rich and full of mercy, that there is no one living on the earth who does not partake of her compassion and favor. This was revealed by our Blessed Lady herself to St. Bridget, saying, "I am the Queen of heaven and the Mother of Mercy; I am the joy of the just, and the door through which sinners are brought to God. There is no sinner on earth so accursed as to be deprived of my mercy; for all, if they receive nothing else through my intercession, receive the grace of being less tempted by the devils than they would otherwise have been". . . . Let us, then, have recourse, and always have recourse, to this most sweet Queen, if we would be certain of salvation; and if

---

5. Alphonsus de Liguori, *The Glories of Mary* (Brooklyn: Redemptorist Fathers, 1931), 153.

we are alarmed and disheartened at the sight of our sins, let us remember that it is in order to save the greatest and most abandoned sinners, who recommend themselves to her, that Mary is made the Queen of Mercy. Such have to be her crown in heaven.[6]

St. Alphonsus' preaching of devotion to Mary took many forms; he advised a daily rosary, a daily visit to a Marian shrine, and the keeping of a statue or painting of our Lady in the home. He also encouraged fasting on bread and water each Saturday—traditionally a day of special devotion to Our Lady—as he did, even in his final years. The charism of this great Doctor of the Church, from a Mariological point of view was oriented towards pastoral formation, the catechesis of which was firmly rooted in the rich tradition of Marian teaching evolving from seventeen hundred years of Catholicism.

With St. Louis de Montfort, however, the emphasis is without doubt directed toward future times. In him we see a prophet in the mold of the great Old Testament prophets; a missionary priest of enormous zeal for whom extending the Kingdom of God through the mediation of Mary was a work without compare. It is significant that running parallel to St. Louis Marie's mission in France were the apparitions of the Blessed Virgin to the visionary Benoite Rencurel, a young shepherdess in the village of Laus, situated in the French Alps.[7]

We could also say that, in a sense, St. Louis was a precursor of Mary and her great interventions in nineteenth-century France.

The ideology of Jansenism was influencing many in France at the

---

6. Ibid., 43.

7. The apparitions of Our Lady of Laus, Refuge of Sinners, were formally approved by the Holy See on May 5, 2008. Astoundingly, the visitations of Mary continued for fifty-four years. There are two prophecies which have remained with the villagers of Laus for three hundred years: The first states that at the close of the apparitions, the events would be forgotten and would only become known again in the end times; secondly, the Shrine would be spared from all chastisements—apparently the French Revolution did not affect it, nor the Second World War.

It is known that locals tend not to sell their houses in Laus due to this second prophecy (from a conversation between Mr. Ferdia McDermott and local villagers in 1995). As to the first prophecy, it cannot be denied that Laus was unknown even to most Marian devotees until the 1990's.

time when St. Louis Marie Grignion de Montfort began his missionary activity. He fought this heresy through preaching confidence in
the mercy of God and his spiritual way of "To Jesus through Mary."
St. Louis de Montfort is a figure of great importance in our evalua-
tion of the dawning of the final battle now taking place; an aspect
that will be dealt with in greater detail in the following chapter.

In his famous book *True Devotion to Mary*, he makes prophetic
announcements on the imminence of the end times:

> . . . because the Most High with his Holy Mother has to form for
> himself great saints who shall surpass most of the other saints in
> sanctity as much as the cedars of Lebanon outgrow the little
> shrubs. . . . These great souls, full of grace and zeal, shall be chosen
> to match themselves against the enemies of God, who shall rage on
> all sides; and they shall be singularly devout to our Blessed Lady,
> illuminated by her light, strengthened by her nourishment, led by
> her spirit, supported by her arm, and sheltered under her protec-
> tion.[8]

He teaches that just as the salvation of the world was begun
through Mary, so it is through Mary that it must be consummated:
"But in the second coming of Jesus Christ, Mary has to be made
known and revealed by the Holy Spirit, in order that through her,
Jesus Christ may be known, loved, and served."[9] For St. Louis,
preaching the consecration of ourselves to Jesus through Mary
would enable us to do "all our actions with Mary," and so enlighten
our souls to be able to follow Mary's path to her Son. It would be
necessary to imitate Our Lady's great virtues of love, purity, humility, and obedience. St. Louis says that: "Mary is the great and exclusive mould of God."[10] In his view, what was needed was the
"apostles of the latter times"[11]—an army of faithful souls, led by
priests, who would fight against Satan and his evil empire. He
explains in detail about the formation of these apostles of the end
times and how they would be taught by their Mother of mercy:

---

8. Louis De Montfort, *True Devotion to Mary* (Rockford, IL: Tan, 1941), 26–27.
9. Ibid., 28.
10. Ibid., 163.
11. Ibid., 34.

They will know the grandeurs of that Queen, and will consecrate themselves entirely to her service as subjects and slaves of love. They will experience her sweetness and her maternal goodness, and they will love her tenderly like well-beloved children. . . . They will have recourse to her in all things, as to their dear advocate and Mediatrix with Jesus Christ . . . but who shall those servants, slaves, and children of Mary be? They shall be the ministers of the Lord who, like a burning fire, shall kindle the fire of divine love everywhere. They shall be "like sharp arrows in the hands of the powerful" Mary to pierce her enemies (Ps.126:4). They shall be the sons of Levi, well purified by the fire of great tribulation. . . . They shall be clouds thundering through the air at the least breath of the Holy Spirit; who, detaching themselves from everything and troubling themselves about nothing, shall shower forth the rain of the Word of God and of life eternal. They shall thunder against sin; they shall storm against the world; they shall strike the devil and his crew. . . . They shall be the true apostles of the end times, to whom the Lord of Hosts shall give the word and the might to work marvels and to carry off with glory the spoils of His enemies.[12]

The following remarks of St. Louis Marie perhaps foreshadow the martyrdom that many will have to undergo in the final persecution of the Antichrist:

They will carry on their shoulders the bloody standard of the Cross, the Crucifix in their right hand and the Rosary in their left, the Sacred names of Jesus and Mary in their hearts, and the modesty and mortification of Jesus Christ in their own behaviour.[13]

Are we not witnesses to the huge army of Mary that has risen in recent times, especially those who have made the consecration to her Immaculate Heart? Are we now seeing the prophecy of de Montfort coming to fruition with the birth of the Legion of Mary, the Marian Movement of Priests, the Marists, as well as the Blue Army of Fatima and the other prayer movements consecrated to Our Lady? St. Louis de Montfort explains that it is in the last, cruel

---

12. Ibid., 33–34.
13. Ibid., 35.

persecution of the Antichrist that we should understand the prophecy given by God in the Book of Genesis: "I will put enmities between thee and the woman and thy seed and her seed; she shall crush thy head and thou shalt lie in wait for her heel" (Gen. 3:15).

Although St. Louis Marie revealed that he did not know exactly when these things would happen, he talks of his own time as "these end times";[14] there are also hints of the beginning of the apostasy: "It is difficult to persevere in justice because of the strange corruption of the world. The world is now so corrupt it seems inevitable that religious hearts should be soiled."[15]

The missionary zeal of this great Marian saint is evident in his many writings. It is as if he knew of the urgency of preaching this spirituality of consecration to Jesus through Mary, leaving us in no doubt that it is God's will that Mary shines forth in the end times; as it is her task to prepare the Church and humanity for the second glorious coming of her Son, Jesus Christ. Virtually all the recent popes since Blessed Pius IX have recommended Montfortian spirituality, and Blessed John Paul II went even as far as to state: "the reading of this book was a decisive turning point in my life. . . . It is from Montfort that I have taken my motto: "Totus tuus" (I am all thine)."[16]

It therefore becomes apparent that the Lord was preparing the Church for these last days with a new form of spirituality—what has now become known as the "School of Mary." A Marian era of grace and mercy; a time of repentance and renewal. With a refocused eschatological dimension, the message of the Gospel was now clearer than ever: "Repent and believe in the Gospel" (Mk. 1:15).

Our Lady also continued to exhort the faithful to repent and convert, most notably in her apparitions given to St. Catherine Laboure at the Rue de Bac in Paris in 1830. The message included the instruction to have a medal struck with the inscription: "O Mary conceived without sin, pray for us who have recourse to thee." The medal rapidly became known as the Miraculous Medal due to the many graces received through it. Two decades later, on December 8, 1854,

14. Ibid., 28.
15. Ibid., 55.
16. Ibid., 6.

at St. Peter's Basilica in Rome, Blessed Pius IX defined as a dogma of the faith, the truth that Mary was born exempt from the stain of original sin. In her revelations to St. Catherine, Our Lady stated that: "The entire world will be overcome by evils of all kinds."

Sixteen years later in the Alps of southern France, Our Blessed Mother again appeared, this time to two shepherd children in the village of La Salette. The uneducated visionaries were warned about severe famines that would soon materialize in Europe as well as scourges of war that would come upon the world. There were also warnings for priests to reform their lives and even mention of the eventual coming of the Antichrist himself.[17] The Catholic Church approved both these apparitions as warnings for people to convert; unfortunately they were not heeded. Revolutions occurred throughout Europe in the middle of the nineteenth century and millions died in the famines that swept across the land. Even the famous apparitions at Lourdes in 1858 to Saint Bernadette Soubirous did not stem the tide of rationalism and apathy towards the Catholic Faith that was seeping into European society as a whole.

Blessed Pius IX, at this time of upheaval and war, was also giving his own warnings stating that: "There will be a great prodigy which will fill the world with awe. But this prodigy will be preceded by the triumph of a revolution during which the Church will go through ordeals that are beyond description."[18] Was this great pope announcing the arrival of the final persecution? It would appear that the Holy Spirit was enlightening him in the quest to discern the signs of the times. After all, the role of the papacy is a prophetic one; one that is intended to guide the people of God in the journey towards the "New Jerusalem" while the Church calmly presses forward "in the midst of the persecutions of the world and the consolations of God."[19]

One of the greatest minds of the Church in the middle of the nineteenth century was that of Blessed John Henry Newman. He

---

17. Rene Laurentin and Michel Corteville, *Découverte du secret de la Salette* (Paris: Fayard, 2002).

18. Birch, *Trial, Tribulation and Triumph Before, During and After Antichrist*, 375.

19. Augustine, *De Civitate Dei.* 18, 59, 2, http://www.newadvent.org/.

was the leader of the Oxford Tractarian Movement and the greatest of the English converts to the Catholic Church at the time. Newman immersed himself in the writings of the Church Fathers and became a great master of Catholic philosophy, theology, morals, and scripture. He was very influential in bringing the Church back to the study of the Fathers, as he was in leading the Church in England through the time when Erastian principles—theories of secular supremacy in religious affairs—were being vigorously promoted. Besides his great intellect, Newman was a prophetic figure who enjoyed deep insights into the future direction of the Church. He once gave a lecture in Dublin entitled *A Form of Infidelity of the Day* in which he seems to have foreseen how liberalism and later modernism would bring about the apostasy that is so prevalent now. He called this heresy the "religion of reason," condemning it as the ruin of all revealed truth and supernatural faith. It is in this light that we are able to understand his reasons for preaching his famous *Advent Sermons on Antichrist*. These sermons were divided into four subjects: The Times of Antichrist; The Religion of Antichrist; The City of Antichrist; The Persecution of Antichrist.

In the first of these homilies, Newman discusses whether there are any signs of an imminent coming of the Antichrist. Without giving a definitive answer, he states that the conditions of humanity at the time give reason to believe that his coming is not far off:

> There are evidences to convince us that we are entering the Age of Apostasy. For apostasy is being formed, gathering forces, gaining ground on the Church every day. Everywhere in the world, but quite visibly in the most peaceful, civilised nations, we are witnessing a supreme effort to govern men and dominate the world without religion. . . . In almost every country there is a united, powerful movement to crush the Church, to strip her of power and place.

Later he examines Satan's role in preparing this apostasy:

> He offers baits to tempt men: he promises liberty, equality, trade and wealth, remission of taxes, reforms. He promises illumination, knowledge, science, philosophy, enlargement of mind. He scoffs at times gone by, at sacred traditions, at every institution that reveres them. He bids man mount aloft, to become a god. He laughs and

26

jokes with men, gets intimate with them, takes their hands, gets his fingers between theirs, grasps them and then they are his.[20]

While the second and third sermons deal with what religion the Antichrist will belong to, and where he will reign, the final sermon is devoted to the understanding of his persecution of the Church. In a sense, all the persecutions to which the Church has been subject have been precursors of the final trial. This trial will be universal, with the notable and terrible prospect of the daily sacrifice, which is the Holy Sacrifice of the Mass, being abolished for three and a half years, as was prophesied by the prophet Daniel (Dan. 12:11). Newman lists four aspects of this final trial: It will be greater, more violent than any before; it will be supported by miraculous signs and wonders; it will abolish the daily workings of the Church, meaning the suffocation of graces necessary for the faithful, especially the reception of the Sacraments; and it will bring about a blasphemous way of life that will be accepted and lived by a great many people. Perhaps the following passage sums up Newman's feelings on the signs of the times:

> Signs do occur in history from time to time, not to fix the day, but to remind us that the Antichrist and the final struggle between the Church and her enemies is daily approaching. Other signs tell us that the universe and the planets are growing old; our earth keeps crumbling away under the forces of nature and the abuse of man. The night is far spent; the day is at hand. Shadows begin to move; the old forms of the Roman Empire, with us from the time of Christ, heave, tremble, and nod toward a fall. When they go, the Antichrist will be released, announced and acclaimed. But he will disappear in a short, dreadful season. And then Christ will come in power and glory.[21]

The situation of the "earth crumbling away" as we know now, is far worse than one hundred and fifty years ago. The old world is gradually giving way to a new birth; a reminder of the words of St. Paul in chapter eight of the Letter to the Romans: "For creation

---

20. John Henry Cardinal Newman, "Advent Sermons on the Antichrist," *Tracts for the Times* (London: J. G. F&J. Rivington, 1840), 12–14.

21. Ibid., 49–50.

awaits with eager expectation the revelation of the children of God; for creation was made subject to futility, not of its own accord but because of the one who subjected it, in hope that creation itself would be set free from slavery to corruption and share in the glorious freedom of the children of God" (Rom. 8:19–21).

Blessed Cardinal Newman has long been considered one of the intellectual giants of Catholicism, and important, especially for those who prefer to ignore the area of eschatology, is the knowledge that his beliefs did not come from private revelations, but from the authentic teachings of the Church—most notably the early Fathers. The teaching of the Antichrist as a person is clearly present in the writings of the Fathers, and this great theologian was prepared to accept the possibility that his era, or soon after, could herald his coming.

Jesus has given us a certain amount of knowledge as to the time of his return in the Gospels; the duty of the Church is to read the signs of the times in every epoch and interpret them. Only in this way can we discover what the "Spirit is saying to the Churches" (Rev. 2:7). St. Luke recounts the words of Jesus; words which seem to relate to the great apostasy: "when the Son of man returns, will he find faith on earth?" (Lk. 18:8). If Blessed John Paul warned of a "silent apostasy" (*Ecclesia in Europa* n.9) then there is reason to believe that he sensed an approaching culmination of this battle. St. Paul stated: "Let no one deceive you in any way. For unless the apostasy comes first and the lawless one is revealed, the one doomed to perdition ... whom the Lord Jesus will kill with the breath of his mouth and render powerless by the manifestation of his coming" (2 Th. 2:3, 8).

As we shall discover, a succession of holy popes have consistently warned about the dangers threatening the world in the last century; dangers which have evolved to take on ever more demonic forms, some of which would even infiltrate the church as a prophetic sign of Satan's desire to ultimately destroy the Catholic Church.

☙ 3 ❧

The Popes of the Marian Era

Children, it is the last hour; and just as you heard that the antichrist
was coming, so now many antichrists have appeared. Thus we know
this is the last hour. They went out from us, but they were not really
of our number; if they had been, they would have remained with us.
Their desertion shows that none of them was of our number. Who is
the liar? Whoever denies that Jesus is the Christ. Whoever denies the
Father and the Son, this is the antichrist. No one who denies the Son
has the Father, but whoever confesses the Son has the Father as well.

(1 Jn. 2:18–19, 22–23)

WHAT IS a "Marian Era" and why does it matter? A possible theological definition of a "Marian era" suggests a particular epoch
within salvation history of eschatological significance, in which
supernatural grace is entrusted to the Virgin Mary by God for the
spiritual maturity of her children. Entrusted and empowered by the
Holy Spirit, the Virgin Mary, in complete submission to the will of
God, becomes intimately associated with Providential activity; the
most vocal proponent of this view of Providence being Saint Louis
de Montfort. According to St. Louis, the providence of God has
entrusted the Blessed Virgin with a special eschatological mission;
essentially, the Mother of Jesus is to produce through the grace
entrusted to her, the saints of the "latter times."[1] This doctrine of
Mary, Mediatrix of all graces, is a long standing and central compo-
nent of papal Mariology which sheds light on her mission as the

1. Cardinal Tarcisio Bertone, the Vatican Secretary of State, further explained
this dimension of the maternal mediation of Mary in this Marian era during a presentation in Rome for the publication of his book, *The Last Seer of Fatima*, on September 21, 2007: "The Virgin Mary's mission in the plan of universal salvation and

29

New Eve. For it was precisely through her obedience that the knot of Eve's disobedience was untied (cf. Saint Irenaeus, *Adversus Haereses*, 3:22). Pope Benedict XIV states: "Our Lady is like a celestial stream through which the flow of all graces and gifts reach the soul of all wretched mortals,"[2] while Benedict XV emphasizes the co-redemptive mystical crucifixion suffered by the Most Holy Virgin:

> For with her suffering and dying son, Mary endured suffering and almost death. . . . One can truly affirm that together with Christ she has redeemed the human race. . . . For this reason, every kind of grace we receive from the treasury of the redemption is ministered as it were through the hands of the same sorrowful Virgin.[3]

More recently, Pope Benedict XVI stated:

> There is no fruit of grace in the history of salvation that does not have as its necessary instrument the mediation of Our Lady. . . . In our day, Our Lady has been given to us as the best defence against the evils that afflict modern life; Marian devotion is the sure guarantee of her maternal protection and safeguard in the hour of temptation.[4]

From a somewhat more historical viewpoint, the argument presented in this chapter is that the period from the proclamation of the dogma of the Immaculate Conception in 1854 through to our own times forms a distinct Marian era in the Church; characterized by a concern with modernism, a deepening Papal reflection on the need for Marian intervention in the World, and the influence of the major Marian apparitions: Rue de Bac, La Salette, Lourdes, Fatima, and Kibeho.

---

in every Christian's life is brought increasingly into the limelight by contemporary Catholicism. . . . Everything in the Virgin's soul that prepares for and prefigures Christ still remains an immediate reality for us today, since the mystery of Christ's gradual coming to all souls and in all nations is taking place before our very eyes." http://www.vatican.va/.

2. Benedict XIV, *Op. Omnia*, v. 16 (Prati, 1846), 428.

3. Benedict XV, Apostolic Letter, *Inter Sodalicia*, AAS 10, (1918): 182; Mass and Office of Mediatrix of all Graces, approved 1921.

4. Benedict XVI, "Homily at Mass for the Canonization of Fr. Antonio Galvao," May 11, 2007, http://www.vatican.va/.

Blessed John Paul II explicitly stated that the Marian era began with the proclamation by Pius IX of the dogma of the Immaculate Conception: "Luigi Marie Monti [the founder of the Sons of the Immaculate Conception] has become an apostle of that new Marian era which was opened by that servant of God Pope Pius IX with the proclamation of the dogma of the Immaculate Conception."[5] John Paul II is alluding to the pious efforts made during the nineteenth century to transform Catholic Marian tradition into dogma; the declaration of the Immaculate Conception dogma is a watershed not because it radically changed Catholic belief but because it represented a victory for those who, following Marian figures such as St. Louis Marie de Montfort and St. Alphonsus Liguori, believed that the re-evangelization of the world depended on an understanding that the Virgin Mary is the surest path to Christ. John Paul II's dating the "new Marian Era" to the papacy of Pius IX is also noteworthy because it recalls a strong association between the papacy, modernism, and Marianism. Pius IX famously condemned many modernist propositions in his *Syllabus of Errors*, which was first published in 1864 on the feast of the Immaculate Conception, on the tenth anniversary of his proclamation of that dogma. As early as 1849, Pius IX had issued the encyclical *Ubi Primum* in which he implores the prayers of all Catholics for the eventual dogmatic definition of the Immaculate Conception. In the text, we see the absolute importance he placed on Mary's mediation in the struggle against the onslaught of evil:

And likewise in our own day, Mary, with the ever merciful affection so characteristic of her maternal heart, wishes, through her efficacious intercession with God, to deliver her children from the sad and grief-laden troubles, from the tribulations, the anxiety, the difficulties, and the punishments of God's anger which afflict the world because of the sins of men. Wishing to restrain and to dispel the violent hurricane of evils which, as We lament from the bottom of Our heart, are everywhere afflicting the Church, Mary desires to transform Our sadness into joy. The foundation of all

---

5. John Paul II, "Address to the Congregation of the Sons of the Immaculate Conception for the Centenary of the Death of its Founder, Luigi Marie Monti," September 24, 1999, http://www.vatican.va/.

31

Our confidence, as you know well, Venerable Brethren, is found in the Blessed Virgin Mary. For, God has committed to Mary the treasury of all good things, in order that everyone may know that through her are obtained every hope, every grace, and all salvation. For this is His will, that we obtain everything through Mary.[6]

In the encyclical *Ubi Nos,* promulgated on May 15, 1871, Pius IX introduces a theme, the Day of Judgment, which as we will discover, also recurs in the thoughts of a succession of Marian popes:

Then request the divine clemency to dispel the blindness of impious minds and convert their hearts to penitence before the great and awful day of the Lord arrives, or to check their lawless plans and show them how foolish those men are who attempt to overthrow the rock founded by Christ and infringe its divine privileges. In these prayers may Our hope be set more strongly on God. . . . Now indeed is the hour of wickedness and the power of darkness. *But it is the final hour* and the power quickly passes away. Christ the strength of God and the wisdom of God is with us, and He is on our side. Have confidence: he has overcome the world.[7]

According to Father Ivan Poyavnik, a former professor at Ljubljana University and a well-known member of the Marian Movement of Priests, the new dogma heralds a new advent. He describes the events surrounding the proclamation:

An occurrence was manifested in St. Peter's Basilica, Rome. There were about 600 bishops and cardinals and many priests and faithful present. The church was full, and the sky was cloudy, completely covered. The Pope began to read the Bull of the Immaculate Conception of Mary. The clouds parted and a beam of sunlight illuminated the person of the Pope. He was in the sun as he read the text. This was a sign from Heaven, namely that the last period of the Second Advent had begun, and also the role of Mary as the mother of the second coming of Christ, the coming of Christ in glory.[8]

6. Pius IX, *Ubi Primum,* Encyclical Letter, February 2, 1849, http://www.papalencyclicals.net/.
7. Pius IX, *Ubi Nos,* Encyclical Letter, May 15, 1871, http://www.papalencyclicals.net/.
8. Fr. Ivan Pujavnik, *The Church and Fatima,* lectures delivered in October 2000. Translated from German and held on file.

As will be shown with reference to a variety of papal writings, the historical developments brought about by liberalism, rationalism, and other modernist forms, caused the popes of the Marian era to consider whether the present conditions were ripe for the appearance of the Antichrist. For Pius IX, Leo XIII, and the other Roman Pontiffs, devotion to the Virgin Mary came to be seen as an efficacious means to alleviate the dangers being introduced to the world by the spread of modernist ideas.

Pius IX convened the First Vatican Council on December 8, 1869 ostensibly to tackle the threats from modern rationalism and atheism. However, the main result of the Council was to define the dogma of papal infallibility.[9] This dogma states that when the pope speaks *ex cathedra* in matters of faith and morals the Holy Spirit preserves his teaching from error.[10] The act of defining Papal infallibility was a striking response to the challenge of modernism; even so, some prominent churchmen, including Cardinal Newman, were uneasy with the timing of its proclamation.[11] The Council broke up on July 19, 1870, due to the start of the Franco-Prussian war. However, the council was not officially concluded until nearly a century later at the opening of the Second Vatican Council. The reign of Pius IX proved to be the longest since the death of the first pope, St. Peter.

After the death of Pius IX, on February 7, 1878, the conclave of cardinals took only three ballots to choose a new pope: Cardinal Pecci of Perugia who became Leo XIII. His first encyclical, *Inscrutabili Dei*, continued his predecessor's attack on modernism and lamented the evils present in society. However, it was a purportedly mystical experience undergone by Leo XIII which seems to have deepened papal anxieties over the future of humanity. Father Domenico Pechenino gave the following account of Leo XIII's reported experience in the *Ephemerides Liturgicae* magazine in 1995:

9. Joseph Kirch, "Vatican Council," *The Catholic Encyclopedia* (New York: Robert Appleton Company, 1912), accessed May 28, 2012, http://www.newadvent.org/cathen/15303a.html/.

10. *Catechism of the Catholic Church*, 2nd ed., 891.

11. *See* Dulles, Avery Cardinal, "Newman on Infallibility," *Theological Studies* 51 (1990).

I do not remember the exact year. One morning the great Pope Leo XIII had celebrated a Mass, and as usual, was attending a Mass of thanksgiving. Suddenly, we saw him raise his head and stare at something above the celebrant's head. He was staring motionlessly, without batting an eye. His expression was one of horror and awe; the color and look on his face changing rapidly. Something unusual and grave was happening to him.

Finally, as though coming to his senses, he lightly but firmly tapped his head and rose to his feet. He headed for his private office. His retinue followed anxiously and solicitously, whispering: "Holy Father, are you not feeling well? Do you need anything?" He answered: "Nothing, nothing." About half an hour later, he called for the secretary of the Congregation of Rites and, handing him a sheet of paper, requested that it be printed and sent to all the ordinaries [bishops] around the world. What was that paper? It was the prayer that we recite at the end of every Mass. It is the plea of Mary and the passionate request to the Prince of the heavenly host, beseeching God to send Satan back to hell.

Pope Leo XIII instructed all present to kneel during the prayer. What we just reported was published in the newspaper *La settimana del clero*, March 30, 1947, but it does not give the source of the information. However we were able to verify that the prayer, which has become widely known to Catholics as the prayer to St. Michael the Archangel, was indeed sent to the ordinaries in 1886, under unusual circumstances. A reliable witness, Cardinal Nasalli Rocca, in his 1946 Lenten Pastoral Letter to the Diocese of Bologna, wrote:

Leo XIII himself wrote that prayer. The sentence, "The evil spirits who wander through the world for the ruin of souls" has a historical explanation that was many times repeated by his private secretary, Monsignor Rinaldo Angelieo. . . . Leo XIII truly saw, in a vision, demonic spirits who were congregating on the Eternal City [Rome]. The prayer that he asked all the Church to recite was the fruit of that experience. He would recite the prayer with a strong, powerful voice: we heard it many a time at the Vatican Basilica. Leo XIII also personally wrote an exorcism that is included in the Roman Ritual. He recommended that bishops and priests read these exorcisms often in their dioceses and parishes. He himself would recite them often throughout the day.[12]

---

12. Gabriele Amorth, *An Exorcist Tells His Story* (San Francisco: Ignatius Press, 1994), 37.

Until the liturgical reforms of the Second Vatican Council, the prayer to St. Michael the Archangel was recited after every Mass.[13]

Leo XIII's strategy for dealing with the evils of modernism was deeply Marian: he published no fewer than thirteen encyclicals on the subject of the rosary. In *Augustissimae Virginis Mariae* he wrote: "this form of prayer [the rosary] appears, under the guidance of Divine Providence, to have been wonderfully developed at the close of the century, for the purpose of stimulating the lagging piety of the faithful."[14] Leo XIII encouraged the faithful to recite the rosary in public and in large numbers; he believed that there was greater efficacy in public prayer than private: "so as to form as it were a single chorus of supplication; as those words of the Acts of the Apostles clearly declare wherein the disciples of Christ, awaiting the coming of the Holy Spirit, are said to have been "persevering with one mind in prayer" (Acts 1:14). Another element of Leo XIII's strategy against modernism was to impress upon the clergy the importance of unity and obedience to the hierarchy of the Church. Leo XIII perceived an emerging problem of dissent and even the blatant rejection of authentic church teachings by some priests:

> If, then, you desire, as you certainly do, beloved sons, that in the formidable contest being waged against the Church by anti-Christian sects and by the city of the evil one, the victory be for God and His Church, it is absolutely necessary for you to fight all together in perfect order and discipline under the command of your hierarchical leaders. Pay no heed to those pernicious men who, though calling themselves Christians and Catholics, throw tares into the field of the Lord and sow division in His Church.... Can he [the priest] ever forget that on the day of his ordination he promised "obedientiam et reverentiam" to his Bishop before the holy altar?[15]

Perhaps the most strikingly prophetic words uttered by Leo XIII

---

13. John Paul II, "Regina Caeli," April 24, 1994, http://www.vatican.va/.

14. Leo XIII, Encyclical Letter *Augustissimae Virginis Mariae*, September 12, 1897, http:// www.vatican.va/.

15. Leo XIII, Encyclical Letter *Depuis Le Jour*, September 8, 1899, no. 37, http:// www.vatican.va/.

came in his encyclical devoted to the Holy Spirit, *Divinum Illud Munus*, in which he quotes St. Paul's Second Letter to the Thessalonians, specifically the passage concerning the times of the Antichrist. Evidently, the Holy Father perceived great enough evils to suggest that the last times had arrived:

> He who resists the truth through malice and turns away from it, sins most grievously against the Holy Ghost. *In our days this sin has become so frequent that those dark times seem to have come which were foretold by St. Paul*, in which men, blinded by the just judgment of God, should take falsehood for truth, and should believe in "the prince of this world", who is a liar and the father thereof, as a teacher of truth: "God shall send them the operation of error, to believe lying" (2 Thess. 2:10). "In the last times some shall depart from the faith, giving heed to spirits of error and the doctrines of devils" (1 Tim. 4:1).[16]

Towards the end of his papacy, in 1899, Pope Leo XIII carried out arguably the most momentous public act of his pontificate. He consecrated the entire world to the Sacred Heart of Jesus. He seems to have regarded this act as unique in Church history, describing it as "the summit and crowning of all the honors which have been customarily paid to the Most Sacred Heart."[17] This consecration invited all people to bind themselves to the mercy of Jesus, the "King of prodigal sons," as Leo XIII put it, and to be led "into the fight of God and his Kingdom" (formula of Consecration):

> We must have recourse to Him who is the Way, the Truth and the Life. We have gone astray and we must return to the right path: darkness has overshadowed our minds, and the gloom must be dispelled by the light of truth. . . . It will at length be possible that our many wounds be healed and all justice spring forth again with the hope of restored authority; that the splendors of peace be renewed, and swords and arms drop from the hand when all men shall acknowledge the empire of Christ and willingly obey His

16. Leo XIII, Encyclical Letter *Divinum Illud Munus*, May 9, 1897, http://www.vatican.va/.

17. Leo XIII, Encyclical Letter *Annum Sacrum*, May 25, 1899, http:// www.vatican.va/.

word, and "Every tongue shall confess that our Lord Jesus Christ is in the glory of God the Father" (Phil. 2:11).[18]

Leo XIII died in 1903. A part of his legacy was the renewal of devotion to the rosary and the act of consecrating the world to the Sacred Heart of Jesus. He also encouraged Catholics to rediscover Sacred Scripture and warned the clergy of the dangers of non-Catholic influences on their spiritual lives. From a prophetic point of view, his papacy seems to point to a greater intervention from the Holy Spirit in assisting the Marian era popes in discerning the eschatological signs of the times.

It could be stated without too much dispute that the twentieth century was blessed by the Lord with three titanic papal figures, each with the unenviable task of leading the Church through the beginning, middle, and end of the century respectively. They are St. Pius X (1903–1914), Pius XII (1939–1958) and Blessed John Paul II (1978–2005), of unforgettable memory. The new century opened with the ever-growing threat of modernism, and the new pope, Pius X, viewed its threat as perhaps the greatest menace facing humanity. The importance of this magnificent pope cannot be stressed highly enough in our understanding of the prophetic roles of the recent pontiffs.

Commenting on Pius X's election, Cardinal Mathieu of France stated:

> We wanted a pope who had never engaged in politics, whose name would signify peace and concord, who had grown old in the care of souls, who would concern himself with the government of the Church in detail, who would above all be a father and shepherd.[19]

The new pope was a pastor and teacher who gave the highest priority to pastoral issues. He had been a parish priest; by contrast, none of his nineteenth century predecessors had worked in parish ministry. The new pope's reason for choosing the name "Pius" was very clear from the beginning of his ministry in the See of Rome; it

---

18. Ibid., no. 11.
19. Eamon Duffy, *Saints and Sinners: A History of the Popes* (New Haven and London: Yale University Press, 1997), 245.

signaled his desire to continue Pius IX and Leo XIII's fight against modernism. Like his immediate predecessor, Pius X expected total loyalty and obedience to the Vicar of Christ and to his teachings: "When we speak of the Vicar of Christ, we must not quibble, we must obey . . . the one hope, the one remedy, is the Pope."[20]

Pius X chose as his papal motto "to restore all things in Christ." This motto is, of course, Pauline in origin. Pius X laid out his vision of the Church and the world at the dawn of the new century in sobering fashion, in his first encyclical, *E Supremi*, promulgated on October 4, 1903. He wrote:

> We are terrified beyond all else by the disastrous state of human society today. *For who can fail to see that society is at the present time, more than in any past age, suffering from a terrible and deep rooted malady which, developing every day and eating into its inmost being, is dragging it to destruction?* You understand, Brethren, what this disease is—*apostasy from God*, than which in truth nothing is more allied with ruin, according to the word of the Prophet: "For behold they that go far from Thee shall perish." We saw therefore that, in virtue of the ministry of the Pontificate, which was to be entrusted to Us, We must hasten to find a remedy for this great evil.[21]

Pius X's program of restoring all things in Christ reflected a deep concern over a general loss of regard for God in human society, in essence the great apostasy. And pursuing this Pauline line of thought, Pius X speculated about the appearance of the "Son of Perdition" in the same prophetic vein as Leo XIII:

> When all this is considered there is good reason to fear lest this great perversity may be as it were a foretaste, and *perhaps the beginning of those evils which are reserved for the last days*; and that there may be already in the world the "Son of Perdition," of whom the Apostle speaks (1 Thess. 2:3). Such, in truth, is the audacity and the wrath employed everywhere in persecuting religion, in combating the dogmas of the faith, in brazen effort to uproot and

20. Ibid., 246.
21. Pius X, Encyclical Letter *E Supremi*, October 4, 1903, no.3, http:// www.vatican.va/.

destroy all relations between man and the Divinity! *While, on the other hand, and this, according to the same apostle, is the distinguishing mark of Antichrist, man has with infinite temerity put himself in the place of God, raising himself above all that is called God.*[22]

In the face of this modern disregard for God, Pius X exhorted the Church to restore the holy laws of God, to defend the sanctity of marriage, to educate and discipline the youth, and to use Christian precepts and customs to restore harmony within society. For Pius X, holy priests meant a faithful laity. He was adamant that a strict process of admission to seminaries was necessary. He quoted St. Paul's First Letter to Timothy, warning the clergy not to be ensnared by the cunning arguments of rationalism: "guard what has been entrusted to you. Avoid profane babbling and the absurdities of so-called knowledge. By professing it, some people have deviated from the faith" (1 Tim. 6:20).

Pius X added to his predecessor's anti-modernist strategy by increasing the laity's access to the Eucharist and the opportunities for lay participation in church life. He lowered the age of first Holy Communion to seven, and also gave his own catechism classes in the Vatican every Sunday, while supporting an active laity within the Church.[23] In the view of the late Fr. Vincent Miceli, S.J., the form of modernism that most concerned Pius X was freemasonry, which he termed the "synthesis of all heresies."[24] He viewed freemasonry as a particular danger to the integrity of the Church. Pius X considered freemasons to be the secret agents of Modernism. The Church had condemned freemasonry since 1738, and those Catholics who associated themselves with freemasonry were subject to automatic excommunication.[25] In a letter to the French Bishops on

22. Ibid.

23. Umberto Benigni, "Pope Pius X," *The Catholic Encyclopedia.* (New York: Robert Appleton Company, 1911), accessed May 28, 2012, http://www.newadvent.org/cathen/12137a.htm.

24. Vincent P. Miceli, S.J., *The Antichrist,* (Harrison, NY: Roman Catholic Books, 1981), 220.

25. Hermann Gruber, "Masonry (Freemasonry)," *The Catholic Encyclopedia* (New York: Robert Appleton Company, 1910), accessed May 27, 2012, http://www.newadvent.org/cathen/09771a.htm.

August 25, 1910, Pius X warned, alluding to freemasonry, that there was an organized movement in all countries that was committed to forming a new "total church," with no hierarchy, dogma, or regulations; all in the name of freedom and human dignity. Pius X suggested that if successful, it would lead to a world empire of great power.[26]

It was not only the pope who warned of the terrible snares of this demonic movement at the time. In a letter from St. Pio of Pietrelcina (Padre Pio) to Padre Agostino on April 7, 1913, the pain of priestly involvement is evident in the words of Jesus Himself:

> The sight of Jesus in distress was very painful to me, so I asked him why he was suffering so much. . . . There was no reply, but his gaze turned on those priests. Shortly afterwards, as if terrified and weary at looking at them, he withdrew his gaze. Then he raised his eyes and looked at me and to my great horror I observed two tears coursing down his cheeks. He drew back from the crowd of priests with an expression of great disgust on his face and cried out: "Butchers!" Then turning to me he said: "*My son, do not think my agony lasted three hours. No, on account of the souls who have received most from me, I shall be in agony until the end of the world.* During my agony, my son, nobody should sleep. My soul goes in search of a drop of human compassion but alas, I am left alone beneath the weight of indifference. The ingratitude and the sleep of my ministers make my agony all the more grievous. Alas, how little they correspond to my love! What afflicts me most is that they add contempt and unbelief to their indifference. Many times I have been on the point of annihilating them, had I not been held back by the Angels and by souls who are filled with love for me. Write to your [spiritual] father and tell him what you have seen and heard from me this morning. Tell him to show your letter to Father Provincial." Jesus continued to speak, but what he said I could never reveal to any creature in this world. This apparition caused me such bodily pain and even greater pain of soul that I was prostrate for the entire day and believed I should die of this suffering. . . . Unfortunately Jesus had reason to complain of our ingratitude! *How many wretched brothers of ours respond to Jesus'*

---

26. Pujavnik, *The Church and Fatima*.

love by casting themselves with open arms into the infamous sect of Freemasonry![27]

As with his immediate predecessor, there seems to have been a mystical aspect to St. Pius X. He is said to have spoken these words to a Roman prelate:

I saw one of my successors taking to flight over the bodies of his brethren. He will take refuge in disguise somewhere; and after a short retirement he will die a cruel death. The present wickedness of the world is only the beginning of the sorrows that are to take place before the end of the world.[28]

Pope Pius X died on the eve of the First World War, his eternal rest in the Lord assured. The great humility and piety of the saintly pope led to his rapid canonization in 1954. He had led the Church with zeal for the salvation of the World, and instigated a series of reforms that would ultimately pave the way for a deepening sanctification of the laity. Perhaps it is in this last aspect, that we can see a process that would find greater expression and fulfillment in the aftermath of the Second Vatican Council.

Benedict XV succeeded Pius X in 1914. From the start of his pontificate, Pope Benedict seems to have shared the views of his immediate predecessors that the Church and the world might well have arrived at the supremely troubled times predicted in Matthew 24.[29] His first encyclical entitled *Ad Beatissimi Apostolorum* refers to the eschatological discourse of Matthew 24:

For what could prevent the soul of the common Father of all being most deeply distressed by the spectacle presented by Europe, nay, by the whole world, perhaps the saddest and most mournful spectacle of which there is any record. Certainly those days would seem to have come upon us of which Christ Our Lord foretold: "*You shall hear of wars and rumours of wars—for nation shall rise against nation, and kingdom against kingdom*" (Matt. 24: 6, 7). . . . On every

---

27. Pio of Pietrelcina, *Letters vol.* 1, San Giovanni Rotondo, Editions Padre Pio Da Pietrelcina, 1984, 395.

28. Birch, *Trial, Tribulation and Triumph Before, During and After Antichrist,* 378.

29. "For there shall be then great tribulation, such as hath not been from the beginning of the world until now, neither shall be" (Matt. 24:21).

side the dread phantom of war holds sway: there is scarce room for another thought in the minds of men. . . . God grant by His mercy and blessing, that the glad tidings the Angels brought at the birth of the divine redeemer of mankind may soon echo forth as we His Vicar enter upon His Work: "on earth peace to men of good will" (Lk. 2:14).[30]

After describing the Great War as a fulfillment of the prophecy of "nation against nation," Benedict XV goes on to identify a deeper (but by now familiar) cause of the international strife, namely the iniquity besetting man because of his entanglement with all forms of modernism:

> But it is not the present sanguinary strife alone that distresses the nations and fills Us with anxiety and care. There is another evil raging in the inmost heart of human society. . . . Forever since the precepts and practices of Christian wisdom ceased to be observed in the ruling of states, it followed that, as they contained the peace and stability of institutions, the very foundations of states necessarily began to be shaken. *Such, moreover, has been the change in the ideas and the morals of men, that unless God comes soon to our help, the end of civilization would seem to be at hand.*[31]

Benedict thus warned against not only the particular "errors" of modernism but a "spirit of modernism," which he believed to have infected the practice of faith at both institutional and personal levels.[32] Benedict XV, like his predecessor, implored the priests to be obedient to the hierarchy:

> There remains one matter which must not be passed over in silence, and that is, to remind the priests of the whole world, as Our most dear sons, how absolutely necessary it is, *for their own salvation*, and for the fruitfulness of their sacred ministry, that they should be most closely united with their Bishop and most loyal to him. The spirit of insubordination and independence, so characteristic of our times has, as We deplored above, not entirely

---

30. Benedict XV, *Ad Beatissimi Apostolorum*, Encyclical Letter Appealing for Peace, November 1, 1914, http://www.vatican.va/.
31. Ibid.
32. Ibid.

spared the ministers of the Sanctuary.... Let those who have so unfortunately failed in their duty, recall to their minds again and again, that the authority of those whom "the Holy Spirit hath placed as Bishops to rule the Church of God" (Acts 20:28) is a divine authority.[33]

Although the era of Benedict's papacy is best known for the First World War, it also saw the famous Marian apparitions of Fatima, Portugal. Benedict XV had issued this plea to the Mother of God on May 5, 1917, only a matter of days before the first Fatima apparition:

> To Mary, then, who is the Mother of Mercy and omnipotent by Grace, let loving and devout appeal go up from every corner of the earth, from noble temples and tiniest temples, from royal palaces and mansions of the rich as from the poorest hut, from every place wherein a faithful soul finds shelter, from blood-drenched plains and seas. Let it bear to her the anguished cries of mothers and wives, the wailing of innocent little ones, the sighs of every generous heart: that her most tender and benign solicitude may be moved and the peace we ask for be obtained for our agitated world.[34]

If Pius IX and Leo XIII, the first popes of the "new Marian era," were especially concerned with the errors of modernism and with the potential of those errors to bring detriment to humanity, the situation faced by Benedict XV and addressed also by the Fatima message, appears as a turning point, namely the large-scale manifestation of those errors contained within communism and other atheistic regimes. The timing of the Fatima apparitions was striking, just prior to the Russian Revolution and occurring during World War I. In all, the Blessed Virgin is reported to have appeared six times between May and October 1917, in the Cova da Iria, Fatima. The visions mostly occurred on the thirteenth of the month. The main message concerning Russia was given after the visionaries were shown a vision of hell:

---

33. Benedict XV, Encyclical Letter *Ad Beatissimi Apostolorum*, November 1, 1914, no. 3, 4, http://www.vatican.va/.

34. Benedict XV, "Letter to Cardinal Pietro Gasparri," May 5, 1917, http://www.vatican.va/holy_father/benedict_xv/letters/documents /hf_ben-xv_let_191705 05_regina-pacis_it.html/ (Italian only).

You have seen hell where the souls of poor sinners go. To save them, God wishes to establish on earth devotion to My Immaculate Heart. If people do what I tell you many souls will be saved and there will be peace. But if it is not done and if the world does not cease offending God, Divine punishment will manifest itself with newer and even greater punishments. Russia will scatter her errors throughout the world, provoking wars and persecutions of the Church. The good will be martyred, the Holy Father will have much to suffer, and various nations will be annihilated.[35]

Like the devotional and sacramental strategies of the popes discussed previously, the message of Fatima also calls for a specific strategy to further the salvation of the world: spreading devotion to the Immaculate Heart of Mary. The text of Fatima's main message also manifests the same concerns with modernist errors as the Marian popes, but with Russia now identified as the agent spreading those errors. Leo XIII had already defined socialism in his encyclical *Quod Apostolici Muneris*, as "the deadly plague that is creeping into the very fibres of human society and leading it on to the verge of destruction."[36] Having lived through the events of the First World War and the apparitions of Fatima, the pontificate of Benedict XV ended in relative peace in 1922.

The successor of Benedict XV was Achille Ratti, who took the name of Pius XI. He had been consecrated as titular Archbishop of Lepanto by Pope Benedict in 1919, and sent as papal nuncio to Poland. His time there had been eventful. The Russian Revolution had raised the specter of a communist takeover of Eastern Europe. Archbishop Ratti found himself besieged in Warsaw in August 1920, by Bolshevik soldiers, after having refused to leave the city. This experience was to have a lasting effect on his papacy. He viewed communism as a grave threat to the Church. He warned the faithful not to be attracted by its ideology, which was contrary to that of the Gospel:

---

35. Lucia, Mary, *Fatima in Lucia's Own Words* (Fatima: Postulation Center, 1989) 162.

36. Leo XIII, *Quod Apostolici Muneris*, Encyclical Letter on Socialism, December 28, 1878, http:// www.vatican.va/.

See to it, Venerable Brethren, that the faithful do not allow themselves to be deceived: Communism is intrinsically evil, and no one who would save Christian civilization may collaborate with it in any undertaking whatsoever. Those who permit themselves to be deceived into lending their aid towards the triumph of Communism in their own country, will be the first to fall victim of its error. And the greater the antiquity and grandeur of the Christian civilization in the regions where Communism successfully penetrates, so, much more devastating will be the hatred displayed by the godless.[37]

Pius XI had also received a powerful example of the threat to Christianity from militant atheism due to the recent savage persecution in Mexico; a persecution that would bring forth many martyrs destined for canonization:

Where Communism has been able to assert its power—and here We are thinking with special affection of the people of Russia and Mexico—it has striven by every possible means, as its champions openly boast, to destroy Christian civilization and the Christian religion by banishing every remembrance of them from the hearts of men, especially of the young. Bishops and priests were exiled, condemned to forced labor, shot and done to death in inhuman fashion; laymen suspected of defending their religion were vexed, persecuted, dragged off to trial and thrown into prison.[38]

For Pius XI, communism was the most urgent manifestation of the destructive atheism that was sweeping across the globe in the first decades of the twentieth century. The Holy Father was also in union with the views of his recent predecessors in discerning the "signs of the times." In his encyclical, *Miserentissimus Redemptor,* promulgated on May 8, 1928, on reparation to the Sacred Heart, he considered the troubled landscape as one ripe for the appearance of the "man of sin":

Now, how great is the necessity of this expiation or reparation, more especially in this our age, will be manifest to everyone who,

---

37. Pius XI, *Divini Redemptoris*, Encyclical Letter on Atheistic Communism, March 19, 1937, http:// www.vatican.va/.
38. Ibid.

as we said at the outset, will examine the world, "seated in wicked-ness" (1 Jn. 19), with his eyes and with his mind. For from all sides the cry of the peoples who are mourning comes up to us, and their princes or rulers have indeed stood up and met together in one against the Lord and against His Church (cf. Ps. 2:2). Throughout those regions indeed, we see that all rights both human and Divine are confounded. Churches are thrown down and over-turned, religious men and sacred virgins are torn from their homes and are afflicted with abuse, with barbarities, with hunger and imprisonment . . . the whole Christian people, sadly disheart-ened and disrupted, are continually in danger of falling away from the faith, or of suffering the most cruel death. *These things in truth are so sad that you might say that such events foreshadow and por-tend the "beginning of sorrows," that is to say of those that shall be brought by the man of sin, "who is lifted up above all that is called God or is worshipped"* (2 Thes. 2:4).[39]

In His eschatological discourse as recounted in St. Matthew's Gospel, Jesus tells us: "and because of the increase of evildoing, the love of many will grow cold" (Matt. 24:12). Interestingly, Pius XI demonstrates in *Miserentissimus Redemptor* that this prophecy is in the process of its fulfillment now, and thus explains the reason for the mystical revelations given to St. Margaret Mary Alaqoque; namely, devotion to the Sacred Heart as the antidote to this evil:

> Among the many proofs of the boundless benignity of our Redeemer, there is one that stands out conspicuously, to wit the fact that when the charity of Christian people was growing cold, the Divine Charity itself was set forth to be honored by a special worship, and the riches of its bounty was made widely manifest by that form of devotion wherein worship is given to the Most Sacred Heart of Jesus.[40]

Pius XI, furthermore, did see signs of hope in the sanctity of those who battled against the prevailing tide of atheism:

---

39. Pius XI, *Miserentissimus Redemptor,* Encyclical Letter on Reparation to the Sacred Heart, May 8, 1928, http:// www.vatican.va/.
40. Ibid.

With heart deeply grateful to the Father of Light, from Whom descends "every best gift and every perfect gift," We see on all sides consoling signs of this spiritual renewal. We see it not only in so many singularly chosen souls who in these last years have been elevated to the sublime heights of sanctity, and in so many others who with generous hearts are making their way towards the same luminous goal, but also in the new flowering of a deep and practical piety in all classes of society, even the most cultured.[41]

The Holy Father's sense of the world closing in on the prophesied tribulations of the last days is also reflected in his encyclical *Divini Redemptoris*. At the end of this encyclical, Pius XI entrusts the battle for the coming of Christ's Kingdom to St. Joseph and returns to the theme of Pius X's motto, *to restore all things in Christ*:

To hasten the advent of that "peace of Christ in the kingdom of Christ" so ardently desired by all, We place the vast campaign of the Church against world Communism under the standard of St. Joseph, her mighty Protector.... With eyes lifted on high, *our Faith sees the new heavens and the new earth described by Our first Predecessor, St. Peter. While the promises of the false prophets of this earth melt away in blood and tears, the great apocalyptic prophecy of the Redeemer shines forth in heavenly splendor:* "Behold, I make all things new."[42]

Pius XI also reiterated in prophetic terms that it is the poor in spirit who will inherit the Kingdom in its fullness at the end of time (cf. Matt. 5:3):

But the poor too.... Let them remember that the world will never be able to rid itself of misery, sorrow, and tribulation, which are the portion even of those who seem most prosperous. *Patience, therefore, is the need of all, that Christian patience, which comforts the heart with the divine assurance of eternal happiness.* "Be patient, therefore, brethren," we repeat with St. James, "until the coming of the Lord." Behold the husbandman waits for the precious fruit of the earth, patiently bearing until he receives the early and the later

---

41. Pius XI, *Divini Redemptoris*, Encyclical Letter on Atheistic Communism, March 19, 1937, http://www.vatican.va/.
42. Ibid.

rain. *Be you therefore also patient and strengthen your hearts, for the coming of the Lord is at hand.* Only thus will be fulfilled the consoling promise of the Lord: "Blessed are the poor."[43]

By the close of his pontificate, Pius XI had already witnessed some of the events that would lead to the outbreak of World War II. In May 1938, Hitler had visited Rome; in response, the pope left the capital for Castel Gandolfo, explaining that he could not bear "to see raised in Rome another cross which is not the cross of Christ."[44] Pius XI died in 1939, having promoted the recitation of the rosary and reparation to the Sacred Heart of Jesus.

The first day of the new conclave, March 2, 1939, saw the election of Cardinal Pacelli to the See of Peter. He took the name Pius XII. He viewed his role as Supreme Pontiff in a mystical light, understanding the gravity of the task that the Lord had entrusted to him, while discerning the eschatological significance of the "Marian era." The new pope was just as apocalyptic as his predecessors, announcing, "The decisive hour of divine judgment of the world."[45] He was known to go down into the crypt of St. Peter's by night and pray among the graves of his predecessors, no doubt asking for assistance and prayers in a time of great tribulation. Although Pius XII was elected at the beginning of World War II, like Pius XI, he saw the Church's deadliest threat coming from Communism, not Nazism. In 1919, when in Munich he had been threatened by a group of armed Communist insurgents, he stood firm in the face of their hatred, but the episode left him with a deep loathing of everything Communism stood for. As a former papal nuncio, he had witnessed first hand the effects of atheism in many areas of the world. Like Pius IX he was to have the rare distinction of proclaiming a Marian dogma. He also proclaimed the Blessed Virgin as Queen of the world, setting a liturgical feast in honor of the title. Pius XII also continued the official acknowledgement of Fatima by the Holy See, responding to a plea issued by the surviving Fatima visionary, Sr. Lucia, purportedly on

---

43. Ibid.
44. Duffy, *Saints and Sinners: A History of the Popes*, 261.
45. Emilia Pacelli, "In The Light Of Fatima," *L'Osservatore Romano* English ed. 12/19 August 1998, 9.

behalf of the Virgin Mary, that the pope should consecrate Russia to the Immaculate Heart of Mary. The Holy Father recited a formula of Consecration on October 31, 1942 in a radio broadcast to Portugal. Moreover, he often spoke favorably of the Fatima apparitions; in fact he himself was consecrated Bishop, and instantly elevated to the rank of Archbishop, on May 13, 1917, the very day of the first apparition. In 1948, Pius XII had indicated that he saw in the consecration of humankind to the Blessed Virgin Mary a sure and effective way for obtaining from God, the end of the "terrible universal conflagration"[46] against which human means had proven ineffective. In his 1943 encyclical, *Divino Afflante Spiritu*, which continued the theme of exhorting Catholics to read the Bible more, Pius XII turned to the terrible events afflicting the world:

> If these things which We have said, Venerable Brethren and beloved sons, are necessary in every age, much more urgently are they needed in our sorrowful times, when almost all peoples and nations are plunged in a sea of calamities, when a cruel war heaps ruins upon ruins and slaughter upon slaughter, when, owing to the most bitter hatred stirred up among the nations, We perceive with greatest sorrow that in not a few has been extinguished the sense not only of Christian moderation and charity, but also of humanity itself.[47]

In 1943, Pius XII also issued the great encyclical *Mystici Corporis Christi*. In it, he encourages those who are outside the flock of Christ to see in its divine unity, the presence of God, and to look for the gifts the Lord makes available for each and every person in the Catholic Church through the Sacraments. Towards the end of the encyclical Pius XII quotes Jesus' words from Matthew 24:

> We know that if all the sorrows and calamities of these stormy times, by which countless multitudes are being sorely tried, are accepted from God's hands with calm submission, they naturally lift souls above the passing things of earth to those of heaven that abide forever, and arouse a certain secret thirst and intense desire

---

46. Ibid.
47. Pius XII, *Divini Afflante Spiritu*, Encyclical Letter on Promoting Biblical Studies, September 30, 1943, http:// www.vatican.va/.

for spiritual things. Thus, urged by the Holy Spirit, men are moved, and as it were, impelled to seek the kingdom of God with greater diligence.... Moreover, We trust that Our exposition of the doctrine of the Mystical Body of Christ will be acceptable and useful to those also who are without the fold of the Church, not only because their good will toward the Church seems to grow from day to day, but also because, *while before their eyes nation rises up against nation, kingdom against kingdom, and discord is sown everywhere together with the seeds of envy and hatred*, if they turn their gaze to the Church, if they contemplate her divinely-given unity—by which all men of every race are united to Christ in the bond of brotherhood—they will be forced to admire this fellowship in charity, and with the guidance and assistance of divine grace will long to share in the same union and charity.[48]

Pius XII also returned to the theme of reparation, which had been given prominence by Pope Pius XI in his encyclical *Miserentissimus Redemptor* of 1928. He states quite clearly that the faithful have a duty, as never before, to offer sacrifices and do penance to God in order to bring to an end that "terrible universal conflagration" afflicting the entire world:

> There never was a time, Venerable Brethren, when the salvation of souls did not impose on all the duty of associating their sufferings with the torments of our Divine Redeemer. But today that duty is more clear than ever, when a gigantic conflict has set almost the whole world on fire and leaves in its wake so much death, so much misery, so much hardship; in the same way today, in a special manner, it is the duty of all to fly from vice, the attraction of the world, the unrestrained pleasures of the body, and also from worldly frivolity and vanity which contribute nothing to the Christian training of the soul nor to the gaining of Heaven. Rather let those weighty words of Our immortal predecessor Leo the Great be deeply engraven upon our minds, that by Baptism we are made flesh of the Crucified, and that beautiful prayer of St. Ambrose: "Carry me, Christ, on the Cross, which is salvation to

---

48. Pius XII, Encyclical Letter *Mystici Corporis Christi*, June 29, 1943, http://www.vatican.va/.

the wanderers, sole rest for the wearied, wherein alone is life for those who die."[49]

As with the other Marian popes, Pius XII was clearly influenced by St. Louis Marie's Mariology, while manifesting an intense personal devotion to the Virgin Mary. This devotion led him, on many occasions, to implore from the Virgin Mary the gift of peace for the Church and the world. One such example is found in *Doctor Mellifluus*, an encyclical devoted to the memory of St. Bernard of Clairvaux:

> Therefore, as the Doctor of Clairvaux sought and obtained from the Virgin Mother Mary help for the troubles of his times, let us all through the same great devotion and prayer so strive to move our divine Mother, that she will obtain from God timely relief from these grave evils which are either already upon us or may yet befall, and that she who is at once kind and most powerful, will, by the help of God, grant that the true, lasting, and fruitful peace of the Church may at last dawn on all nations and peoples.[50]

Pius XII believed that the Blessed Virgin would bring about the instillation of the Kingdom of Christ, echoing a theological opinion that had been powerfully expressed by St. Louis de Montfort. He also thought of the nineteenth century as the beginning of a "Marian era," as John Paul II has also done, stating in his encyclical *Le Pelerinage de Lourdes*: In many ways the nineteenth century was to become, after the turmoil of the [French] Revolution, a century of Marian favors.[51]

Pius XII also echoes in this encyclical on the anniversary of the Lourdes apparitions one of the well-known statements from those same apparitions: "penance, penance, penance." The same exhortation was also revealed to be a part of the text of the third secret of Fatima released by the Vatican in 2000:

---

49. Ibid.

50. Pius XII, Encyclical Letter *Doctor Mellifluus*, May 24, 1953, http:// www.vatican.va/.

51. Pius XII, Encyclical Letter *Le Pelerinage de Lourdes*, July 2, 1957, http:// www.vatican.va/.

In a society which is barely conscious of the ills which assail it, which conceals its miseries and injustices beneath a prosperous, glittering, and trouble-free exterior, the Immaculate Virgin, whom sin has never touched, manifests herself to an innocent child. With a mother's compassion she looks upon this world redeemed by her Son's blood, where sin accomplishes so much ruin daily, and three times makes her urgent appeal: "Penance, penance, penance!" She even appeals for outward expressions: "Go kiss the earth in penance for sinners." And to this gesture must be added a prayer: "Pray to God for sinners." As in the days of John the Baptist, as at the start of Jesus' ministry, this command, strong and rigorous, shows men the way which leads back to God: "Repent!" Who would dare to say that this appeal for the conversion of hearts is untimely today. . . . "May blind spirits . . . be illumined by the light of truth and justice", Pius XI asked during the Marian feasts of the Jubilee of the Redemption, "so that those who have gone astray into error may be brought back to the straight path, that a just liberty may be granted the Church everywhere, and that an era of peace and true prosperity may come upon all the nations."[52]

Pius XII insisted that to bring about a better future, human beings would have to keep the horrors of war etched into their memories as a warning of what can happen when divisions and cracks appear in international relations. However, he was full of hope for the coming of better times as expressed in his 1944 Christmas address:

> Blessed be the Lord! Out from the mournful groans of sorrow, from the very depths of the heart-rending anguish of oppressed individuals and countries there arises an aura of hope. To an ever-increasing number of noble souls there comes the thought, the will, ever clearer and stronger, to make of this world, this universal upheaval, a starting point for a new era of far-reaching renovation, the complete reorganization of the world. If ever a generation has had to appreciate in the depths of its conscience the call: "war on war," it is certainly the present generation. . . . Having passed, as it has, through an ocean of blood and tears in a form perhaps never experienced in past ages, it has lived through the indescribable

52. Ibid.

atrocities with an intensity such that the recollection of so many horrors must remain stamped in its memory, and even in the deepest recesses of its soul, like a picture of a hell against which anyone who cherishes a sense of humanity desires more than anything else to close the door forever.[53]

Pius XII realized that people in the aftermath of the war years needed hope in the dark hours through which they were living. The significant Marian acts of Pius XII's pontificate, especially the consecration of Russia to the Immaculate Heart of Mary, the proclamation of the dogma of the Assumption and the proclamation of the Queenship of Mary, have as a backdrop this desire of the Pontiff to nurture a Christian hope that would reinvigorate the faithful.

It is against this historic setting that we can especially understand the reason for the proclamation of the dogma of the Blessed Virgin's Assumption into Heaven, body and soul. What does this truth say to the Church of the Marian era? It could seem like a theological clarification of interest only to scholars and academics, but seen in the light of the Church's journey to the New Jerusalem, it becomes the foretaste of our own ultimate liberation. Hope becomes the key word in understanding the dogma because it reveals the final, ultimate victory of God's creatures. Mary, by sharing in Christ's sufferings in a unique way as Co-redemptrix, deserved to share in the resurrection of the saints before the rest of the redeemed; as the Preface to the Mass of the Assumption says: "For today the Virgin Mother of God was assumed into heaven as the beginning and image of your Church's coming to perfection."[54]

It is appropriate here to digest Pope John Paul's teaching on this matter, from a general audience on March 14, 2001:

Certainly, in historical time the Church can be forced to seek refuge in the desert, like ancient Israel on its way to the promised land. Among other things, the desert is the traditional refuge of those pursued, the secret, tranquil place where divine protection is offered (cf. Gn. 21:14–19; 1 Kgs. 19:4–7). However, as the Book of

---

53. Pius XII, "Christmas Radio Message 1944," The Pope Teaches, December 24, 1944.

54. *The CTS New Sunday Missal* (London: Catholic Truth Society, 2011), 1178.

Revelation stresses (cf. 12:6, 14), the woman remains in this refuge for only a limited period. The time of anguish, persecution and trial, then is not indefinite: in the end liberation will come and the hour of glory. *In contemplating this mystery in a Marian perspective, we can say that Mary, at the side of her Son, is the most perfect image of freedom and of the liberation of humanity and of the universe. It is to her as Mother and Model that the Church must look in order to understand in its completeness the meaning of her own mission.* Let us fix our gaze, then, on Mary, the icon of the pilgrim Church in the wilderness of history but on her way to the glorious destination of the heavenly Jerusalem, where she will shine as the Bride of the Lamb, Christ the Lord. The Mother of God, as the Church of the East celebrates her, is the *Hodegetria,* she who "shows the way," that is, Christ, the only mediator for fully encountering the Father. A French poet sees her as "creation in its first honour and its final flowering, as it came forth from God at the dawn of its original splendor" (Claudel, *La vierge à midi,* ed. Pleiade, 540).[55]

It is clear how the traditional teaching of the Church has seen Mary as the "eschatological icon of the Church," and for those weighed down by troubles in the past century, the Lord has given the gift of raising the doctrine of the Assumption to the status of dogma; to be held as belief by all Catholics. As with Leo XIII's vision recounted earlier, there are also certain mystical aspects surrounding the proclamation of the Assumption dogma. Pius XII wrote down the following account of a vision and sent it to one of his cardinals. While walking in the Vatican gardens two days prior to the proclamation he recalled:

> Having lifted up my eyes above the papers I had in my hand, I was struck by a phenomenon I had never seen before. The sun, which was fairly high, looked like a pale yellow opaque globe completely surrounded by a luminous halo, which nevertheless did not prevent me from staring attentively at the sun without the slightest discomfort. A very light cloud was before it. The opaque globe began to move outward, slowly turning over upon itself, and

55. John Paul II, "Mary the Eschatological Icon of the Church," General Audience, March 22, 2001, http://www.vatican.va/.

going from left to right and vice-versa. But within the globe very strong movements could be seen in all clarity and without interruption. The same phenomenon repeated itself the following day, October 31.[56]

Pius XII is reported to have witnessed the purported miracle twice more; on the day of the proclamation and a week later.

One year later, in 1951, Pius XII issued another encyclical, *Evangelii Praecones*, on the promotion of missions throughout the world in which he gave one of his gravest assessments of the state of the world:

> Venerable Brethren, you are well aware that almost the whole human race is today allowing itself to be driven into two opposing camps, for Christ or against Christ. *The human race is involved today in a supreme crisis, which will issue in its salvation by Christ, or in its dire destruction.* The preachers of the Gospel are using their talents and energy to extend the Kingdom of Christ; but there are other preachers who, since they profess materialism and reject all hope of eternal happiness, are trying to drag men down to an abject condition.[57]

Pius XII continued to encourage the faithful to increase their love and devotion to the Virgin Mary through their consecration to her Immaculate Heart. In a speech to the clergy and faithful at Saragossa during a National Congress for the celebration of the Marian year His Holiness stated:

> We believe that today *more than ever*, the whole of humanity ought to run to this port of salvation, which We have indicated at the end of this Marian year, the Most Pure Heart of the Virgin, precisely because the clouds obscure the horizon, because at certain moments the darkness seems to blot out the roads even more because the audacity of the ministers of hell continues to increase. Humanity ought to take refuge in this fortress, it ought to confide

---

56. Michael H. Brown, *The Final Hour* (Milford, OH: Faith Publishing Company, 1992), 102.

57. Pius XII, Encyclical Letter *Evangelii Praecones*, June 2, 1951, no. 70, http://www.vatican.va/.

in this most sweet Heart which, to save us, asks only prayer and penance, asks only on our part a little correspondence.[58]

The same day, addressing the crowd participating in the Archdiocesan Congress of Montevideo, Pius XII said:

> The world passes through a dark hour and the clouds do not manage to disperse completely. Quite the contrary, here and there resound from time to time the cries by which the enemies of the Church celebrate their victories while the good seem greatly confused, deprived, perhaps, of needed union. For this reason our hope is more strong, *and our prayer to the Queen of the heavens is more fervent, as though from her hand alone we hoped for all our salvation.* She has never ceased to be the help of Christians, *Auxilium Christianorum.*[59]

While addressing the crowd of the Tenth International Marian Congress at Lourdes on September 17, 1958, Cardinal Tisserant, Legate of Pope Pius XII, confirmed the pope's thinking on the importance of the act of consecration to the Immaculate Heart of Mary: "He expects from it a definite alleviation of the painful situation in which the Holy Church now finds itself."[60]

These last three papal excerpts were taken from a conference given by Fr. Augustin Fuentes (Postulator for the beatification of Francisco and Jacinta Marto of Fatima) in Jalapa, Mexico on April 21, 1959, shortly after he had interviewed Sr. Lucia, the sole surviving visionary of Fatima. After talking about the value Sr. Lucia placed on suffering, he turned his attention to Pope Pius XII:

> The second part of the message refers to the Holy Father [Pope Pius XII]. He himself did not deny that in 1956 he was miraculously cured by Our Lord. He was gravely ill and praying the "Soul of Christ, sanctify me." When he came to the words, "and bid me come to Thee," he heard Our Lord say to him, "No, your hour has not yet come." The Holy Father arose from his bed and said Mass. Since then he has given everyone the impression of someone who

58. Pius XII, "Address to National Congress in Saragossa during Marian Year of 1954," *Fatima Findings*, vol. XIV, no. 2 (June 1959): 9.
59. Ibid., 10.
60. Ibid., 13.

is working with little time left and is making known his last desires with great urgency. He does not deny that he has seen the Blessed Virgin. He also witnessed the miracle of the sun the day before the proclamation of the dogma of the Assumption. The Holy Father suffers very much at the present time. A proof of this is the following incident. He recently received the primate of Poland, Stefan Wyszynski, in private audience. They spoke over an hour and a half at the end of which he took the Cardinal by the hand to a group who were conversing together. Pius XII then said:

"I love Poland very much because all through the ages she has given proof of her staunch faith with the blood of her bishops and priests, of her faithful of every category and in these times with the sufferings of the Cardinal Primate. How much the Church has suffered! But the Vicar of Christ suffers all these trials in his heart, these and the trials of the entire world. The Pope suffers from all the hate and rancor of humanity and his cross is becoming so heavy that his weak shoulders can no longer carry it." On saying these words, he let go of the Cardinal's hand and, burying his face in his hands, he wept bitterly. Is this not proof of how much the Holy Father needs our support and our prayers, he who carries the Cross of Christ, the cross of the entire human race on his shoulders?[61]

Several speeches by Pius XII give an indication of his thinking about the future of humanity. In 1954 he stated, "You know too Our conviction that the moments through which We are now living are among the most crucial in history. . . . It is our firm conviction that in less time than could be humanly foreseen, evil will be stopped in its tracks."[62] And again to the youth of Italian Catholic Action:

Observe, beloved children, the world in which we live; consider the time which many signs indicate as the most decisive in the history of Christianity. Moreover, it already seems that God is preparing something truly unexpected for the whole of humanity.[63]

61. Ibid., 5.

62. Pius XII, "Message to Young Women's Section of Italian Catholic Action," December 8, 1954, *The Pope Speaks*, 67.

63. Pius XII, "Address to Italian Catholic Action," October 2, 1955, *Acta Apostolicae Sedis*, Pope Pius XII, 723.

This prophetic charism present within the magisterium of Pius XII, contains many references to the glorious future promised by God at the conclusion of history when Jesus returns in glory at His second coming: for instance, certain texts foretell the work of the Holy Spirit in bringing to fruition the new heaven and new earth (cf. Rev. 21:1):

> *You, Lord, see how urgent the times are, and how they grow ever more ready for a deep renewal; send therefore your Spirit and renew the face of the earth: Emitte Spiritum tuum . . . et renovabis faciem terrae. And make this world alive, giving to it a form and a soul,* whilst on the moving waters of the world your Spirit is already freed, oh Lord, just as in the beginning when you created the sky and the earth. And in fact, just as in the beginning Christ sent his Paraclete to the first Apostles, so in these times of decisive changes in the history of the Church, He is calling together multitudes of ever more numerous new apostles for the harvest, to renew them and transform them into capable and ardent builders of a different and better world.[64]

On the Feast of the Immaculate Conception, 1954, Pius XII would again suggest, while imploring the gift of the Holy Spirit, that a glorious future lay ahead for the Church and the world, in a way which could be seen to anticipate Pope John XXIII's prayer for a new Pentecost at the Second Vatican Council:

> We pray Jesus to hasten the day—which must come—in which a new mysterious effusion of the Holy Spirit will come down upon all the soldiers of Christ and He will send them all out among the miseries of the earth, as bearers of salvation. Then there will be better days for the Church; there will be—through the Church— better days for the world.[65]

Six months before his death, Pius XII spoke in the most prophetic terms, seemingly directing us to a time when after a great "winter" of persecution and tribulation, a fruitful and light-filled

---

64. Pius XII, "Address to Italian Catholic Action," May 24, 1953, *Acta Apostolicae Sedis*, Pope Pius XII, 412.

65. Pius XII, "Message to Young Women's Section of Italian Catholic Action," December 8, 1954, *The Pope Speaks*, 69.

summer would come: "The summer is near" (cf. Matt. 24:32). Once again, as with his predecessors, the eschatological discourse of Jesus was the point of reference:

A thousand modern errors have been punished by their own failure: you have seen the pride of some smashed to nothing; certain giant fortunes fail without warning; the mud of wantonness often mixed in the river of tears and blood which have coursed through the world in the past. Other errors, O youth, will have to disappear; other high seats will have to fall; other uncontrolled ambitions will have to crash. The dizzying speed of their ruin will depend upon their boldness in competing with God. *Summer will come, beloved sons; it will come with a rich yield. The earth drenched with tears will smile with pearls of love, and from soil bedewed with blood of martyrs, Christians will spring forth.*[66]

The popes of the Marian era, with the assistance of the Holy Spirit and the intervention of the Blessed Virgin Mary, carefully discerned the signs of the times and courageously proclaimed the reality that for the Church, its final, great struggle against the forces of evil was at hand. By recognizing the maternal mediation of Mary, they placed before the faithful the image of the *Hodegetria*, she who "shows the way" to the Sun of Justice, Jesus Christ. In Mary Most Holy, the Roman Pontiffs perceived the role of the Mother of the Second Advent, who would stay at the foot of the Cross, dispensing the graces necessary for the Church to accept its own crucifixion.

66. Pius XII, "The Springtime of History," Address to the Youth of Italian Catholic Action, March 19, 1958, *The Pope Speaks*, 429.

🌿4🌿
The Second Vatican Council:
The Vision of Eschatological Hope

And do this because you know the time; it is the hour now for you to awake from sleep. For our salvation is nearer now than when we first believed; the night is advanced, the day is at hand. Let us then throw off the works of darkness and put on the armor of light; let us conduct ourselves properly as in the day, not in orgies and drunkenness, not in promiscuity and licentiousness, not in rivalry and jealousy. But put on the Lord Jesus Christ, and make no provision for the desires of the flesh. (Rom. 13:11–14)

POPE PIUS XII died on October 9, 1958 after two decades in the See of Peter. Two weeks later, the Conclave elected the seventy-seven year old Patriarch of Venice, Angelo Roncalli, a Vatican diplomat who was known for his holiness and peaceful character. Seemingly, the idea behind his election was to give the Church some time to reflect on the legacy left by Pope Pius XII, before a younger, more energetic cardinal would ascend St. Peter's Throne. If proof were ever needed that the Holy Spirit "blows where He wills" (cf. Jn. 3:8), then here was the evidence.

The new pope, taking the name John XXIII, decided that he would be the one to set the agenda for the Church in the second half of the twentieth century; doing this most spectacularly with the calling of an Ecumenical Council, less than three months after his election. Pope John XXIII wanted to open up the Church to the modern world, not by embracing the ideals of the world, but rather by confronting them in a pastoral way. Reconciliation and brotherhood were strong themes of his pontificate. The Second Vatican Council would be ecumenical; it would renew the liturgy and would address the area of collegiality between the pope and the bishops of the world. Before looking at the Council in an eschatological light, it is appropriate to look deeper into the mind of the new pope to discover what his thoughts were, and above all what the Holy Spirit was saying to him.

It cannot be denied that the new pope seemed to have a great deal more optimism than his predecessors in terms of the direction of the Church and the world. It appears that the Lord was gradually reminding the Church after the terrible years of World War II that better days were coming, a reminder that for the Christian, joy and hope should be central pillars of their spiritual life, for with every passing day, the Kingdom of God draws ever closer to humanity. In an ironic sense, the more the world goes away from God, the closer he draws it to himself; preparing in a decisive way, its complete renewal at the end of time. It would seem that the Holy Spirit was guiding the pontiff in this direction; after all, the liturgy at Mass says: "as we await the blessed hope and the coming of our Savior, Jesus Christ."[1] The nuclear age had dawned and there was the real possibility of the total destruction of the planet, especially with the Cuban Missile Crisis of the early sixties. The peoples of the world needed a new message to inspire them, and Pope John XXIII was universally recognized for his ability to deliver it.

The choice of the name "John," is important in our understanding of his role in this eschatological drama, for in a speech given on December 23, 1959, the Holy Father gave some very interesting insights as to why he chose the name:

A year ago the new successor of St. Peter, still trembling under the first emotions of the lofty mission conferred on him as pastor of the Universal Church, somewhat shy about the name of John which he had chosen for himself in token of a good will that was at once anxious yet firm with regard to the programme *for preparing the ways of the Lord,* suddenly thought of the valleys to be filled and the mountains to be brought low, and he began to advance on his way. And then, day-by-day, he was to recognize in great humility of spirit that truly the hand of the Most High was with him. . . .

1. *The CTS New Sunday Missal* (London: Catholic Truth Society, 2011), 633.

The task of humble Pope John is to "prepare for the Lord a perfect people," which is exactly like the task of the Baptist, who is his patron and from whom he takes his name. And it is not possible to imagine a higher and more precious perfection than that of the triumph of Christian peace, which is peace of heart, peace in the social order, in life, in wellbeing, in mutual respect, and in the brotherhood of all nations.[2]

We know that St. John the Baptist's role was to prepare the way for the first coming of Jesus,[3] therefore it is significant that the pope saw his role in a similar light. The insinuation is that Pope John sensed the triumph of Christ nearing, and so his papacy and the Ecumenical Council would be two means of preparing the way of the Lord. On November 13, 1960, the pope explained that the Council's aim was to restore the Church to its original beauty, as it was when the Holy Spirit descended on the Apostles and the Blessed Virgin in that first cenacle of prayer. There is a tradition that just as the Church began with a small faithful group, so it would end in the same way with a remnant who would await the return of Jesus in glory amidst the final persecutions of the world:

> Everything that the new Ecumenical Council is to do is really aimed at restoring to full splendor the simple and pure lines that the face of the Church of Jesus had at its birth, and at presenting it as its divine founder made it: *sine macula et sine ruga . . .* the highest and noblest aim of the Ecumenical Council . . . is to pause a little in a loving study of the Church and try to rediscover the lines of her more fervent youth, and to reconstruct them in a way that will reveal their power over modern minds that are tempted and deceived by the false theories of the prince of this world, the open or hidden adversary of the Son of God, Redeemer and Savior.[4]

---

2. John XXIII, "Address of 23 December 1959," *The Encyclicals and Other Messages of John XXIII* (The Pope Speaks Press, 1964).

3. In the wilderness prepare the way of the Lord! Make straight in the wasteland a highway for our God! Every valley shall be lifted up, every mountain and hill made low; the rugged land shall be a plain, the rough country, a broad valley. Then the glory of the Lord shall be revealed, and all flesh shall see it together; for the mouth of the Lord has spoken (Is. 40: 3–5).

4. John XXIII, *The Encyclicals and Other Messages of John XXIII.*

The Vision of Eschatological Hope

A year later on September 10, 1961, the Holy Father expanded his thoughts on the value of the Council, by suggesting that it would promote the gathering of all nations under the sovereignty of Christ. Reiterating the absolute importance of the Marian era, Blessed John XXIII petitioned the Blessed Virgin, proclaiming: "This is your hour, O Mary!" imploring her intercession for the peace of Christ to be granted to the world:

> Reflect that the Catholic Church, scattered throughout a world that is today, alas, troubled and divided, is preparing for a universal gathering—the ecumenical council—which is aimed at the promotion of that true brotherhood of nations which exalts Christ Jesus, the glorious and immortal King of ages and of peoples, light of the world, and the way, the truth, and the life. And finally we turn to you, O Blessed Virgin Mary, mother of Jesus and our mother also. How can we, with trembling hearts, apply ourselves to this greatest problem of life or death, which overshadows all mankind, without confiding ourselves to your intercession to preserve us *a periculis cunctis? This is your hour, O Mary!* Blessed Jesus entrusted us to you in the supreme moment of His bloody sacrifice. *We are certain of your intervention.* . . . O our most sweet mother, O Queen of the World! Of victorious war or of a conquered people there is no need, but of a renewed and more robust state of safety, of fruitful and serene peace. Of this there is need, and for this we cry out in a loud voice: *salutis exordium et pacis incrementum. Amen. Amen.*[5]

Without doubt, the most prophetic admissions concerning the Council's eschatological orientation came from the radio address he gave on September 11, 1962, exactly one month before the Council convened:

> The prophetic words of Jesus, pronounced in view of the *final consummation of the world,* inspire the good and generous dispositions of men—*especially at certain periods in history*—to a fresh start toward the highest peaks: "Lift up your heads, because your redemption is at hand" (cf. Lk. 21:28–33). Considered in its spiritual preparation; *the Council which is to meet in a few weeks, seems*

5. Ibid.

to merit that invitation of Our Lord: "Behold the fig tree, and all the trees. When they put forth their buds, you know that summer is near. Even so, when you see these things coming to pass, know that the kingdom of God is near."[6]

The analogy of the "summer" (cf. Matt. 24:32), we may recall, was used by Pope Pius XII several years earlier and would later be used by Pope John Paul II.[7] It is a most beautiful analogy because it directs our hearts to the brilliant light of God that will disperse the dark clouds of sin and death, illuminating the renewed creation at the end of time in the Kingdom of God. For Pope John XXIII to speak of the *final consummation* in the context of the Council is certainly striking; and in the context of his knowledge of the Fatima third secret, most enlightening.

Returning to the idea that Pope John viewed his own papacy as a prophetic one, we have clear evidence of this not only from his explanation of why he chose the name "John," but also from his Easter Urbi et Orbi Blessing of 1962, echoing the remarkably direct words from his great predecessor's Easter 1957 exclamation[8] concerning the nearness of the second coming:

> Accept this blessing [Urbi et Orbi blessing]; take it to your families, your homes and extend it there especially, where there is suffering, misfortune, but also hope and confidence. *It truly signals the return of the victorious Christ, the Bearer everywhere of peace, serenity, and fraternal love.*[9]

Pope John XXIII had a great devotion to the Mother of God; his encyclical *Grata Recordatio* bears testimony to that, as does the

---

6. John XXIII, "Nuntius Radiophonicus: Universis catholici orbis christifidelibus, mense ante quam Oecumenicum Concilium sumeret initium." *AAS* 54 (1962): 678–685. See English translation: John XXIII, "Opening Address," *Catholic Documents*, 4 (1964), 21–27.

7. John Paul II, "Address at the Ordinary Public Consistory," *L'Osservatore Romano*, English. ed. February 25, 1998, 2.

8. "Come Lord Jesus, there are numerous signs that Thy return is not far off" *AAS* (1957): 280.

9. John XXIII, "Easter Urbi et Orbi address," April 22, 1962, *AAS* 54 (1962): 281–286.

well-known rosary meditations that he composed. In his Apostolic Letter *The Rosary* he states:

> The rosary of Mary assumes the dignity of a great public and universal prayer, to express the ordinary and extraordinary needs of Holy Church, of the nations and of the whole world. In the history of the most powerful states of Europe there have been some periods of great, indeed of the greatest danger, because of a series of events which have stained them with tears and blood. Those who study the developments of political events from the historical point of view know well the influence exerted by Marian devotions in preserving the nations from the calamities which threatened them, in the restoration of prosperity and social order and in the achievements of spiritual victories.[10]

Although Pope John was optimistic, he was nevertheless not blind to the reality of a deepening crisis instigated by the enemies of Christ. His encyclical *Aeterna Dei Sapientia*, dedicated to the memory of Pope Leo the Great, clearly displays the same distress at the state of mankind felt by his predecessors:

> Venerable Brethren, the fifteenth centenary of the death of St. Leo the Great, finds the Catholic Church in much the same plight as she was at the turn of the fifth century. The same waves of bitter hostility break upon her. How many violent storms does she not enter in these days of ours—storms which trouble Our fatherly heart, even though our Divine Redeemer clearly forewarned us of them! On every side We see "the faith of the gospel" imperiled. In some quarters an attempt is being made—usually to no avail—to induce bishops, priests, and faithful to withdraw their allegiance from this See of Rome, the stronghold of Catholic unity. To rid the Church of these dangers We confidently invoke the patronage of that most vigilant of Popes who labored and wrote and suffered so much for the cause of Catholic unity.... *Then let the battle commence in earnest, as we strive with might and main to resist the adversary's assaults who in so many parts of the world is threatening to annihilate our Christian faith.*[11]

10. John XXIII, *Journal of a Soul* (Geoffrey Chapman, 1965), 429.
11. John XXIII, Encyclical Letter *Aeterna Dei Sapientia*, 1961, no. 70–73, http://www.vatican.va/.

These somber words spoken in 1961 portray a picture of a battle being waged for souls; for the pope to suggest that the enemy is threatening the annihilation of Christianity is further evidence that his views are in union with his predecessors. In terms of the Council, the Holy Father was taking a far-sighted view as to whether it would ultimately be successful. To a group of seminarians, he said: "You see how the Church operates: she sows in one century and reaps in subsequent ones by means of her councils, her synods, and her canonical rulings."[12] Interestingly, in the same speech he exhorted them to take the Book of Revelation as their guide:

> "Take the scroll and eat it up" (Rev. 10:9). *Always keep the prophetic symbols of the Apocalypse before your eyes*: it is the angel standing on the sea and the earth who, obeying the command uttered by the voice from heaven, offers the Sacred Book to you, just as he offered it to John the Apostle. What a meaningful symbol this is for the Church, who reaches across continents and hands you her precious treasure! The Book indicates the will of God for each one of us: it points to the right conduct of life and to the secret of success in any effective form of the apostolate; in other words, the kind of apostolate which does not crave human results—indeed, such may not be forthcoming.... New soldiers of the modern age...*you will, with ardent desire and action, devote yourselves to the unification of all humanity in Christ.*[13]

At this point, a deeper discussion of the Second Vatican Council and its meaning for the Church is necessary. We have already seen some of Pope John XXIII's reasons for calling the Council, but in the light of the journey in which the Church is following Christ, towards the new heaven and new earth (Rev. 21:1), it is clear that it is of paramount importance. Firstly, it is appropriate to mention the debate that has raged in recent years as to whether the Council was good or bad for the Church; some even refuse to accept it at all. The Council came from God, of that there is no doubt. Every pope since the Council has reaffirmed its relevance and has tried constantly to

---

12. John XXIII, "Address to Seminarians," *The Encyclicals and Other Messages of John XXIII* (The Pope Speaks Press, 1964), 102–111.

13. Ibid.

implement its teaching, restating that is not what the Council Fathers taught that has caused the problems; rather the dubious interpretations that many Catholics including priests and bishops have given it.[14] In *Tertio Millennio Adveniente*, the Apostolic Letter of Pope John Paul II, he stated: "The Second Vatican Council was a providential event, whereby the Church began the more immediate preparation for the Jubilee of the Second Millennium." He added, "The best preparation for the new millennium, therefore, can only be expressed in a renewed commitment *to apply*, as faithfully as possible, *the teachings of* Vatican II *to the life of every individual and of the whole Church*."[15]

We may recall that Blessed John XXIII prayed that God would grant us a "Second Pentecost" at the opening of the Council; in fact he also suggested that the Lord was preparing a new era for mankind:

In the present order of things, Divine Providence is leading us to a new order of human relations which, by men's own efforts and even beyond their very expectations, are directed toward the *fulfillment of God's superior and inscrutable designs*. And everything, even human differences, leads to the greater good of the Church.[16]

What, we may ask are God's superior and inscrutable designs? They are the restoration of all things in Christ "in heaven and on earth." (Eph. 1:10). The pope went even further in his explanation of the Council's importance in his apostolic exhortation *Sacrae Laudis*:

The Ecumenical Council will surely be, even more than a new and magnificent Pentecost, *a real and new Epiphany*, one of the many revelations which have been renewed and are continually being renewed in the course of history, *but one of the greatest of all. . . . We may already say that we all feel we are within sight of a new era*,

14. Of relevance here is the important address of Pope Benedict XVI to the Roman Curia on December 22, 2005, available at http://www.vatican.va/.

15. John Paul II, Apostolic Letter *Tertio Millenio Adveniente*, November 10, 1994, London, Catholic Truth Society nos. 18, 20.

16. John XXIII, "Address at the Opening of Second Vatican Council," October 11, 1962, http://www.vatican.va/.

founded on our fidelity to our ancient treasury of faith, and opening on to the wonders of real spiritual progress: a progress which from Christ alone, the glorious and immortal King of all ages and peoples, can draw dignity, prosperity, and blessing.[17]

In his opening address of Vatican II on October 11, 1962, Pope John reiterated the desire of the Council to help bring about the spiritual renewal of the Church and the world so that it would be ready to receive the heavenly city at the end of time:

> Venerable brothers, such is the aim of the Second Vatican Ecumenical Council, which, while bringing together the Church's best energies and striving to have men welcome more favorably the good tidings of salvation, *prepares*, as it were, and consolidates the path toward that unity of mankind which is required as a necessary foundation, in order that the earthly city may be brought to the resemblance of that heavenly city where truth reigns, charity is the law, and whose extent is eternity (cf. Augustine, Epistle 138, 3).[18]

Although the years since the Council have seen considerable internal tensions concerning the value of it, there are certainly positive fruits which have yielded a rich harvest in vocations to the religious life. The Church has witnessed the birth of many prayer groups, religious associations and movements since Vatican II. Several years before his election, our present Pontiff, Benedict XVI shed some light on their development within the Church:

> What sounds full of hope throughout the Universal Church—and this even in the midst of the crisis that the Church is going through in the Western world—is the upsurge of new movements that no one has planned and no one called into being.... I am thinking for instance of the Charismatic Renewal movement, the Neocatechumenals, the Cursillo movement, the Focolarini, Communion and Liberation, and so on.... In the heart of a world desiccated by rationalistic skepticism a new experience of the Holy Spirit has come about, amounting to a worldwide renewal move-

---

17. John XXIII, *Sacrae Laudis*, Apostolic Exhortation, *John XXIII, Journal of a Soul* (Geoffrey Chapman, 1965), 509.

18. John XXIII, "Address at the Opening of Second Vatican Council," October 11, 1962, http://www.vatican.va/.

ment. What the New Testament describes, with reference to the charisms, as visible signs of the coming of the Spirit, is no longer merely ancient, past history: this history is becoming a burning reality today.[19]

The Holy Spirit is the agent of that new missionary endeavor begun by the Council; it is he who guides the Church onwards towards its eternal destiny. Jesus Christ himself gave the Apostles the gift of the Holy Spirit in the Upper Room after his Resurrection. In fact, he suggested the necessity of his ascension in order for the "Advocate" to come: "It is better for you that I go. Because if I do not go, the Advocate will not come to you" (Jn. 16:7). In a mysterious development, after completing the work of the redemption, Jesus enlightens the Apostles understanding, that the Holy Spirit's task is to bring about the sanctification of the Church. The Savior returns to heaven in order to plead for us at the right hand of the Father while the Spirit of Love and Truth works to bring the new creation inaugurated by the Resurrection to the rest of humanity. Thus we can truly say that through the infinite merits of Jesus' redemptive passion, the Holy Spirit, the Spirit of the Father and the Son, is poured into the hearts of every faithful follower of Christ to teach and inspire, until the work of salvation reaches a universal dimension through the proclamation of the Gospel *ad Gentes*.

The Paschal Mystery of Christ is made present to us through the sacraments, and so, in a sense, there is always a "new coming" of Jesus, as explained by St. Bernard as the *adventus medius*.[20] But unlike his mission on earth before the passion, this new coming takes place through the action of the Holy Spirit. The Lord said to his Apostles at the Last Supper, "I will not leave you orphans, I will come back to you" (Jn. 14:18). Of course the sacrament par excellence is the Eucharist, the Body, Blood, Soul, and Divinity of Jesus. This sacramental presence of the Lord is accomplished by the power of the Holy Spirit, as the Second Eucharistic Prayer says: "Make

---

19. Joseph Cardinal Ratzinger, *The Ratzinger Report* (San Francisco: Ignatius Press, 1985), 43, 151.

20. Bernard of Clairvaux, "Sermo 5, In Adventu Domini, 1–3," *Opera Omnia*, Edit. Cisterc. 4 (1966), 188–190.

holy, therefore, these gifts, we pray, by sending down your Spirit upon them like the dewfall, so that they may become for us the Body and Blood of our Lord Jesus Christ."[21] It is his overwhelming love which is capable of burning away all evil from the face of the earth, as the Psalmist says: "Send forth your spirit, they are created and you renew the face of the earth." (Ps. 104:30) To this we can add: "The Spirit and the Bride say, 'Come'" (Rev. 22:17). It becomes clear that the Paraclete inspires the prayer of the Church to hasten the second advent of Jesus when he will come in glory as King and Judge; these new movements are all gifts from the Holy Spirit, bringing forth a new and deeper awareness of His presence, especially among the laity.

The Blessed Virgin Mary, spouse of the Holy Spirit, teaches us to have confidence in His ability to change hearts, to bring about conversions in families and to obtain the joy and peace of Christ. It is correct to say that there are different aspects of the same mystery at work where spirituality is concerned within Charismatic and Marian movements. Many feel threatened by the Charismatic Renewal and the gifts associated with it, but its presence in the Church as with Marian groups, under the guidance of and in obedience to the hierarchy, will be essential in the task of the new evangelization. In time, many of their number could well be asked to offer up the ultimate sacrifice.

In certain documents of the Second Vatican Council, there are explicit references to the times in which the Council took place, and those to come in the future. It was a prophetic Council, an area that seems to have been forgotten amongst the arguments about liberalism in the Church. The decree on the Church's missionary activity, *Ad Gentes*, clearly demonstrates that the Council's mission was to prepare for the Lord's return while recognizing a "new situation" developing in the world:

> In the present state of affairs, out of which there is arising a new situation for mankind, the Church, being the salt of the earth and the light of the world (cf. Matt. 5:13–14), is *more urgently called*

---

21. *The CTS New Sunday Missal*, 605.

*upon to save and renew every creature, that all things may be restored in Chris*t and all men may constitute one family in Him and one people of God.... Therefore, this sacred synod, while rendering thanks to God for the excellent results that have been achieved through the whole Church's great-hearted endeavor, desires to sketch the principles of missionary activity and to rally the forces of all the faithful in order that the people of God, marching along the narrow way of the Cross, may spread everywhere the reign of Christ, Lord and overseer of the ages (cf. Ecc. 36:19), *and may prepare the way for his coming.* ... And so the time for missionary activity extends between the first coming of the Lord and the second, in which latter the Church will be gathered from the four winds like a harvest into the kingdom of God. For the Gospel must be preached to all nations before the Lord shall come (cf. Mark 13:10).[22]

Other texts also speak of our apocalyptic times. The Pastoral Constitution of the Church *Gaudium et Spes* recalls the idea that the Church is the Kingdom of God in its initial stage and that, in itself, it is a "sacrament" charged with the responsibility of bringing the salvation won for us by Jesus Christ to all humanity, without exception:

Coming forth from the eternal Father's love, founded in time by Christ the Redeemer and made one in the Holy Spirit, the Church has a saving and an eschatological purpose which can be fully attained only in the future world. But she is already present in this world, and is composed of men, that is, of members of the earthly city who have a call to form the family of God's children during the present history of the human race, and to keep increasing it until the Lord returns. While helping the world and receiving many benefits from it, *the Church has a single intention: that God's kingdom may come, and that the salvation of the whole human race may come to pass.* ... The Lord is the goal of human history, the focal point of the longings of history and of civilization, the center of the human race, the joy of every heart and the answer to all its yearnings. He it is whom the Father raised from the dead, lifted on

22. Second Vatican Council, Missionary Decree *Ad Gentes*, nos. 1, 9, http://www.vatican.va/.

high and stationed at His right hand, making Him judge of the living and the dead. Enlivened and united in His Spirit, we journey toward the consummation of human history, one which fully accords with the counsel of God's love: "To re-establish all things in Christ, both those in the heavens and those on the earth" (Eph. 1:10).[23]

The document further warns in stark terms that unless the world converts, there is a danger that the destruction of humanity beckons:

Unless enmities and hatred are put away and firm, honest agreements concerning world peace are reached in the future, humanity, which already is in the middle of a grave crisis, even though it is endowed with remarkable knowledge, will perhaps be brought to that dismal hour in which it will experience no peace other than the dreadful peace of death. But, while we say this, the Church of Christ, present in the midst of the anxiety of this age, does not cease to hope most firmly. She intends to propose to our age over and over again, in season and out of season, this apostolic message: "Behold, now is the acceptable time for a change of heart; behold! Now is the day of salvation."[24]

However, a prophetic message of hope reminds us of ultimate victory. The Lord himself speaks: "Behold, I am coming soon. I bring with me the recompense I will give to each according to his deeds. I am the Alpha and the Omega, the first and the last, the beginning and the end" (Rev. 22:12–13).[25]

The Dogmatic Constitution *Lumen Gentium,* enlarges the scope of the contribution made by the Council Fathers to this subject, recalling the truth that we are in the end times already, leaving no room for heretical millenarianist views:

Already the final age of the world has come upon us and the renovation of the world is irrevocably decreed and is already anticipated in some kind of a real way; for the Church already on this earth is

---

23. Second Vatican Council, Pastoral Constitution *Gaudium et Spes,* no. 40, http://www.vatican.va/.
24. Ibid., nos. 81, 82.
25. Ibid., no. 45.

signed with a sanctity which is real although imperfect. However, until there shall be new heavens and a new earth in which justice dwells, the pilgrim Church in her sacraments and institutions, which pertain to this present time, has the appearance of this world which is passing and she herself dwells among creatures who groan and travail in pain until now and await the revelation of the sons of God. . . . Reckoning therefore that "the sufferings of the present time are not worthy to be compared with the glory to come that will be revealed in us," strong in faith *we look for the "blessed hope and the glorious coming of our great God and Savior, Jesus Christ who will refashion the body of our lowliness, conforming it to the body of His glory."* And who will come "to be glorified in His saints and to be marveled at in all those who have believed."[26]

Vatican II also reaffirmed the role of our Blessed Mother in preparing the Church for the second coming of the risen Christ:

In the interim just as the Mother of Jesus, glorified in body and soul in heaven, is the image and beginning of the Church as it is to be perfected in the world to come, so too does she shine forth on earth, until the day of the Lord shall come, as a sign of sure hope and solace to the people of God during its sojourn on earth.[27]

Pope John Paul II, in his 1987 encyclical *Redemptoris Mater,* taught that Mary would be present in the Church until the end of the world: "*She also has that specifically maternal role of mediatrix of mercy at his final coming.*"[28]

The Mariology of the end times as taught by the popes and the Council reflects the seriousness of the message of Fatima, in which Our Lord stated his desire to Sr. Lucia that the Church place devotion to the Immaculate Heart of Mary alongside the already established devotion to his Sacred Heart. Sr. Lucia expressed her view that the Lord was preparing the world for the end in an interview with Fr. Augustin Fuentes, the former postulator of the Causes for

26. Second Vatican Council, Dogmatic Constitution *Lumen Gentium*, no. 48, http://www.vatican.va/.

27. Ibid., no. 68.

28. John Paul II, Encyclical Letter *Redemptoris Mater*, March 25, 1987, http://www.vatican.va/.

Beatification of Jacinta and Francisco Marto. The interview took place on December 26, 1957. Fr. Fuentes quotes Our Lady's words to Sr. Lucia: "The last means that God will give to the world for its salvation are the Holy Rosary and My Immaculate Heart."[29] He mentions that Sr. Lucia was given to understand by Our Lady that the world was living in the last phase of the end times[30] for two other reasons: Firstly, because the world was going through a decisive battle in which there would be no room for sitting on the fence; people would have to choose between either God, or Satan. And secondly, that whenever Our Lord determines to chastise the world, he first uses every means to save humanity, and seeing that this fails, he sends the Blessed Virgin and Mother as the last anchor of salvation.

This sheds further light on the eschatological Marian era. It is part of the new evangelization in which God has called upon apostles in love with Mary's Immaculate Heart to help spread the devotion as rapidly as possible. In fact the Polish pontiff had on many occasions called Our Lady the "Star of the New Evangelization." It is known that Our Lady told Sr. Lucia that God wished her to remain on earth for much longer than her cousins to help promote the message of salvation through Mary. There have been other wonderful examples of Marian apostles, most notably St. Maximilian Kolbe, the great martyr of Auschwitz who took the place of a family man condemned to death by starvation in that infamous concentration camp. At the Basilica of St. Mary Major on December 8, 1982, the year of St. Maximilian's canonization, Pope John Paul stated:

> Maximilian Kolbe pondered with extraordinary acumen the mystery of the Immaculate Conception of Mary in the light of Sacred Scripture, the Magisterium and Liturgy of the Church, finding therein wondrous lessons for life. *He has appeared in our times as prophet and apostle of a new "Marian era,"* destined to spread splendor throughout the world on Jesus Christ and his Gospel. This mission which he promoted with such ardor and dedication

---

29. Augustin Fuentes, "Interview with Sr. Lucia," December 26, 1957, *Fatima Findings*, Vol. XIV, 5, no. 2.

30. From a theological point of view, the end times formally began with Pentecost and the birth of the Church in Jerusalem.

"classifies him," as Pope Paul VI affirmed in the homily for his beatification, "among the great Saints and discerning spirits who have understood, venerated, and sung the mystery of Mary."[31]

Anyone who loves Mary and tries to imitate her will surely grow in those great virtues so present in the beauty of her soul, thus learning to love Jesus as she does. For where hatred reigns, Mary teaches love. Where pride reigns, Mary teaches humility. Where impurity reigns, Mary teaches purity. Where disobedience reigns, Mary teaches obedience. These are the standards set by the Blessed Virgin, because she does not want us to settle for mediocrity. She has taken to heart the words of Jesus: "Be perfect just as your heavenly Father is perfect" (Matt. 5:48) and her maternal love desires to present each one of her children to Jesus at their particular judgment spotless and pure. As this is true for the individual judgment, so it is true for the Last Judgment when her role as Mediatrix of mercy will shine forth for the final time. This helps to explain Pope Paul VI's decision to proclaim Mary "Mother of the Church" at the end of the Second Vatican Council; for just as Mary is the Mother of the Redeemer, so she is also Mother of the redeemed. This act of Paul VI confirmed the confidence that the Council had in Mary's ability to protect and intercede for the Church on its pilgrim way.

The papacy of John XXIII ended on June 3, 1963, after only five years. It was the shortest reign for two centuries, and yet remarkably changed the course of history for the Church and the world. The pope had focused the Church's attention towards the new era, reminding his flock of the plan of salvation, and perhaps especially, the glory of its completion. It was the emphasis of hope and optimism that was his lasting legacy. In view of his great reputation for holiness, John XXIII was declared Blessed alongside Pope Pius IX on September 3, 2000, in St. Peter's Square by Pope John Paul II.[32]

---

31. *Kolbe, Saint of the Immaculata* (New Bedford: Franciscans of the Immaculate, 2001), 221.

32. Pope John Paul stated in the beatification homily: "The Council was a truly prophetic insight of this elderly Pontiff who, even amid many difficulties, opened a season of hope for Christians and for humanity." Available at http://www.vatican.va/.

On June 21, 1963, the papal torch was handed on to Cardinal Giovanni Battista Montini, the Archbishop of Milan. He took the name Paul VI, and to him was given the task of completing the Council and implementing its teachings. He would also speak prophetically of the coming of the Kingdom, as well as of Satan's growing activity within the Catholic Church.

From the very beginning of his pontificate, Pope Paul VI suggested that there would be three specific issues within the Church that he would address; the first, that the Church look within itself, to discover anew its mystery; the mystery hidden in God from the beginning of time until the birth of the Church at Pentecost. Secondly, to bring the members of the Church to a clearer realization of their own duty to correct faults, to strive for perfection and so bring forth the renewal of the Church. Thirdly, the mission to bring men together in mutual love through the power of that kingdom of justice and peace which Christ inaugurated by His coming into the world. It was a programme of renewal intimately linked with the Council, notably the insistence on the self-examination of the laity. For the Kingdom to spread, the laity would have to participate in a greater, more radical way, especially as the number of vocations to the priesthood would continue to diminish.

In many ways, it was Pope Paul VI who began the second evangelization. He began the papal pilgrimages, visiting among other places India, America, and the Holy Land. His rallying call to prepare for the coming of the Kingdom came from the earliest days of his reign. For example, while in India in 1964 at the episcopal ordination of several bishops, he said:

> Just as Christ, Whose ministry We now personify, said to His disciples when He had made them Apostles, that is, messengers of His word and His grace, so We say to you, who are consecrated to that same mission: Go, preach the message: *The kingdom of heaven is at hand!*. . . . Go, then, Shepherds, on all the roads of the earth; go, reveal to the peoples their dignity, their freedom, their mission on this earth and in the next world. Your journey will not be an easy one, but do not fear, for the Lord is with you . . . *you will mark off each hour of human history, until the end of time, with this supreme*

desire and this supreme certitude: "Come, Lord Jesus. Come!" (Rev. 22:20).[33]

Again, in imitation of his illustrious predecessor, the new pope was spreading joy and hope. The days of the Ecumenical Council were being marked by a staggering amount of enthusiasm from the whole world, as if the Holy Spirit were inspiring mankind with his gifts. Pope Paul VI saw joy as essential in evangelizing; after all, the saints have always been known for their cheerfulness even when confronted by the harshest of trials. In *Gaudete in Domino*, the apostolic letter on Christian joy, the Holy Father calls the youth to be at the forefront of the evangelization, co-workers for the Kingdom. Strikingly, in this passage is the pope's suggestion that the "field is ready for a harvest"; similar words are to be found in the New Testament (Matt. 13:39) and the Book of Revelation (Rev. 14:15):

We are sure that grace will not fail the Christian people, and we hope that they themselves will not fail grace, or reject—as some today are gravely tempted to do—the inheritance of truth and holiness handed down to this *decisive moment in the history of the world*. And—this is the point—we think that we have every reason to have confidence in Christian youth: youth will not fail the Church if within the Church there are enough older people able to understand it, to love it, to guide it and to open up to it a future by passing on to it with complete fidelity the Truth which endures. Then new workers, resolute and fervent, will in their turn enter upon spiritual and apostolic work in the fields which are white and ready for the harvest. Then the sower and the reaper will share the same joy of the kingdom. . . . *One must also recognize a prophetic intuition on the part of our predecessor John XXIII, who envisaged a kind of new Pentecost as a fruit of the Council.* We too have wished to place ourself in the same perspective and in the same attitude of expectation. Not that Pentecost has ever ceased to be an actuality during the whole history of the Church, but so great are the needs and the perils of the present age, so vast the horizon of mankind drawn towards world coexistence and powerless to achieve it, that there is no salvation for it except in a new outpouring of the gift of

---

33. Paul VI, "Homily at Episcopal Ordinations," India, December 3, 1964, http://www.vatican.va/.

God. Let Him then come, the Creating Spirit, to renew the face of the earth![34]

When addressing the Episcopal Commission for seminaries, Pope Paul VI discussed the calling of young men to the priesthood: "We all remember how the Second Ecumenical Council of the Vatican, reading the *signs of a new age,* devoted not a little care to the question."[35] This new age would be the triumph of good over evil, fulfilling Isaiah's prophecy: "The wolf lives with the lamb, the panther lies down with the kid, calf and lion cub feed together with a little boy to lead them" (Is. 11: 6–7). The Holy Father furthermore evoked the prophetic sentiments of John XXIII's radio address a month before the Council, in a speech on October 23, 1965: "The expectation of the people is more anxious than ever, the sadness of times, the dangers incurred by peace lead us to think that *God's time is near.*"[36]

We may recall that the missionary decree *Ad Gentes* explicitly stated that the Council's duty was to help prepare for the coming of the Lord. Pope Paul VI alluded to this dimension as well in September 1968 when adding further insights of his own:

> The Council sought to enlarge the horizons of the Church, to recompose its unity, to dispose it for new defenses and for new contacts with the world, putting it into closer contact with its sources and, finally, *to hasten it on its pilgrim journey towards its eschatological goal—its final, open and glorious encounter with Christ, Our Lord. This is a great and difficult task.*[37]

Although the task would be demanding, there was no way the Church could avoid it, if it was to be faithful to its Master. The eschatological direction of the Church is clear as it hurries towards its meeting with the Lord, but first it must pass through its own Gethsemane.

---

34. Paul VI, Apostolic Exhortation *Gaudete in Domino,* May 9, 1975, http://www.ewtn.com/.

35. Paul VI, "Address to Episcopal Commission for Seminaries," *L'Osservatore Romano* English ed., April 10, 1969, 5.

36. Paul VI, *Acta Apostolicae Sedis,* 1965, 923.

37. Paul VI, "General Audience A Church Always Young and New," *L'Osservatore Romano* English ed., September 19, 1968, 1.

There is a comparison to be made between the mystical passion of the Church and the passion of Jesus that began in the Garden of Gethsemane. Just as Jesus prayed in his abandonment for the Father's will to be done, so the Church prays and suffers that same abandonment in the world. The betrayal of Judas—one of the Lord's own chosen—is constantly repeated through the apostasy of many within the Mystical Body of Christ. The joyful entry of the Lord on Palm Sunday before his Passion was a foreshadowing of the same false worship of those who would only accept a Messiah formulated by their own standards of truth. The Church, after having been accepted by millions throughout the ages, now endures this process of betrayal and eventual crucifixion. As the pope represents the Church, the Mystical Body can make its own the prophetic words Jesus addressed to Peter concerning his future martyrdom:

> Amen, amen, I say to you, when you were younger, you used to dress yourself and go where you wanted; but when you grow old, you will stretch out your hands, and someone else will dress you and lead you where you do not want to go. (Jn.21:18)

There is an interesting insight concerning the Second Vatican Council given by Fr. Marie-Dominique Philippe, founder of the Community of St. John, in which he discusses the gentle tone preached by the Council Fathers. He explains that unlike previous Councils where the Church was aggressive in its defense of the faith against heresy and sinfulness, the new Council was different:

> When we see today all the struggles of the Church, we understand why the Second Vatican Council is the Council of fraternal charity, the Council of mercy. Doesn't this Council announce the last week of the Church, when the Church no longer condemns, like Jesus during the last week, as it is shown by St. John; Christ no longer condemns during the last week; in the same way the Church condemns as little as possible, and at that moment accepts to live the mystery of the Cross. I deeply think that this is what we really live: this mystery of a divine renewal is the great victory of love through apparent weaknesses, defeats.[38]

38. Marie Dominique Philippe, "Radio Talk," transcript available at http://www.stjean.com/.

The near silence of Jesus at his trial before the Sanhedrin reveals his acceptance of the Father's divine will; there is no need for a defense, only the strength to bear the sufferings to come. The Church is learning the same lesson now. Although the Catholic Church continues to exhort humanity to convert, it also accepts the condemnation and ridicule of the world. At the coming of the Antichrist, the Church will, more than ever, face the accusation of leading people away from freedom and the right to choose their own destiny. When that day comes, the time for teaching will have passed, leaving only the silent witness of martyrdom for the remnant flock of Christ.

Pope Paul VI shared his predecessors' confidence in the powerful intercession of Mary, as did the Council Fathers. In his encyclical *Christi Matri* promulgated in September 1966, he implored the help of the Blessed Virgin, citing several evils that needed to be destroyed through her intercession. As mediatrix and advocate, our Blessed Mother could hasten the defeat of Satan and usher in the new age:

> Look down with maternal clemency, Most Blessed Virgin, upon all your children. Consider the anxiety of bishops who fear that their flocks will be tormented by a terrible storm of evils. . . . Through your intercession, may God, the avenger of injuries, turn to mercy. May He give back to nations the tranquility they seek and bring them to a lasting age of genuine prosperity.[39]

The pope viewed his proclamation "Mary, Mother of the Church"[40] as highly important at a time when, in some quarters of the Church, devotion to the Mother of God was beginning to crumble. Knowing that his time was short, Satan had begun a systematic attempt to downplay the significance of Mary's role in salvation history. The battle that had begun in Genesis, the first book of the

---

39. Paul VI, Encyclical Letter *Christi Matri*, September 15, 1966, no. 13, http://www.vatican.va/.

40. Pope Paul VI proclaimed this title in his speech at the end of the Council's third session (November 21, 1964), also asking that, "henceforth the Blessed Virgin be honoured and invoked with this title by all the Christian people" (*Acta Apostolicae Sedis*, 1964, no. 37).

Bible, had now reached its peak in the last book; Satan was fighting hard to drown out Mary's plea for total consecration to her Immaculate Heart. The Holy Father addressed the reason for Mary's new title in August 1968:

> What, in fact, does the Church accomplish through the example of Our Lady? What has Our Lady done? She has given birth to Christ; she has given Christ to the world. And what must the Church do? It must bring forth new Christians, and make men sons and brothers of Christ. What the Church does in every Man, Our Lady has done in her Son. Thus we call her Mother of the Church, because she gives birth to us in the supernatural order in the same way in which she brought forth Christ the Lord into being.[41]

Returning to the question of the battle between Mary and the Devil at the end of the second millennium after Christ, the pope gave a compelling account of Satan's work of destruction in a general audience in 1972 which caused a great deal of public interest. In it, he tells of the Church's struggles against the menacing increase of evil. It is worth recalling a large portion of the address in view of the valuable spiritual direction contained within:

> What are the Church's greatest needs at the present time? Don't be surprised at our answer and don't write it off as simplistic or even superstitious: one of the Church's greatest needs is to be defended against the evil we call the Devil. . . . Don't we see how much evil there is in the world—especially moral evil, which goes against man and against God at one and the same time, although in different ways? Isn't this a sad spectacle, an unexplainable mystery? And aren't we—the lovers of the Word, the people who sing of the Good, we believers—aren't we the ones who are most sensitive and most upset by our observation and experience of evil?
>
> We come face to face with sin which is a perversion of human freedom and the profound cause of death because it involves detachment from God, the source of life. And then sin in its turn becomes the occasion and the effect of interference in us and our work by a dark, hostile agent, the Devil. *Evil is not merely an*

---

41. Paul VI, Homily, "The Mother of God in the Mystery of Salvation," *L'Osservatore Romano* English ed., August 29, 1968, 2.

absence of something but an active force, a living, spiritual being that is perverted and that perverts others. It is a terrible reality, mysterious and frightening. It is a departure from the picture provided by biblical Church teaching to refuse to acknowledge the Devil's existence; to regard him as a self-sustaining principle who, unlike other creatures, does not owe his origin to God; or to explain the Devil as a pseudo-reality, a conceptual, fanciful personification of the unknown causes of our misfortunes. When the problem of evil is seen in all its complexity and in its absurdity from the point of view of our limited minds, it becomes an obsession. It poses the greatest single obstacle to our religious understanding of the universe. It is no accident that St. Augustine was bothered by this for years: "I sought the source of evil, and I found no explanation."

The lurking shadow of this wicked presence is pointed up in many, many passages of the New Testament. St. Paul calls him the "god of this world," and warns us of the struggle we Christians must carry on in the dark, not only against one Devil, but against a frightening multiplicity of them. "I put on the armor of God," the Apostle tells us, "that you may be able to stand against the wiles of the devil. For our wrestling is not against flesh and blood, but against the Principalities and the Powers, against the world—rulers of this darkness, against the spiritual forces of wickedness on high."

Many passages in the Gospel show us that we are dealing not just with one Devil, but with many. But the principal one is Satan, which means the adversary, the enemy; and along with him are many others, all of them creatures of God, but fallen because they rebelled and were damned—a whole mysterious world, convulsed by a most unfortunate drama about which we know very little. There are many things we do know, however, about this diabolical world, things that touch on our lives and on the whole history of mankind. The Devil is at the origin of mankind's first misfortune, he was the wily, fatal tempter involved in the first sin, the original sin. That fall of Adam gave the Devil a certain dominion over man, from which only Christ's Redemption can free us. It is a history that is still going on: let us recall the exorcisms at Baptism, and the frequent references in Sacred Scripture and in the liturgy to the aggressive and oppressive "power of darkness." The Devil is the number one enemy, the pre-eminent tempter.

So we know that this dark disturbing being exists and that he is still at work with his treacherous cunning; he is the hidden enemy who sows errors and misfortunes in human history. . . . He is "a murderer from the beginning . . . and the father of lies," as Christ defines him. He undermines man's moral equilibrium with his sophistry. He is the malign, clever seducer who knows how to make his way into us through the senses, the imagination and the libido, through utopian logic, or through disordered social contacts in the give and take of our activities, so that he can bring about in us deviations that are all the more harmful because they seem to conform to our physical or mental makeup, or to our profound, instinctive aspirations.

People are afraid of falling back into old Manichean theories, or into frightening deviations of fancy and superstition. Nowadays they prefer to appear strong and unprejudiced, to pose as positivists, while at the same time lending faith to many unfounded magical or popular superstitions or, worse still, exposing their souls—their baptized souls, visited so often by the Eucharistic Presence and inhabited by the Holy Spirit!—to licentious sensual experiences and to harmful drugs, as well as to the ideological seductions of fashionable errors. These are cracks through which the Evil One can easily penetrate and change the human mind. This is not to say that every sin is directly due to diabolical action; *but it is true that those who do not keep watch over themselves with a certain moral rigor are exposed to the influence of the "mystery of iniquity"* cited by St. Paul which raises serious questions about our salvation. Our doctrine becomes uncertain, obscured as it is by the darkness surrounding the Devil. But our curiosity, excited by the certainty of his multiple existence, has a right to raise two questions. Are there signs, and what are they, of the presence of diabolical action? And what means of defense do we have against such an insidious danger? We have to be cautious about answering the first question, even though the signs of the Evil One seem to be very obvious at times. We can presume that his sinister action is at work where the denial of God becomes radical, subtle, and absurd; where lies become powerful and hypocritical in the face of evident truth; where love is smothered by cold, cruel selfishness; where Christ's name is attacked with conscious, rebellious hatred; where the spirit of the Gospel is watered down and rejected; where despair is affirmed as the last word; and so forth. . . . *The Christian must be a militant; he must be vigilant and strong; and he must at*

83

times make use of special ascetical practices to escape from certain diabolical attacks. Jesus teaches us this by pointing to "prayer and fasting" as the remedy. And the Apostle suggests the main line we should follow: "Be not overcome by evil, but overcome evil with good." *With an awareness therefore, of the opposition that individual souls, the Church, and the world must face at the present time,* we will try to give both meaning and effectiveness to the familiar invocation in our principal prayer: Our Father . . . deliver us from evil![42]

Pope Paul VI even went further suggesting that, "the smoke of Satan has entered into the Church."[43] An explosive revelation certainly, revealing the worrying development of abuses within the Catholic clergy. The Holy Father must have begun to feel isolated and betrayed as obedience to the magisterium was questioned.

It is important to note that Pope Paul VI reigned at the time of the sexual revolution. Impurity was rampant, especially among the young, the abortion laws were being passed in the western world and a culture of drug abuse was beginning. Family life was gradually eroded as divorce and remarriage became frequent. Satan focused on attacking the family, and thus causing a rapid breakdown in society, causing a monumental crime epidemic even involving children. The Holy Father's 1968 encyclical *Humanae Vitae* on birth control once again confirmed the Church's position that artificial contraception was intrinsically evil. Many bishops and priests had opposed this total ban, but the pope knew that to give in would send a signal that life was cheap and that chastity in marriage was consigned to the past. In relation to the devaluing of life he stated:

To experience the gift of married love while respecting the laws of conception is to acknowledge that one is not the master of the sources of life but rather the minister of the design established by

42. Paul VI, "General Audience Confronting the Devil's Power," November 15, 1972, http://www.ewtn.com/.
43. Cardinal Virgilio Noe gave a most enlightening account as to why Paul VI used this famous phrase. See http://wdtprs.com/blog/2008/05/petrus-amazing-interview-with-card-noe-paul-vis-smoke-of-satan-remark-concerned-liturgy/.

the Creator. . . . Human life is sacred—all men must recognize that fact.[44]

The importance of chastity is also underlined:

The right and lawful ordering of birth demands, first of all, that spouses fully recognize and value the true blessings of family life and that they acquire complete mastery over themselves and their emotions. . . . This is especially clear in the practice of periodic continence. Self-discipline of this kind is a shining witness to the chastity of husband and wife and, far from being a hindrance to their love of one another, transforms it by giving it a more truly human character.[45]

No matter what time or season the Church was living in, the truth would always remain the same; "heaven and earth will pass away, but my words will not pass away" (Matt. 24:35). This was the truth that the pope would cling to even when the temptations of the evil one would rise to entice the Church to loosen its grip on morals and purity. The world was changing rapidly as free love reigned supreme and it was at this point in history that the Church's voice seemed to begin to fade, when people closed their ears to the splendor of the truth. It is not surprising therefore, that while recognizing that the sands of time were running out, the pope would call for a new missionary period: a second evangelization.

The apostolic exhortation *Evangelii Nuntiandi*, issued on the Feast of the Immaculate Conception in the Holy Year 1975, was the command to begin this new missionary activity. It would be the Holy Spirit's work, as Pope Paul VI said, with the aim of evangelizing even those areas where Christianity had been rooted out many centuries ago. The Catholic Church itself would also need to be renewed through this evangelization in order to be an authentic witness to mankind. Once again a joyful message of hope was prevalent throughout the document:

---

44. Paul VI, Encyclical Letter *Humanae Vitae*, July 25, 1968, http://www.vatican.va/.

45. Ibid., no. 21.

We live in the Church at a privileged moment of the Spirit. Everywhere people are trying to know Him better, as the Scripture reveals Him. They are happy to place themselves under His inspiration. They are gathering about Him; they want to let themselves be led by Him. Now if the Spirit of God has a pre-eminent place in the whole life of the Church, it is in her evangelizing mission that He is most active. It is not by chance that the great inauguration of evangelization took place on the morning of Pentecost, under the inspiration of the Spirit.... *He is the goal of evangelization: He alone stirs up the new creation, the new humanity of which evangelization is to be the result.*[46]

It could be stated that the popes of the past century, not only promoting devotion to the Blessed Virgin and defining mariological doctrines, have awakened in the hearts of the faithful a renewed appreciation of the Holy Spirit as "the Lord, the giver of life" (cf. Nicene Creed). The intention is to deepen the love and devotion that by right is owed to Divine Love himself, in such a way that Christians truly become "temples of the Holy Spirit" (cf. 1 Cor. 6:19), burning with a missionary zeal, and enriched by a greater degree of holiness which propels them onto the frontline of evangelization. Pope Leo XIII, in his encyclical *Divinum Illud Munus*, spoke beautifully of the invocation of the Divine Paraclete, proclaiming that the Church:

> ... addresses Him in humble supplication, calling upon Him by the sweetest of names: "Come, Father of the poor! Come, Giver of gifts! Come, Light of our hearts! O, best of Consolers, sweet Guest of the soul, our refreshment!" (Hymn, Veni Sancte Spiritus). She earnestly implores Him to wash, heal, water our minds and hearts, and to give to us who trust in Him "the merit of virtue, the acquirement of salvation, and joy everlasting."[47]

The successors of St. Peter desire and expect from those docile to the Spirit of truth, an acceptance of his gifts, to be used for the spiritual regeneration of the Church, as an antidote to the prevailing

---

46. Paul VI, Apostolic Exhortation *Evangelii Nuntiandi*, December 8, 1975, no. 75.
47. Leo XIII, Encyclical Letter *Divinum Illud Munus*, May 9, 1897, http://www.vatican.va/.

apostasy evident especially, but not exclusively, in the West. Pope Paul VI impressed upon the faithful the urgency of this theme a matter of four weeks later, hinting at the lateness of the hour:

> The personal awareness of the joint responsibility that every Catholic must feel with regard to the needs of our time, the dialectical meeting of the present day Church with the problems, the polemics, the hostilities, the possible catastrophes of a godless society, *the drama of which the Church is experiencing today in the full tension of her history,* the discovery of unexpected evangelical possibilities in human souls, sorely tried by the hard and disappointing experiences of modern progress, and *finally certain secrets of divine mercy, in which moving resources of the Kingdom of God are revealed: everything tells us that this is a great and decisive hour which we must have the courage to live with open eyes and undaunted hearts.*[48]

One year before his death, Pope Paul VI gave his clearest warnings about the end times. In this passage, he seems to point to the apostasy itself as being the greatest concern:

> There is, at this time, a great turmoil in the world and in the Church, and what is in question is the faith. . . . And now it comes to me to repeat the obscure phrase of Jesus in the Gospel of Saint Luke: "When the Son of man returns, will he still find faith on earth?" There are books coming out in which the faith is in retreat on some important points, the bishops are remaining silent and these books are not found strange. In my view this is strange. Sometimes I re-read the Gospel on the end of times and I notice that, at this moment, there are emerging some signs of this end. Are we close to the end? This is something we shall never know. What is necessary is that we always remain ready, but everything can last a lot longer still. What strikes me when I consider the Catholic world, is that, in the heart of Catholicism, it sometimes appears that a pattern of thought prevails which is not Catholic in character, and it can come about that this non-Catholic pattern of thought, at the heart of Catholicism, could become the more powerful one at some time in the future. But it will never represent the

---

48. Paul VI, General Audience, "Time Now To Evangelize!" *L'Osservatore Romano* English ed., January 15, 1976, 1.

thought of the Church. It is necessary that a little flock should remain, however little it be.[49]

The *charism of assistance* (cf. Lk. 22:32) given by the Holy Spirit to the popes, is for the benefit of the Universal Church to see in the signs of the present, a way of approaching the future with the blessing and assistance of God.[50] It is true that we can all read Sacred Scripture and notice the presence of eschatological signs in the world, but when confronted by the authority of the pope we must listen, if we are to be saved from the tide of unbelief that threatens to sweep away vast numbers of the faithful. It is worth recalling the Gospel passage where St. Peter begins to walk towards Jesus on the water during the great storm. (cf. Matt. 14:24–31) Is this not representative of the Church's journey towards the end of the world? The Lord holds out his hand ready to save Peter, but what Jesus requires is faith and trust. The same can be said for the Church; yes, it continues to be tossed about by the sea of indifference and evil, but Jesus is walking ever closer as we look patiently towards the second coming. The pope, as successor to St. Peter, is the helmsman, guiding our boat onto the shore of the New Jerusalem. What is required from us is obedience to his commands, otherwise we will risk shipwreck in the faith and be lost in the sea of apostasy. A ship does not have two masters; the same applies to the Church, for if the Lord has chosen one leader out of the apostles, then it is for us, in humility, to submit to divine wisdom and offer prayerful support for his Vicar on earth.

49. Jean Guitton, *The Secret Paul VI*, 152–153, cited from *To the Priests, Our Lady's Beloved Sons* (St. Francis, ME), 14.

50. Pope John Paul II explained how this charism of assistance is related to discerning the signs of the times in an eschatological sense: "... the essential task of the papal Magisterium is to explain the doctrine of the faith, and to promote knowledge of the mystery of God and the work of salvation, bringing out all the aspects of the divine plan as it unfolds in human history under the action of the Holy Spirit" (General Audience, March 10, 1993). Furthermore, in an earlier address, he had been even more specific: "The perspective in which Peter's responsibility—like the Church's whole mission—must be considered is therefore both historical and eschatological" (General Audience, December 2, 1992). Both available at http://www.vatican.va/.

The Holy Father died on the Feast of the Transfiguration, August 6, 1978 at Castel Gandolfo. His successor was immediately known as the "Smiling Pope." He was the Patriarch of Venice, a simple, humble, and holy man who set the tone for his pontificate by refusing to be crowned. It was a great sign of humility and solidarity with his people. Albino Luciani took the name of John Paul and he was universally accepted with great enthusiasm. Within days, however, thirty-three to be precise, and to the dismay of millions, the Holy Father died, leaving the Church in shock. He had no time to set his ideas in encyclicals or apostolic letters and so the faithful wondered; where was the Holy Spirit working in all of this?

We do have a certain amount of knowledge as to whether John Paul I felt the same way as his predecessors concerning the approaching days of justice. Certainly, what is clear from his time as Cardinal Patriarch of Venice was his understanding of the Marian era, with its dual principles, Petrine and Marian:

> If Peter holds the keys of the Church, Mary holds the keys of God's Heart; if Peter binds and unbinds, Mary also binds with chains of love; she also unbinds with the art of forgiveness. If Peter is the guardian and minister of indulgences, Mary is the magnanimous and skilful treasurer of the divine favours. Those who look for grace but have not recourse to the Virgin Mary to accomplish their journey, are looking to fly without wings.[51]

In terms of a more specific attitude to the signs of the times Cardianl Luciani delivered a startling message in his homily for the Feast of Santa Maria della Salute, on November 21, 1971:

> The Madonna, from all time, is a virgin and totally pure. When she looks on our society, termed permissive because it permits and excuses everything in matters of immorality, the Virgin Mary becomes a "weeping Madonna." She weeps on account of the evil we commit and tolerate, *and on account of the chastisements we are heading for.*[52]

---

51. Albino Luciani, "Speech of April 21, 1949," cited from *The Whole Truth about Fatima*, available at http://www.catholicvoice.co.uk/fatima4/.
52. Albino Luciani, "Homily for the Feast of Santa Maria della Salute," on November 21, 1971. *Opera omnia*, vol. 5, 291.

In 1977 the Cardinal visited Sr. Lucia of Fatima who made a great impression on him. According to Andrea Tornielli, in a stunning prophecy "Sister Lucy apparently greeted him by calling him Holy Father."[53] A month later, in a Letter to the Prior of Pietralba on August 15, 1977, Cardinal Luciani affirmed the importance of these interventions of Our Lady, stressing as many popes before him had done the dangers of ignoring these maternal pleas:

> At Lourdes, Fatima, La Salette, and elsewhere, the Madonna helps and guides us by saying almost only one thing: Prayer and Penance. She echoes Jesus' admonition: "Unless you do penance, you will all perish".... You should pray without ceasing.[54]

In terms of his magisterium, Pope Luciani's Urbi et Orbi address delivered one day after his election, confirms a complete understanding of the eschatological realism which all the popes of the Marian era have been called to proclaim:

> A dawn of hope spreads over the earth, although it is sometimes touched by sinister merchants of hatred, bloodshed, and war with a darkness which sometimes threatens to obscure the dawn.... We make no distinction as to race or ideology *but seek to secure for the world the dawn of a more serene and joyful day. Only Christ could cause this dawn of a light which will never set, because he is the "sun of justice"* (cf. Mal. 4:2). He will indeed oversee the work of all. *He will not fail us.*[55]

Pope John Paul I's spirituality can be summed up in these words quoted by Pope Benedict XVI in a speech from October 2006. They offer further evidence that this gentle soul was a true Marian pontiff in the tradition of the great 20th century popes: "*It is impossible to conceive of our life, the life of the Church, without the Rosary, the Marian feasts, Marian shrines, and images of Our Lady.*"[56]

53. Andrea Tornielli, *Papa Luciani. Il parroco del mondo*, Segno, 1998, 114.

54. Albino Luciani, "Letter to the Prior of Pietralba of August 15, 1977," extracts. *Opera omnia*, vol. 8, 190.

55. John Paul I, "Urbi et Orbi Address," August 27, 1978, http://www.vatican.va/.

56. Benedict XVI, "Address at the preview of the film 'Pope Luciani, God's Smile,'" October 8, 2006, http://www.vatican.va/.

Is there a deeper element to the timing of the deaths of both Paul VI and John Paul I? To begin with, Pope Paul VI died on the feast of the Transfiguration. In the Gospel, the Transfiguration of Jesus occurs just before he enters Jerusalem for the Passover and his Passion—a sign to show Peter, James, and John his divinity before they witness his cruel sufferings. Could this be the same for the Church as she enters the stage of the final Passover? Pope John Paul I died after thirty-three days. Perhaps we could see in this a reference to the thirty-three years of Jesus's life.[57] We know that many great mystics have died aged thirty-three, notably St. Faustina Kowalska, St. Catherine of Siena, Blessed Mariam Baouardy, St. Michael of the Saints, Sr. Josefa Menendez, and the Servant of God Domenica Lazzeri. Does this suggest that with the reign of Pope John Paul II, linking two millenniums, the Church prepares to enter the time of its ultimate trial, a season of grace and mercy before its meeting with its Lord and Savior? The evidence suggests that Pope John Paul II viewed his role in leading the Church towards the second coming of Jesus as critical and urgent. The second part of this book will aim to show that this theme was ever present during the extraordinary Pontificate of this great Marian pope, a true servant of the Lord, the Church, and all humanity.

---

57. Although not a revealed truth, tradition has it that the Lord lived to thirty-three years of age. Luke 3:23 states: "When Jesus began his ministry he was about thirty years of age," while St. John's Gospel mentions the occurrence of three Passovers during the years of Jesus' ministry (2:23, 6:4, and 12:1).

PART II

Blessed John Paul II:
Herald of the Second Advent

5

The Church
Experiences the New Advent

Let no one deceive you in any way. For unless the apostasy comes first and the lawless one is revealed, the one doomed to perdition, who opposes and exalts himself above every so-called god and object of worship, so as to seat himself in the temple of God, claiming that he is a god—do you not recall that while I was still with you I told you these things? And now you know what is restraining, that he may be revealed in his time. For the mystery of lawlessness is already at work. But the one who restrains is to do so only for the present, until he is removed from the scene. And then the lawless one will be revealed, whom the Lord Jesus will kill with the breath of his mouth and render powerless by the manifestation of his coming.   (2 Thes. 2:3–8)

THE YEAR 1978 will always be remembered as the year of the three popes. In the aftermath of the terrible sadness caused by the sudden death of Pope John Paul I, the remarkable series of events in Rome took another completely unexpected turn with the election of the Polish Cardinal Karol Wojtyla. The two favored Italian cardinals, Giuseppe Siri, the Archbishop of Genoa, and Giovanni Benelli, the Archbishop of Florence cancelled each other out, leaving the path clear for a compromise candidate. With the influential Archbishop of Vienna, Cardinal Franz Konig championing the young Polish Cardinal and the majority of American cardinals led by Cardinal Krol also rallying behind him, the Holy Spirit's decision was finally ratified on the eighth ballot of the second day of voting. Taking the name of his immediate predecessor, John Paul II became the first non-Italian pope since the Dutch Adrian VI, who reigned from 1522 to 1523.

95

Heralds of the Second Coming

Even before His Holiness, Pope John Paul II ascended the Throne of St. Peter in October 1978, he had already spoken several times of the final battle looming over humanity. His words were, in a sense, a glimpse of his eschatological understanding as the second millennium drew to a close. In a homily on the First Sunday of Advent in 1974 he seemed to encourage the faithful to discern the signs for themselves—something he would often do as pope:

> The moment which we are living and which we must "know" is maybe very similar to the moment described in today's Gospel reading (Lk. 21:25–33),[1] so that it too gives rise to much reflection, some of it deeply pessimistic and fearful of catastrophe. . . . I would urge you to strive to "know what hour it is," because this hour is also the time of the Lord's coming.[2]

At the conclusion of a trip to the United States of America in 1976, the Polish Cardinal, Karol Wojtyla, the Archbishop of Krakow, spoke in similar terms:

> We are now standing in the face of the greatest historical confrontation humanity has gone through. I do not think the wide circle of the American society or the wide circle of the Christian community realize this fully. We are now facing the final confrontation between the Church and the Anti-Church, of the Gospel versus the Anti-Gospel. This confrontation lies within the plans of divine providence; it is a trial which the whole Church, and the Polish Church in particular, must take up.[3]

---

1. "There will be signs in the sun, the moon, and the stars, and on earth nations will be in dismay, perplexed by the roaring of the sea and the waves. People will die of fright in anticipation of what is coming upon the world, for the powers of the heavens will be shaken. And then they will see the Son of Man coming in a cloud with power and great glory. But when these signs begin to happen, stand erect and raise your heads because your redemption is at hand. He taught them a lesson. 'Consider the fig tree and all the other trees. When their buds burst open, you see for yourselves and know that summer is now near; in the same way, when you see these things happening, know that the kingdom of God is near. Amen, I say to you, this generation will not pass away until all these things have taken place. Heaven and earth will pass away, but my words will not pass away.'"

2. Karol Wojtyla, *The Word Made Flesh* (San Francisco: Harper & Row, 1985), 7.

3. Vincent P. Miceli, *The Antichrist* (Harrison, NY: Roman Catholic Books, 1981), 5.

The Church Experiences the New Advent

The storm clouds gathering over humanity in the final decades of the twentieth century were becoming ever more menacing; however, the Church and the world had been blessed by the Holy Spirit with a new pope formed in the Immaculate Heart of Mary, a prophetic voice for the greatest triumph ever, a sign of the Blessed Virgin's increasing maternal mediation for the Church in her hour of need.

In this opening chapter of part two, I would like to focus on the arrival of the "New Advent," a theme which curiously does not seem to appear in any previous pontificate.[4] With the new pope, the phrase is used frequently, in fact from the opening section of his first encyclical *Redemptor Hominis* published in March 1979. Let us look at what Pope John Paul says:

> We also are in a certain way in a season of a new Advent, a season of expectation: "In many and various ways God spoke of old to our fathers by the prophets; but in these last days he has spoken to us by a Son. . . ."
>
> While the ways on which the Council of this century has set the Church going, ways indicated by the late Pope Paul VI in his first Encyclical, will continue to be for a long time the ways that all of us must follow, we can at the same time rightly ask at this new stage: How, in what manner should we continue? What should we do, in order that this new advent of the Church connected with the approaching end of the second millennium may bring us closer to him whom Sacred Scripture calls "Everlasting Father," *Pater futuri saeculi?*
>
> *Nevertheless, it is certain that the Church of the new Advent, the Church that is continually preparing for the new coming of the Lord, must be the Church of the Eucharist and of Penance.* Only when viewed in this spiritual aspect of her life and activity is she seen to be the Church of the divine mission, the Church in *statu missionis,* as the Second Vatican Council has shown her to be.[5]

---

4. As Archbishop of Krakow, Cardinal Wojtyla had referred to a "new advent" in his closing remarks during the retreat he preached to Pope Paul VI in March 1976.

5. John Paul II, Encyclical Letter *Redemptor Hominis*, March 4, 1979, http://www.vatican.va/.

Therefore, from the first important document,[6] even the first page, the pope is categorical: the Church is now in a season of Advent, awaiting the new coming of the Lord. And what will be the strength of the faithful in this time? The Eucharist and the sacrament of Confession; the two greatest means given by Jesus for the sanctification of the mystical body of Christ.

The Holy Father calls for an intensification of prayer, united to that of Mary, in order to live this new advent:

> We feel not only the need but even a categorical imperative for great, intense and growing prayer by all the Church. Only prayer can prevent all these great succeeding tasks and difficulties from becoming a source of crisis and make them instead the occasion and, as it were, the foundation for ever more mature achievements on the People of God's march towards the Promised Land in this stage of history approaching the end of the second millennium. . . . Above all, I implore Mary, the heavenly Mother of the Church, to be so good as to devote herself to this prayer of humanity's new Advent, together with us who make up the Church, that is to say the Mystical Body of her Only Son. I hope that through this prayer we shall be able to receive the Holy Spirit coming upon us and thus become Christ's witnesses "to the end of the earth," like those who went forth from the Upper Room in Jerusalem on the day of Pentecost.[7]

The pope reflects on varying aspects of the world situation, from the terrible abortions to the environmental catastrophes. The continuous cycle of wars and terrorism cause him to reflect that creation seems to be groaning in a greater way than ever before. We may recall that in chapter eight of St. Paul's Letter to the Romans, he speaks of this groaning of creation, as if it is a giant act of giving birth to the new era of peace and renewal. The psalms also sing of this time: "Love and truth will meet; justice and peace will kiss" (Ps. 85:10). We may ponder how much greater the Holy Father's words spoken so many years ago apply to our age now:

---

6. Even more significant is the fact that a new pope's first encyclical is often referred to as the manifesto of his papacy.

7. Ibid., no. 22.

Are we of the twentieth century not convinced of the overpower-ingly eloquent words of the Apostle of the Gentiles concerning the "creation that has been groaning in travail together until now" and "waits with eager longing for the revelation of the sons of God," the creation that "was subjected to futility"? Does not the previously unknown immense progress—which has taken place especially in the course of this century—in the field of man's dominion over the world itself reveal—to a previously unknown degree—that manifold subjection "to futility"? It is enough to recall certain phenomena, such as the threat of pollution of the natural environment in areas of rapid industrialization, or the armed conflicts continually breaking out over and over again, or the prospectives of self-destruction through the use of atomic, hydrogen, neutron, and similar weapons, or the lack of respect for the life of the unborn. The world of the new age, the world of space flights, the world of the previously unattained conquests of science and technology—is it not also the world "groaning in travail" that "waits with eager longing for the revealing of the sons of God"?[8]

The earthquakes, floods, heat waves, and other natural disasters tell of an old world dying. The seasons appear to be intermingling more with every passing year. All this has come about through the abuse and neglect of God given resources. The world is now experiencing the backlash from nature itself, as it struggles to stem the tide of industrialization and materialism.

The term "Advent," which means "coming," calls to mind the joyful expectation of God's people. In the Old Testament it was the expectation of the Messiah, and in the New, the expectation of the coming of the Son of man, in judgment and glory at the end of time.

Although there was an expectation of an imminent return of the Lord in the early Church that eventually cooled, the Church has always continued to look forward to the second coming, and the liberation from all evil that would be the result of it. The keyword for the Church remains "watch." The Holy Father continually addressed this to the cardinals, while also reminding them that their purple vestments recall the blood of the martyrs:

8. Ibid.

The whole Church is called to keep watch. In the Church the cardinalate too is a particular sign of this watchfulness. You are called, dear Brothers, to keep watch in expectation of the Lord's coming, just as the shepherds kept watch on Bethlehem night. And just as the Apostles whom Christ took with him to Gethsemane the night before his Passion had to keep watch. You are called to keep watch beside the mystery of Christmas and at the same time in the perspective of the paschal mystery, when the saving coming of the Redeemer of the world will reach its supreme fulfillment. If today the Bishop of Rome calls you, Shepherds of the Church, to this eminent dignity, *he wishes in this way to call the whole Church to that watchfulness* which Christ enjoined on his Apostles.... In the Church the dignity of the Cardinalate corresponds to a double tradition. First of all, to the tradition of the martyrs, those who did not hesitate to shed their blood for Christ. This is reflected in your very dress, for purple is the color of blood. As you receive the cardinalate purple, each of you hears the call to be ready to shed your blood, should Christ require it.[9]

In this time of watching, the Mother of Jesus is present, teaching us to discern the signs and to be attentive to what the Holy Spirit is telling the Churches (cf. Rev. 3:22). For the Holy Father, Mary's role is vital in the new Advent. In his best-selling book *Crossing the Threshold of Hope,* he states that it is God's will that the future victories of the Church will come through Mary.[10] For just as the Blessed Virgin shone like a star in the firmament before the coming of the Messiah, so too does she rise in the sky of history as the *Stella Matutina,* that is "Morning Star," before the Day of the Lord arrives. In *Redemptoris Mater,* the encyclical devoted to the teachings of the Second Vatican Council concerning Mary, the pope compares the second advent with the first and explains that Mary is the light shining in the darkness of both:

9. John Paul II, Homily, "Serve the Gospel of Life and Love," *L'Osservatore Romano* English ed., November 30, 1994, 3.

10. See the last testament of Pope John Paul II in which he quotes Cardinal Stefan Wyszynski: "When victory is won, it will be a victory through Mary," words which actually originated from Cardinal August Hlond, Wyszynski's predecessor. Available at http://www.vatican.va/.

The Church Experiences the New Advent

The Church has constantly been aware that Mary *appeared* on the horizon of *salvation history before Christ*.... The fact that she "preceded" the coming of Christ is reflected every year *in the liturgy of Advent*. Therefore, if to that ancient historical expectation of the Savior we compare these years which are bringing us closer to the end of the second millennium after Christ and to the beginning of the third, it becomes fully comprehensible that in this present period we wish to turn in a special way to her, the one who in the "night" of the Advent expectation began to shine like a true "Morning Star."[11]

To those who regard Marian devotion as outdated, the pope's message is clear: if we want to be fully prepared for the final coming of Jesus then we should imitate Mary's example of love and trust, while being docile to the action of the Holy Spirit. It is essential that we recall that the Blessed Virgin is already the *eschatological fulfillment of the Church* because, free from the stain of original sin and being obedient to the divine will, she perfected her role as Co-redemptrix with the Savior, and thus gained through the infinite merits of her Son, the singular privilege of participating body and soul in the Kingdom of God before the rest of the redeemed.[12] It is no surprise then, that our Queen desires her children to reach the same fulfillment, and this explains the frequency of modern day apparitions. Just as the Advent liturgy calls us to prepare for the Last Judgment, so Mary reminds us and exhorts us to be converted before the retribution comes (cf. 1 Thess. 1:10).

Pope John Paul II speaks again of this fact in the same encyclical:

---

11. John Paul II, Encyclical Letter *Redemptoris Mater*, March 25, 1987, no.3, http://www.vatican.va/.

12. Although a controversial theological term, Cardinal Wojtyla explains the doctrine of the Co-redemptrix: "Mary's holiness, and the whole process of her sanctification, must be viewed in the framework of her complete and active participation in the redemptive work of her Son. In her, the forces of grace were not directed (or at least not to any great extent) toward overcoming the consequences of original sin . . . she used them, instead, in order to link herself personally, with her whole life, to the work of redemption. The role of Co-redemptrix (*alma socia Redemptoris*) which is recognized as proper to the Mother of Christ, gives us a new and more complete way of understanding the mystery of the Immaculate Conception" (Wojtyla, *Sign of Contradiction*, 17).

For, if as Virgin and Mother, she was singularly united with him *in his first coming*, so through her continued collaboration with him she will also be united with him in expectation of the second; "redeemed in an especially sublime manner by reason of the merits of her Son," she also has that specifically maternal role of mediatrix of mercy *at his final coming* when all those who belong to Christ "shall be made alive," when "the last enemy to be destroyed is death" (1 Cor. 15:26).[13]

The pope invited the whole Church to reflect on the maternal mediation of Mary in preparing the way of the Lord. In 1994, at his sixth Ordinary Public Consistory, these words were addressed to all the faithful:

In my recent Apostolic Letter *Tertio millennio adveniente,* I emphasized how "Christians are called to prepare for the Great Jubilee of the beginning of the third millennium by *renewing their hope in the definitive coming of the Kingdom of God*, preparing for it daily in their hearts, in the Christian community to which they belong, in their particular social context, and in world history itself" (n. 46). The Church is called to show all humanity, by word and example, that its journey in time is really a journey towards Christ, a mysterious spiritual journey which ends in God. I entrust this demanding journey to the Virgin Mother of the Redeemer, who is particularly present in the Advent liturgy. She is the perfect image of the Church, which awaits with hope the coming of the Son of God. Mary goes before us on the road towards Christ, firm in faith and ready to fulfill the word of God. Her total adherence to the salvific plan is a model for every believer who lives in active anticipation of the return of the Lord in glory.[14]

In his Angelus address of November 27, 1994, the Holy Father said:

May the Virgin of Advent guide us all in this period of expectation in which we contemplate the mystery of the first coming that was fulfilled in the Incarnation, we turn our gaze to the last day when the Lord will come again "with all his holy ones" (1 Thes. 3:13).[15]

---

13. Ibid., no. 41
14. John Paul II, "Address at Sixth Ordinary Consistory, Called to a Demanding Service of Love," *L'Osservatore Romano* English ed., November 30, 1994, 2.
15. Ibid., 1.

I would like to return briefly to the idea of the Church staying awake, and how it relates to the apostasy. The pope made reference in his speech to the new cardinals that the Apostles needed to stay awake in the Garden of Gethsemane. The Church is living her own Gethsemane now, but the general state of apostasy, the "silent apostasy" (*Ecclesia in Europa*) tells us that many are asleep. What does this mean for the Church? It means that Jesus' prophecy concerning men and women living lives unfettered by the signs of the end times is currently being fulfilled.[16] The Lord is warning that many will continue to be asleep to the call to convert, unaware of the necessity to keep watch.

Fr. Marie-Dominique Philippe relates how many years ago the Holy Father addressed the French bishops. He talked of a Church struggling to stay awake:

> The Church is actually living a metatemptation; in the philosophical language of the Pope, a metatemptation is a temptation which goes beyond all the temptations which might have been encountered before. The Holy Father does not hesitate to say that the "temptation which the Church is undergoing today is stronger than ever." He explains that this metatemptation is a kind of temptation "par excellence," a temptation which gives meaning to all the other ones. People in today's world would like to bypass God and be saved by themselves. They reject Jesus as Savior, and they believe that, thanks to the progress of science and technology, they will be able to save themselves, and hence will no longer need a Savior.[17]

In this context, we may remember the words of Jesus to his Apostles: "Watch and pray that you may not undergo the test. The spirit is willing, but the flesh is weak" (Matt. 26:41). Here the Lord links two facets of spiritual formation: first the need to stay awake, and second, the need to pray in the face of temptation. In a speech given

---

16. "For as it was in the days of Noah, so it will be at the coming of the Son of Man. In those days before the flood, they were eating and drinking, marrying and giving in marriage, up to the day that Noah entered the ark. They did not know until the flood came and carried them all away. So will it be also at the coming of the Son of Man" (Matt. 24:37–39).

17. Marie Dominique Philippe, "The Struggles of the Church," http://www. st jean.com/.

to religious priests at the Marian shrine of Altotting, Germany, in 1980, the Holy Father also warned his priests that they would face the greatest temptations:

> You are called to share in a special way in this spiritual struggle. You are called to this constant combat that Mother Church is engaged upon and which fashions it into the image of the Woman, the Mother of the Lord. You have at the heart of your vocation the adoration of Holy God; but by the same token you are particularly exposed to the temptations of the Evil One, as is evident in the temptations of the Lord.[18]

Without prayer to combat the temptation, spiritual lethargy will set in and the clarity of the Gospel message will fade. This goes some way to explain why many Catholics today seem totally indifferent. They appear not to care, and have become lukewarm souls. The Lord's warning to the Church in Laodicea should resound in all our hearts: "I know your works; I know that you are neither cold nor hot. I wish you were either cold or hot. So, because you are lukewarm, neither hot nor cold, I will spit you out of my mouth" (Rev. 3:15). In many ways these souls are more repugnant to Jesus than his enemies because they know the faith, and profess it, and yet never allow Jesus to reside in their hearts. How many show proper respect for the true presence of Jesus in the Blessed Sacrament? Truly it is the God of love and mercy we come face to face with at the moment of the Consecration at Holy Mass, the Creator of the universe who in unfathomable humility allows himself to remain in cold tabernacles day and night waiting for someone to come and open the door of their heart to him. This is the deep sleep that has descended on the Church, and it seems to point towards the time when the Holy Sacrifice will be abolished during the reign of the Antichrist (cf. Dn. 12:11). Tradition teaches us that the apostasy will lay the foundation for these terrible future events that will last for three and a half years.

The Great Jubilee, for which the pope called the Church to prepare for many years, can also be understood in the light of the

---

18. Peter Hebblethwaite, *Introducing John Paul II* (London: Fount Paperbacks, 1982), 36.

Advent season. The message of the year 2000 was to thank the Lord for all the benefits of the last millennium, while focusing our eyes on the remainder of the journey. The Second Vatican Council as we know prepared the ground for the new times, and Pope John Paul alluded to its significance in *Tertio millenio adveniente*:

> If we look for an analogy in the liturgy, it could be said that the yearly *Advent liturgy* is the season nearest to the spirit of the Council. *For Advent prepares us to meet the One who was, who is and who is to come* (cf. Rev. 4:8). . . . It is certainly not a matter of indulging in a new millenarianism, as occurred in some quarters at the end of the first millennium; rather, it is *aimed at an increased sensitivity to all that the Spirit is saying to the Church and the Churches* (cf. Rev. 2:7).[19]

What does the Spirit say to the Churches? He prepares the people to hear Jesus' message: "Yes, I am coming soon" (Rev. 22:20). In the encyclical *Dominum et Vivificantum* on the Holy Spirit, promulgated in 1986, the twin themes of the Jubilee and the new Advent were dwelt upon: "in preparing for the great jubilee we must emphasize the 'desires of the spirit,' as exhortations echoing in the night *of a new time of advent, at the end of which, like two thousand years ago, 'every man will see the salvation of God.'*"[20] Pope John Paul states that the Church can only live the Advent season properly by being attentive to the inspirations of the Holy Spirit, as he is its agent; continually renewing humanity and preparing its final, universal restoration at the end of time. The Holy Father adds:

> In the time leading up to the third Millennium after Christ, while "the Spirit and the Bride say to the Lord Jesus: Come!" this prayer of theirs is filled, as always, *with an eschatological significance, which is destined to give fullness of meaning to the celebration of the great jubilee.* It is a prayer concerned with the salvific destinies toward which the Holy Spirit by his action opens hearts throughout the history of man on earth.[21]

19. John Paul II, Apostolic Letter *Tertio Millenio Adveniente*, November 10, 1994, London, Catholic Truth Society, nos. 20, 23.

20. John Paul II, Encyclical Letter *Dominum et Vivificantum*, May 18, 1986, no. 56.

21. Ibid., no. 66.

Some of the most enlightening comments from Pope John Paul II concerning the new Advent come from an *ad Limina* address that he gave to the bishops of Texas, Oklahoma, and Arkansas on April 16, 1988. The entire speech is a reflection on preparation for the third Millennium. It is highly prophetic in character:

> Our present pastoral efforts as bishops . . . should be directed to creating that *profound and dynamic vision which must characterize the Church in the year* 2000. The Church of the Millennium must have an increased consciousness of being the Kingdom of God in its initial stage. She must show that she is *vitally concerned with being faithful to Christ*; hence she must strive mightily to the great challenges of holiness, evangelization and service. At the same time the Church of the Millennium must emerge *as a clear sign of her own eschatological state*, living by the mystery that is yet to be revealed.
>
> The Church of the Millennium will still be *the Church undergoing purification through suffering*—the salvific value of which she fully knows. Yet in her purifying experiences the Church will still be able to cry out that the sufferings of this time are "as nothing to be compared with the glory to be revealed in us" (Rom. 8:18). As a Church living in expectation of glory to be revealed she will find ever greater strength *to proclaim the value of celibacy* that is lived for the Kingdom of God, *the final state of which is in preparation: "Thy Kingdom Come!" At such an important juncture of her life, the Church of the Millennium must declare that she is ready at any moment to meet the Lord, just as she is ready to go on faithfully in joyful hope awaiting his coming. . . .* The Church is convinced of her right to be with Jesus, who, seated at the right hand of the Father, has already united her to himself in glory. *This makes it easy for the Church as she lives the new Advent to accept with keen conviction the words of her victorious Redeemer: "Remember, I am coming soon" (Rev. 22:12). During the Millennium the Church is called upon to remember. It is also the special hour for the Church to respond with fidelity and confidence, proclaiming by her actions and by her whole life: "Come Lord Jesus!". . . . Living in the Spirit sent by Christ, the Church looks forward to the Millennium as a time of vast interior renewal. By his power the Holy Spirit is truly able to effect in the Church a new Pentecost.* On the part of all of us, however, this requires *new attitudes* of humility, generosity, and openness to the purifying action of the Holy Spirit. The whole concept of renewal

must be seen in its relationship to *penance* and the *Eucharist*. In *Redemptor Hominis* I emphasized, *"that the Church of the new Advent . . . must be the Church of the Eucharist and Penance"*. . . . *The Millennium is the supreme moment for the glorification of the Cross of Christ and for the proclamation of forgiveness through his blood.*[22]

The sobriety with which the Holy Father spoke in this address is startling. He demonstrates within the text a clear understanding of the destiny of the Church in the near future, even if exact dates are hidden in the secrets of the Father. The final statement says: "The Millennium is the supreme moment for the glorification of the Cross of Christ." In the Church's recent history, does this not perhaps show the glorification of the many martyrs, and point to an increase in suffering for the Church? For as the bloody sacrifice of Jesus was necessary for his resurrection, so too the bloody sacrifice of the Church's martyrs will be necessary for its own resurrection.

In 1993, in an *ad Limina* address to Polish bishops, Pope John Paul made further interesting comments about our times. They mirror claims from visionaries that we are living in a time of grace and mercy, before the chastisement comes:

On the threshold of the Third Millennium of redemption, the love of Christ is arousing a new apostolic ardour in the Church and all her members. *Ours is a particular time, truly the "Kairos," that is, a time of grace.* By the power of the Holy Spirit many great things are happening in the world. As a Church let us be sensitive to these signs of the times; let us study them and respond to them in a spirit of faith. May they inspire us with new hope.[23]

It is interesting that in a general audience which Pope John Paul gave on September 23, 1998 he spoke of *"times"* (*chronoi*) *and "seasons"* (*Kairoi*) in relation to the end times, reminding us that they were not for us to know. It seems certain, however, that the successor of St. Peter, who obtains the papal charism of assistance from

---

22. John Paul II, *ad Limina* Address, "The Church of the Millennium Bears Witness to Christ with No Fear of Displeasing the World," *L'Osservatore Romano* English ed., April 25, 1988, 5, 8.

23. John Paul II, *ad Limina* Address, "The Hour of the Laity has Struck for the Church in Poland too," *L'Osservatore Romano* English ed., February 3, 1993, 8.

the Holy Spirit, is granted certain insights into his particular historical era and thus is able to discern the *Kairos* in a way that is not open to others. The doctrine of the charism of assistance was explained by Pope John Paul at the general audience of March 17, 1993; the theological basis of which derives from Jesus' words to Peter: "I have prayed for you" (Lk. 22:32).[24]

A clear concept of the new Advent is essential to our understanding of the pontificate of John Paul II, and statements explaining it appear throughout the twenty-seven years of his reign, clearly presenting to us the unveiling of a mystery concerning the future of the Church. This mystery, however, is only revealed to those who listen to and obey the pope; only to those who are attentive to the inspirations of the Holy Spirit and the interventions of his Spouse, the Blessed Virgin. On his travels, the message was the same: prepare for the Lord's return. During his apostolic voyage to Lebanon in May 1997, the pope's vision of the future was clear:

> The whole Church awaits his coming, from East to West. The sons and daughters of Lebanon await His new coming. *We are all living in the Advent of the last days of history, and all trying to prepare for the Coming of Christ,* to build the Kingdom of God which he proclaimed.[25]

Although a separate chapter will be devoted to his message for the youth, it is appropriate to give his closing comments at the World Youth Day in Denver in 1993:

> This pilgrimage must continue—it must continue in our lives; it must continue in the life of the Church as she looks forward to the Third Christian Millennium. *It must continue as a new advent, a moment of hope and expectation until the return of the Lord in glory.* Your celebration of this World Youth Day has been a pause along

---

24. "The Bishop of Rome is also the heir to Peter in the charism of special assistance that Jesus promised him when he said: 'I have prayed for you' (Lk. 22:32). This signifies the Holy Spirit's continual help in the whole exercise of the teaching mission, meant to explain revealed truth and its consequences in human life." Pope John Paul II, General Audience, March 17, 1993, http://www.vatican.va/.

25. John Paul II, "Homily at Naval Esplanade Beirut," Lebanon, May 11, 1997, http://www.vatican.va/.

the journey, a moment of prayer and of refreshment, but a journey that must take us even further.[26]

The Marian year of 1987–88 was a significant step on the journey of the new Advent. The pope urged the faithful to raise their eyes to Mary, and to place their trust in her maternal heart. Its beginning on the Feast of Pentecost is significant because it recalled our Blessed Mother's place among the Apostles in the cenacle of the upper room, reminding us that Mary is uniquely related to the Holy Spirit as His Spouse and urging the Church to look towards the return of Christ: "The Spirit and the Bride say, 'Come'" (Rev. 22:17). The year ended on the Feast of Mary's Assumption, reaffirming her perfection in heaven and encouraging the Church along its own journey to perfection. In the Holy Father's homily at the close of this Marian year, addressing Mary, he said:

> We have begun our pilgrimage of faith with you, we, the generation which is drawing near *to the beginning of the third Millennium* after Christ. We have begun to walk with you, we, a generation which bears *a certain resemblance to that first Advent*, when on the horizon of human longing for the coming of the Messiah, a mysterious light was enkindled: *the Morning Star*—the Virgin of Nazareth, prepared by the Most Holy Trinity to be the Mother of the Son of God: *Alma Redemptoris Mater.*[27]

The Holy Father concluded the Marian year with a prayer to the Most Holy Virgin which included this plea for her maternal intercession:

> Mercifully accompany our steps towards the frontiers of a redeemed and peaceful humanity and make our heart glad and secure in the certainty that the Dragon is not stronger than your Beauty, gentle and eternal woman, first among the redeemed and friend of every creature, who still groans and hopes in the world. Amen.[28]

---

26. John Paul II, "Angelus Address for World Youth Day, Cherry Creek State Park," *L'Osservatore Romano* English ed., August 18, 1993.

27. John Paul II, Homily, "During the Past Year We have Followed You, O Mother, on Our Pilgrimage of Faith," *L'Osservatore Romano* English ed., August 22, 1988, 2.

28. Ibid., 2.

It is fitting to close this chapter on the new Advent with perhaps the most prophetic prayer ever composed by Pope John Paul II. It is important because he reveals the eschatological destination facing the world, and clearly states that the new birth of Jesus is almost upon us; that is to say, the final coming. We know this because of the reference to the approaching *Eternal* Kingdom of Christ. Certainly the pope knows time is short for us and calls us to watch and pray:

> *Lord on the night of your birth*
> *the poor shepherds of Bethlehem*
> *heard the promise of peace.*
> *We have brought life into being*
> *and believe that if the convulsions of our century*
> *are the death pangs of an old world,*
> *they are also the birth pangs of your new birth.*
> *We perceive that the hour of birth is approaching*
> *for the young mother of the new Advent,*
> *and that the Father wishes to spread by our means*
> *the rainbow of his Covenant of Reconciliation.*
> *Lord, may the angels soon sing of the beatitude*
> *for those who are poor in spirit on this earth.*
> *And so, full of faith, they shall discover that for them*
> *your eternal and universal Kingdom is approaching,*
> *the Kingdom of Truth and Life,*
> *the Kingdom of Sanctity and Grace*
> *the Kingdom of Justice, Love, and Peace.*
> *Amen.*[29]

29. John Paul II, "Pope's Prayer with Young People for Peace," *L'Osservatore Romano* English ed., April 9, 1985, 4.

6

The Pope of Fatima

It performed great signs, even making fire come down from heaven to earth in the sight of everyone. It deceived the inhabitants of the earth with the signs it was allowed to perform in the sight of the first beast, telling them to make an image for the beast who had been wounded by the sword and revived. It was then permitted to breathe life into the beast's image, so that the beast's image could speak and could have anyone who did not worship it put to death. It forced all the people, small and great, rich and poor, free and slave, to be given a stamped image on their right hands or their foreheads, so that no one could buy or sell except one who had the stamped image of the beast's name or the number that stood for its name. (Rev. 13:13–17)

THE RELATIONSHIP between Pope John Paul II and the great Marian apparitions of Fatima, Portugal is of paramount importance to this discussion. As stated in the introduction, the influence of these supernatural events on the Church as a whole, and on the popes in particular, is so profound that they warrant a deeper reflection. Some apparitions are approved and left for the individual to gain spiritually from their message. Fatima is different; it could not be ignored by the Church. The prophetic nature was such that to close our eyes to its contents would have had catastrophic implications for mankind. Cardinal Ratzinger (now Pope Benedict XVI) stated on June 26, 2000, when releasing the "third secret," that Fatima was "undoubtedly the most prophetic of modern apparitions."[1] It is not my intention to study the actual apparitions, as there are plenty of books on the subject, but rather to reveal the role they have played in the pontificate of John Paul II.

1. "The Message of Fatima," June 26, 2000, http://www.vatican.va/.

Firstly, Fatima is apocalyptic; the sensational miracle of the sun on October 13, 1917 was a symbolic sign of the "Woman clothed with the Sun" (Rev. 12:1) and her battle with the "huge red dragon" (Rev. 12:3). In fact, Pope Paul VI even saw in this miraculous event a fore-shadowing of the last judgment scene: "It was eschatological in the sense that it was like a repetition or an annunciation of a scene at the end of time for all humanity assembled together."[2] With the revealing of the third secret in June 2000, we have a vivid picture of the message imparted to Sr. Lucia. The secret contains a vision in which an angel is about to set fire to the world with a flaming sword. He shouts: "Penance, Penance, Penance!" Next the Blessed Virgin is seen; her outstretched right hand radiates such power that the flames die out. The pope is then seen walking through a city in ruins, with corpses littering the streets. He bends down in pain and sorrow; praying for their souls. He then proceeds up a steep mountain, with a procession of bishops, priests, religious, laymen, and women in train. At the top of the mountain there is a large Cross, and when the Holy Father reaches it he falls to his knees. Suddenly he is killed by a group of soldiers with bullets and arrows, and immediately after, his entourage are also killed one after another. Beneath the two arms of the Cross there are two angels each with a crystal aspersorium in which they gather up the blood of the Martyrs. They then sprinkle the souls making their way to God with the blood.

The Vatican's interpretation of the secret (although not binding) suggests that the assassination attempt on the life of Pope John Paul II on May 13, 1981, the very date of the first apparition in 1917, fulfills the prophecy of the pope at the top of the mountain. We know that the Holy Father had publicly stated that Our Lady saved his life: "It was a motherly hand that guided the bullet's path, and the agonizing Pope, rushed to the Gemelli Polyclinic, halted at the threshold of death."[3] Medical reports from the time suggest that the bullet miraculously changed direction in his body, missing vital organs by

2. Francis Johnston, *Fatima: The Great Sign* (Rockford: Tan Books, 1980), 69.
3. John Paul II, Address to Italian Bishops, "The World Awaits Our Service," *L'Osservatore Romano* English ed., June 1, 1994, 3.

a fraction.[4] Sr. Lucia commented on the third secret in a letter to Pope John Paul II on May 12, 1982. She stated:

> The third part of the secret refers to Our Lady's words: "If not, Russia will spread her errors throughout the world, causing wars and persecutions of the Church. The good will be martyred; the Holy Father will have much to suffer; various nations will be annihilated." The third part of the secret is a symbolic revelation, referring to this part of the Message, conditioned by whether we accept or not what the Message itself asks of us: "If my requests are heeded, Russia will be converted, and there will be peace".... *And if we have not yet seen the complete fulfillment of the final part of this prophecy, we are going towards it little by little.*[5]

The final part refers to whole nations being annihilated; is this what is soon to transpire as part of the great tribulation?

The pope made three pilgrimages to the shrine of Fatima, and on each occasion gave many insights into its significance in these end times. The first visit was exactly one year after the assassination attempt. He went to say thank you to Divine Providence for saving his life. In his homily at Mass, he spoke of Mary's maternal love for us all: "Mary's motherhood in our regard is manifested in a particular way in the places where she meets us: *her dwelling places*; places in which a special presence of the Mother is felt." He added: "Mary's spiritual motherhood is therefore a sharing in the *power of the Holy Spirit*, of 'the giver of life.'" The pope stresses that the message of Fatima is basically the same as the Gospel message: "Repent, for the Kingdom of Heaven is at hand" (Matt. 3:2):

> This call was uttered at the beginning of the twentieth century, and it was addressed particularly to the present century. *The Lady*

---

4. The pope's surgeon Professor Crucitti observed something "absolutely anomalous and inexplicable." The bullet had moved in a zigzag from the pope's stomach missing vital organs. It came within a hairsbreadth of the central aorta and also missed the dorsal spine and all the other principle nerve centers. The professor's conclusion? "It seems that the bullet was guided so as to avoid irreparable damage." Renzo Allegri, *The Pope of Fatima* (Milan: Mondadori, 2006), 271.

5. Lucia, "letter to Pope John Paul II," May 12, 1982, *The Message of Fatima*, June 26, 2000, http://www.vatican.va/.

of the message seems to have read with special insight the "signs of the times", the signs of our time. . . . And so while the message of Our Lady of Fatima is a motherly one, it is also strong and decisive. It sounds like John the Baptist speaking on the banks of the Jordan. It invites to repentance. It gives a warning. It calls to prayer. It recommends the Rosary.

The Holy Father later turned to the eschatological dimension of the Fatima message:

The people of God is a pilgrim along the ways of this world *in an eschatological direction.* It is making its pilgrimage towards the eternal Jerusalem, towards "the dwelling of God with men." God will there *"wipe away every tear* from their eyes, and death shall be no more, neither shall there be mourning nor crying nor pain any more, for the former things have passed away." But at the present "the former things" *are still in existence.* They it is that constitute the temporal setting of our pilgrimage.

For this reason we look towards him who sits upon the throne and says, "Behold, I make all things new" (cf. Rev. 21:15). And together with the Evangelist and Apostle we try to see with the eyes of faith "the new heaven and new earth," for the first heaven and first earth have passed away. But "the first heaven and first earth" still exist about us and within us. We cannot ignore it. But this enables us to recognize what an immense *grace* was being granted to us human beings when, in the midst of our pilgrimage, *there shone forth on the horizon of the faith of our times this "great portent. A woman"* (cf. Rev. 12:1).[6]

At his general audience the day before leaving for Fatima, the pope said: "That message is revealed today as more relevant than ever."[7] It is noticeable that the Pontiff equates Mary's role with that of John the Baptist; the message from both is clear: "This is the time of fulfillment. The kingdom of God is at hand. Repent, and believe in the gospel" (Mk. 1:15). As John the Baptist prepared the way for the first coming, so Mary prepares the way for the second coming;

---

6. John Paul II, Homily, "The Message of Mary's Maternal Love," *L'Osservatore Romano* English ed., May 17, 1982, 1, 3, 12.

7. Ibid., 12.

using the same language—"strong and decisive," as confirmed by Pope John Paul.

The figure of the pope is essential to the entire message of Fatima; evidently for several reasons. Firstly, the prophetic element of the secret mentions that the pope will have much to suffer; secondly, there is the request for him to consecrate Russia to the Immaculate Heart of Mary; and thirdly, as head of the Church, the pontiff must above all recognize the importance and urgency of the message. For this great Marian pope, the third reason was made abundantly clear with the events of May 13, 1981. He himself called it a "great divine trial," and explained his innermost feelings at his first two general audiences after his recovery:

> During the last few months God has allowed me to experience suffering, and to experience the danger of losing my life. At the same time he has allowed me to understand clearly that this *is a special grace of his for me myself as a man, and at the same time—considering the service I am carrying out as Bishop of Rome—a grace for the Church.* . . . With deep gratitude to the Holy Spirit, I think of that weakness that he permitted me to experience since May 13, believing and humbly trusting that it may have served for the strengthening of the Church and also that of my human person.[8]

If we look back at the early history of the Church, we see the many martyrs who sacrificed their lives for the growth of the Kingdom. This number included many popes who bore testimony to the crucified and risen Christ. There is also an interesting parallel between John Paul II and the first pope, St. Peter. We read in the Acts of the Apostles chapter 12, of the miraculous escape of St. Peter from Herod's prison; was this not also the case with Blessed John Paul? Did not the Lord come to his rescue just before death struck? The pope seems to imply that the "divine trial" was necessary for his ministry and for the entire Church. We will only know in eternity the enormity of what occurred that day, but we can be certain that the Lord blessed the Church at that moment. In Poland, the Solidarity Movement was wrestling with Communism; in East and

---

8. John Paul II, General Audience, "The 13 May Event a Great Divine Trial," *L'Osservatore Romano* English ed., October 19, 1981, 3.

West, the Cold War was at its height threatening a nuclear disaster, and within the Church the apostasy was rapidly spreading. Into this arena entered the suffering pope, offering up his life for the salvation of the world. It is a fact that suffering brings us closer to God, which explains why the Lord allows so much to afflict us; and suffering offered up in union with the Passion of Christ takes on an entirely new meaning, as is evident in the "victim-souls,"[9] who live a continuous *Via Crucis*.

It becomes apparent that the assassination attempt opened the spiritual eyes of Pope John Paul II even more to the message of Fatima. Very soon after the attack, he thought of consecrating the world to the Immaculate Heart of Mary, and the opportunity arose on June 7, 1981, the Solemnity of Pentecost. He entrusted the "whole human family" to Mary, and included this invocation in the prayer: "O Mother. May there dawn for everyone the time of peace and freedom, the time of truth, of justice, and of hope."[10] In order to respond more fully to the request of Our Lady, the pope wrote to all the bishops of the world to ask them to join him in consecrating all men and women and all peoples to the Immaculate Heart of Mary. The pope decided to recite the formula of Consecration in the Jubilee Year of the Redemption, on the Feast of the Annunciation, March 25, 1984. The prayer itself was much publicized, but what was not so well known was the pope's prayer in front of the statue of Our Lady of Fatima recited later that same day. The relevance of Fatima to the *novissimis* and the prospects of a renewed world are evident in the text:

> So today we have wanted to entrust the fate of the world, of individuals, of peoples, to your Immaculate Heart in order to arrive at the very center of the mystery of the Redemption, the mystery that is stronger than all the sins of man and of the world, the mystery in which one can conquer sin in its various forms, *in which one can inaugurate a new world*. And we so need this new world because we

---

9. Those souls who accept lives of continual suffering, forming a deep mystical union with the Lord—St. Gemma Galgani being a perfect example.

10. John Paul II, "Act of Entrustment to the Immaculate Heart of Mary," *The Message of Fatima*, June 26, 2000, http://www.vatican.va/.

experience more and more that the old world, the world of sin, oppresses us, frightens us, brings various forms of injustice.[11]

This is at the core of the Fatima message; that after the trials have passed, an era of peace will come in the form of a new world, a world where Jesus reigns and death is no more. Our Lady specifically said that, "*in the end* my Immaculate Heart will triumph . . . and a period of peace will be granted to the world." In order to reach this goal, the request for the Consecration had to be met; unfortunately, it is known that many bishops did not obey the Holy Father's desire, and much confusion arose as to whether the conditions set down by Our Lady were met. It cannot be denied that Russia was not mentioned in the text and perhaps one day a future pope will renew the consecration with the explicit mention of that nation; however, just as no prayer is ever wasted, we can assume that the Lord accepted it in the same way that He accepted the 1942 Consecration performed by Pius XII. Sr. Lucia had confirmed this to be the case: "The good Lord has already shown me His contentment with the act performed by the Holy Father (Pius XII) . . . although it was incomplete according to His desire."[12] It is in this light that we can understand the sudden collapse of Communism in Eastern Europe in 1989. For those of us who knew the power of that Consecration and trusted the Blessed Virgin, the great events of that year came as no real surprise. When the Lord promises something it is binding, although of course these peaceful revolutions were only a precursor to the ultimate triumph still in the future.

The Holy Father returned to Fatima nine years later, again on the anniversary, in May 1991. Much had occurred in the world in the intervening years, most notably the collapse of Communism and the easing of tensions between the Soviet Union and the United States. Pope John Paul once more reflected on Fatima's relevance to the eschatological journey of the Church. It becomes clear when reading the papal homilies and addresses given at the Shrine, that

11. John Paul II, "Prayer to Our Lady of Fatima," *L'Osservatore Romano* English ed., April 2, 1984, 10.
12. Antonio Socci, *The Fourth Secret of Fatima* (Loreto Publications: Fitzwilliam, NH, 2006), 187.

the pope wanted to enlighten our understanding of where the Blessed Virgin is leading the Church: to the "new heavens and the new earth." He returned to the theme of a "new world" in recalling St. Augustine's response to a group of Christians from Hippo who were under attack from the Vandals: "Don't be afraid, dear children. This is not an old world that is ending. It is a new world that begins. A new dawn seems to be rising in the sky of history, inviting Christians to be the light and soul to the world that has enormous need for Christ, Redeemer of man."[13]

The pope's homily on May 13, 1991, centered on the Cross of Christ as the center of history, the depth of man's mystery revolving around Golgotha. The history of the Cross is the history of sin and death. But a new perspective is revealed with the death of Jesus; it is the passing away of the "first heaven and first earth" and with the rolling away of the tomb, the inauguration of the "new heaven and new earth." The pope explained beautifully: "By his death he was sown in the womb of the earth, the invisible power of new life; his death *is the beginning of resurrection*: 'Where, O death, is your victory; Where, O death, is your sting?' (1 Cor. 15:55)."[14] The Holy Father reflected that the message of Fatima emphasizes the maternal mediation of Mary as essential to the Church of our times, as it struggles with the curse of unbelief and apostasy:

> Mary, who was near the Cross of her Son had to accept one more time the will of Christ, Son of God. But while on Golgotha, the Son pointed out one man only, John, the beloved disciple, she *has had to receive* everyone—all of us, the *men and women of this century* and of its difficult and dramatic history. . . . The inheritance of sin shows itself as an insane aspiration *to build the world*—a world created by humanity—*as if God did not exist*. And also as if there were no Cross on Golgotha where "death and life contended in that combat stupendous (Easter Sequence)."[15]

13. John Paul II, "Address in Portugal, May 11, 1991," *Queen of Peace Special Edition II*, Spring 1995 (McKees Rocks, PA: St. Andrew's Productions).

14. John Paul II, Homily, "At the Foot of the Cross, Mary Receives Every Person in this Difficult and Dramatic Century," *L'Osservatore Romano* English ed., May 20, 1991, 6–7.

15. Ibid.

This goal to create a world without God is the great desire of the Antichrist; it is his agents that lay the foundations for the great recapitulation of all evil that will be manifest within him. Fatima tells us that consecration to the Immaculate Heart of Mary is the greatest weapon in defending the Church and the world against this onslaught of evil.

The Holy Father made his third visit to the Shrine in May 2000, for the beatification of two of the three visionaries, Jacinta and Francisco Marto. Once again he alluded to the battle between Mary and Satan:

> According to the divine plan, "a woman clothed with the sun" (Rev. 12:1) came down from heaven to this earth to visit the privileged children of the Father. She speaks to them with a mother's voice and heart: she asks them to offer themselves as victims of reparation, saying that she was ready to lead them safely to God.... "Another portent appeared in heaven; behold, a great red dragon" (Rev. 12:3). These words from the first reading of the Mass make us think of the great struggle between good and evil, showing how, when man puts God aside, he cannot achieve happiness, but ends up destroying himself. How many victims there have been throughout the last century of the second millennium! We remember the horrors of the First and Second World Wars and the other wars in so many parts of the world, the concentration and extermination camps, the gulags, ethnic cleansings and persecutions, terrorism, kidnappings, drugs, the attacks on unborn life and the family. The message of Fatima is a call to conversion, alerting humanity to have nothing to do with the "dragon" whose "tail swept down a third of the stars of heaven, and cast them to the earth" (Rev. 12:4). Man's final goal is heaven, his true home, where the heavenly Father awaits everyone with his merciful love.[16]

While Pope John Paul spoke of the tribulation of the past century and the many martyrs who suffered, he explained that the new *beati* would spread the light of Christ helping Christians to dispel the darkness from the earth:

---

16. John Paul II, "Homily for the Beatification of Francisco and Jacinta Marto at Fatima," May 13, 2000, http://www.vatican.va/.

Today Jesus' praise takes the solemn form of the beatification of the little shepherds, Francisco and Jacinta. With this rite the Church wishes to put on the candelabrum these two candles, which God lit to illumine humanity in its dark and anxious hours.[17]

Finally, the pope made reference to the special value of devotion to the Mother of Jesus, and its powers to advance one's spiritual life:

> My last words are for the children . . . ask your parents and teachers to enroll you in the "school" of Our Lady, so that she can teach you to be like the little shepherds, who tried to do whatever she asked them. I tell you that *"one makes more progress in a short time of submission and dependence on Mary than during entire years of personal initiatives, relying on oneself alone"* (St. Louis de Montfort, *The True Devotion to the Blessed Virgin Mary*, n. 155).[18]

In essence, Blessed John Paul II was the greatest apostle of Fatima; bearing the hallmarks of the apostles of the end times as described by St. Louis de Montfort. He bore witness to the message through his sufferings and his obedience to the demands of the Blessed Virgin. Throughout the years of his pontificate, he renewed the consecration to the Immaculate Heart of Mary using a variety of specially composed prayers. However, from a purely eschatological point of view, and in the context of Fatima's prophetic revelations, it is the original Consecration of 1981 in the form of an "Act of Entrustment" that perhaps portrays more than any other, the importance of Fatima in helping prepare the Church for the second coming of Jesus. In the prayer, the Holy Father calls on Mary for her help to set free creation from its bondage of sin and death:

> Take under your motherly protection the whole human family which we consecrate to you, O Mother, with affectionate rapture. May the time of peace and freedom, the time of truth, justice and hope approach for everyone. O You, who through the mystery of Your particular holiness, free of all stain from the moment of Your conception feel in a particular deep way that "the whole creation has been groaning in travail" (Rom. 8:22), while, "subject to futility," it hopes that it will be "set free from its bondage to decay"

17. Ibid.
18. Ibid.

(Rom. 8:20–21). *You contribute unceasingly to the "revealing of the sons of God" for whom "the creation waits with eager longing"* (Rom. 8:19), to enter the freedom of their joy (cf. Rom. 8:21). O Mother of Jesus, now glorified in heaven in body and soul, as the image and beginning of the Church, which is to have its *fulfillment in the future age here on earth*, until the day of the Lord comes (cf. 2 Pet. 3:10), do not cease to shine before the pilgrim people of God as a sign of sure hope and consolation (cf. *Lumen Gentium,* 68).... "The Spirit and the Bride say to the Lord Jesus 'Come'" (cf. Rev. 22:17). "Thus the Church is seen to be a people brought into unity of the Father, the Son, and the Holy Spirit" (*Lumen Gentium,* 4). Thus we repeat today: "Come," trusting in your motherly intercession, O Clement, O Loving, O sweet Virgin Mary.[19]

Interestingly, Cardinal Ratzinger (now Pope Benedict XVI) stated in 1996 that, "we hear today the groaning of creation as no one has heard it before."[20]

Looking back over the history of the Fatima apparitions we can see that only the last chapter remains to be written; that is the bloody persecution seen in the third secret (pertaining to the Antichrist's final assault on the Church of Christ, and the coming of the Kingdom through the triumph of the Immaculate Heart of Mary). We leave this present chapter with these words spoken by Pope John Paul II in *Crossing the Threshold of Hope,* published in 1994: "Mary appeared to three children at Fatima in Portugal and spoke to them the words that now, at the end of this century, seem close to their fulfillment."[21]

---

19. John Paul II, "Radio message during the Ceremony of Veneration, Thanksgiving and Entrustment to the Virgin Mary Theotokos in the Basilica of Saint Mary Major": *Insegnamenti di Giovanni Paolo II, IV,* 1, Vatican City, 1981, 1246.
20. Ratzinger, *Salt of the Earth,* 231.
21. John Paul II, *Crossing the Threshold of Hope,* 221.

7

The Spark from Poland?

Now I am sending my messenger—he will prepare the way before me; And the lord whom you seek will come suddenly to his temple; The messenger of the covenant whom you desire—see, he is coming! says the LORD of hosts.
But who can endure the day of his coming? Who can stand firm when he appears? For he will be like a refiner's fire, like fullers' lye. He will sit refining and purifying silver, and he will purify the Levites, Refining them like gold or silver, that they may bring offerings to the Lord in righteousness. Then the offering of Judah and Jerusalem will please the Lord, as in ancient days, as in years gone by.
(Mal. 3:1–4)

FATIMA is not the only private revelation that molded Pope John Paul's eschatology. Whereas it only came to be an essential part of the pontificate after the assassination attempt in 1981, the revelations and mystical experiences of St. Faustina Kowalska (1905–1938) were meditated upon by the pope many years before his election to the See of Peter. In fact after twenty years of suspicion by the Vatican, it was Karol Cardinal Wojtyla who opened a new investigation in his Diocese of Krakow into the life of Sister Faustina. The intervention by the Cardinal led to the lifting of the ban imposed on the Polish mystic's writings just six months before his election in 1978. The ban had been imposed because of a faulty translation of her writings; nevertheless Cardinal Wojtyla continued to quietly build up the case for Sr. Faustina's eventual canonization. Finally, to the joy of thousands around the world, he himself proclaimed the "Apostle of Divine Mercy" as the first saint of the new millennium on April 30, 2000 in St. Peter's Square.[1]

1. The devotion Pope John Paul II felt towards St. Faustina was emphasized by his comment on this occasion to Dr. Valentine Fuster (a pre-eminent cardiologist

The Spark from Poland?

In order to understand why St. Faustina's message is important, it is necessary to give a brief summary of the teachings given to her by Our Lord. The entire content of St. Faustina's revelations revolves around devotion to the Divine Mercy; that is devotion to Jesus who is mercy personified. It is, in reality, an extension of the devotion to the Sacred Heart, because the mercy of Jesus flows from the love of his Heart, pierced by the lance for our salvation. It was from the side of Christ that the Church was born—the blood and water that flowed out at that moment became the source of divine mercy, proclaimed most wonderfully in the sacrament of reconciliation. We may recall that Pope Pius XI emphasized that the Sacred Heart devotion in the form promoted by St. Margaret Mary, was given to the Church because of the gradual onset of the last days, when the love of many would grow cold. The new aspect of divine mercy was given specifically to our times because sin and evil had grown to such heights that there was a danger that trust in the mercy of God could evaporate in many of the faithful. Jesus came to reveal that devotion to His divine mercy was the last hope of salvation. He told St. Faustina that the greater the sinner, the greater the right that sinner would have to receive His mercy. The Lord instructed St. Faustina to have an image painted showing two rays emanating from his pierced heart. The two rays, according to what Jesus told her, "represent the blood and the water."[2] The blood—from the sacrifice on Golgotha, and the water—the grace of baptism and rebirth. Under the image, He asked for the words to be inscribed: "Jesus I trust in Thee!"

This image would help those doubting the forgiveness of God to trust more in his mercy; it speaks of a tender love from a God who continually goes in search of the lost sheep, and of his burning desire to forgive sins and raise up repentant souls out of the abyss of despair. We need to bear in mind that with the devil's extended

who had studied the miraculous cure of Fr. Ron Pytel in his capacity as a medical consultant for the Congregation for the Causes of Saints): "*This is the happiest day of my life.*" See George W. Kosicki, *Pope John Paul II: The Great Mercy Pope* (Stockbridge: John Paul II Institute of Divine Mercy, 2001), 17.

2. Faustina Kowalska, *Divine Mercy in my Soul* (Stockbridge: Marians of the Immaculate Conception, 1987), 132.

power in the twentieth century, his ability to seduce people obviously grew; therefore, for those who would continually struggle to remain pure in the eyes of God, a new encouraging message of mercy was going to be extremely helpful. This goes some way towards explaining why this devotion has spread so rapidly in recent decades.

There is another aspect of the divine mercy message, which is of paramount importance to this discussion. It is clear and unambiguous in the words of Jesus that the end is approaching rapidly. I would like to offer some extracts from St. Faustina's diary entitled, *Divine Mercy in my Soul*, in which she recorded the words of Jesus, all under the orders of her spiritual director. These revelations are all eschatological in nature:

> Secretary of My mercy, write, tell souls about this great mercy of Mine, because the awful day, *the day of my justice, is near*. (Diary 965)

> Speak to the world about My mercy; let all mankind recognize My unfathomable mercy. *It is a sign for the end times, after it will come the day of justice*. (Diary 848)

> *You will prepare the world for My final coming*. (Diary 429)

The Blessed Virgin also spoke on this grave subject:

> Your lives must be like mine: quiet and hidden, in unceasing union with God, pleading for humanity and *preparing the world for the second coming of God*. (Diary 625)

> I gave the Savior to the world; as for you, you have to speak to the world about his great mercy *and prepare the world for the second coming of Him who will come not as a merciful savior, but as a just Judge*. Speak to souls about this great mercy while it is still time for granting mercy. If you keep silent now, you will be answering for a great number of souls on that terrible day. (Diary 635)

Perhaps the message that relates to the importance of Pope John Paul II in preparing the world for the final coming of Jesus, is this prophecy given by the Lord to his faithful apostle of divine mercy:

> As I was praying for Poland, I heard these words: "I bear a special love for Poland, and if she will be obedient to my will, I will exalt

her in might and holiness. *From her will come forth the spark that will prepare the world for My final coming.*" (Diary 1732)

The "spark" to which the Lord refers was in the opinion of the great apostle of Fatima, Bishop Pavel Hnilica, none other than the Polish Pontiff;[3] a view seemingly shared by many. Pope Benedict, adding further weight to that opinion stated in Blessed John Paul's beatification homily: "Throughout the long journey of preparation for the great Jubilee he directed Christianity once again to the future, the future of God, which transcends history . . . to be lived in history in an "Advent spirit."[4] Benedict had also stated in *Light of the World*: "Indeed, it was a concern of John Paul II to make clear that we are looking ahead to the coming of Christ."[5]

Blessed John Paul accomplished an incredible amount to impress upon the faithful the message of mercy. His second encyclical, *Dives in Misericordia*, issued in 1980 dealt specifically with the mercy of God and, over the twenty-five years until his death, he preached about, and implemented the requests Jesus made to St. Faustina concerning the spreading of the devotion. The greatest example of this came on the day of St. Faustina's canonization, when the Holy Father announced that from henceforth the Second Sunday of Easter would be known as "Divine Mercy Sunday." On that day, Jesus had promised St. Faustina that anyone who would go to confession and receive Holy Communion would be granted a complete pardon of sin and the temporal punishment due for them. In essence what the Lord was promising was a kind of renewal of baptism; not a new sacrament or second baptism, but the restoration of the purity of the soul that is present at the moment of baptism. It is one of the greatest, if not *the* greatest promise associated with a private revelation. It reflects the seriousness of the message, and calls us to take the opportunity to embrace divine mercy "while it is still time for granting mercy" (Diary 635).

---

3. Pavel Hnilica, "Letter to all Marian groups, 1995," *Queen of Peace Special Edition III*, Spring 1995 (McKees Rocks, PA: St. Andrew's Productions).
4. Benedict XVI, "Homily for the Beatification of Blessed John Paul II," May 1, 2011, http://www.vatican.va/.
5. Benedict XVI, *Light of the World* (London: Catholic Truth Society, 2010), 63.

The pope gave this interpretation on his relationship with the spreading of the Divine Mercy devotion in an Angelus Address at the Sanctuary of Merciful Love at Collevalenza, Italy in 1981:

Right from the beginning of my ministry in St. Peter's See in Rome, I considered this message my special task. *Providence has assigned it to me in the present situation of man, the Church, and the world.* It could also be said that precisely this situation assigned that message to me as my task before God, who is Providence, who is inscrutable mystery, the mystery of Love and Truth, of Truth and Love.[6]

Many years later, while visiting the Shrine of Divine Mercy in Poland he returned to the theme:

The message of Divine mercy has always been near and dear to me. It is as if history had inscribed it in the tragic experience of the Second World War. In those difficult years it was *a particular support and an inexhaustible source of hope*, not only for the people of Krakow but for the entire nation. This was also my personal experience, which I took with me to the See of Peter and which, in a sense, *forms the image of this pontificate.*[7]

The encyclical on mercy, although not mentioning the revelations given by the Lord to St. Faustina (probably because her cause for canonization was very far from completion at the time), still took its foundation from the messages. We know this from the statement made by George Weigel in his excellent biography of Pope John Paul II, *Witness to Hope:*

As Archbishop of Krakow, Wojtyla had defended Sister Faustina when her orthodoxy was being posthumously questioned in Rome, due in large part to a faulty Italian translation of her diary, and had promoted the cause of her beatification. John Paul II, who said that he felt spiritually "very near to Sister Faustina," had been thinking about her for a long time when he began *Dives in Misericordia.*[8]

---

6. John Paul II, "Pope's Pilgrimage to Collevalenza and Todi," *L'Osservatore Romano* English ed., November 30, 1981, 5.
7. Kosicki, *Pope John Paul II: The Great Mercy Pope*, 108.
8. George Weigel, *Witness To Hope* (New York: Harper Collins, 1999), 387.

It becomes apparent that the pope was well aware of the fundamental importance of placing this new devotion before the universal Church.[9] Do we not see in these facts confirmation that the pope knew deep within himself that he was specially chosen by God to prepare the world for the return of Jesus through spreading the devotion? That he was to be the "spark" that would ignite the dawning of the new day? Let us look in detail at this splendid encyclical, which reveals God, who is "rich in mercy" (Eph. 2:4).

The pope opens the Letter with his reasons for choosing the theme of mercy:

> Following the teaching of the Second Vatican Council and paying close attention to the special needs of our times, I devoted the encyclical *Redemptor hominis* to the truth about man, a truth that is revealed to us in its fullness and depth in Christ. A no less important need in these critical and difficult times impels me to draw attention once again in Christ to the countenance of the "Father of mercies and God of all comfort" (2 Cor. 1:3).... The present-day mentality, more perhaps than that of people in the past, seems opposed to a God of mercy, and in fact tends to exclude from life and to remove from the human heart the very idea of mercy. The word and the concept of "mercy" seem to cause uneasiness in man, who, thanks to the enormous development of science and technology, never before known in history, has become the master of the earth and has subdued and dominated it.... The truth, revealed in Christ, about God the "Father of mercies," enables us to "see" Him as particularly close to man especially when man is suffering, when he is under threat at the very heart of his existence and dignity. And this is why, in the situation of the Church and the world today, many individuals and groups guided by a lively sense of faith are turning, I would say almost spontaneously, to the mercy of God. They are certainly being moved to do this by Christ Himself, who through His Spirit works within human hearts. *For the mystery of God the "Father of mercies"*

---

9. Pope John Paul's knowledge of Sr. Faustina can be traced back to his youth during the Second World War: "I often visited the grave of Sister Faustina.... Everything about her was extraordinary, impossible to foresee in such a simple girl." John Paul II, *Rise Let Us Be On Our Way* (London: Jonathan Cape, 2004), 194.

revealed by Christ becomes, in the context of today's threats to man, as it were a unique appeal addressed to the Church.[10]

This last sentence confirms the conviction that the appeal of mercy is especially relevant to the last stage of the Church's journey. It is noticeable that the pope, even many years ago was aware that the devotion was being taken up by the faithful in great numbers. The Holy Father teaches that the "Paschal Mystery is the culmination of this revealing and effecting of mercy, which is able to justify man, to restore justice in the sense of that salvific order which God willed from the beginning in man and through man in the world." The eschatological dimension of mercy, and one which is most relevant to this discussion, is taken up later in the document. The Pontiff explains:

> The cross is like a touch of eternal love upon the most painful wounds of man's earthly existence; it is the total fulfillment of the messianic programme that Christ once formulated in the synagogue at Nazareth and then repeated to the messengers sent by John the Baptist. According to the words once written in the prophecy of Isaiah, this programme consisted in the revelation of merciful love for the poor, the suffering and prisoners, for the blind, the oppressed and sinners. In the paschal mystery the limits of the many sided evil in which man becomes a sharer during his earthly existence are surpassed: the cross of Christ, in fact, makes us understand the deepest roots of evil, which are fixed in sin and death; thus the cross becomes an eschatological sign. Only in the eschatological fulfillment and definitive renewal of the world will love conquer, in all the elect, the deepest sources of evil, bringing as its fully mature fruit the kingdom of life and holiness and glorious immortality. The foundation of this eschatological fulfillment is already contained in the cross of Christ and in His death. The fact that Christ "was raised the third day" (1 Cor. 15:4) constitutes the final sign of the messianic mission, a sign that perfects the entire revelation of merciful love in a world that is subject to evil. At the same time it constitutes the sign that foretells "a new heaven

10. John Paul II, Encyclical Letter *Dives in Misericordia*, November 30, 1980, nos. 1, 2, http://www.vatican.va/.

and a new earth" (Rev. 21:1) when it "will wipe away every tear from their eyes, there will be no more death, or mourning, no crying, nor pain, for the former things have passed away" (Rev. 21:4).[11]

The Church's duty is to practice mercy in order to encourage others to do the same. Only in this way can a new era for humanity dawn. The practice of the prayer of mercy for the pope is an important means of bringing peace to our times:

However, at no time and in no historical period—especially at a moment as critical as our own—can the Church forget the prayer that is a cry for the mercy of God amid the many forms of evil which weigh upon humanity and threaten it. Precisely this is the fundamental right and duty of the Church in Christ Jesus, her right and duty towards God and towards humanity. The more the human conscience succumbs to secularization, loses its sense of the very meaning of the word "mercy," moves away from God and distances itself from the mystery of mercy, the more the Church has the right and the duty to appeal to the God of mercy "with loud cries" (Cf. Heb 5:7). *These "loud cries" should be the mark of the Church of our times, cries uttered to God to implore His mercy, the certain manifestation of which she professes and proclaims as having already come in Jesus crucified and risen, that is, in the Paschal Mystery.*[12]

These words of the Holy Father recall the reason for the Chaplet of Divine Mercy that Jesus dictated to St. Faustina. The Chaplet to be recited on the beads of the rosary consists of two prayers:

Eternal Father, I offer you the Body, Blood, Soul and Divinity of your beloved Son Our Lord Jesus Christ, in atonement for our sins and those of the whole world. (On large beads)

For the sake of his sorrowful Passion, have mercy on us and on the whole world. (On small beads)

11. Ibid., no. 8.
12. Ibid., no. 15.

In conclusion the following invocation is recited three times:

Holy God, Holy mighty One, Holy Immortal One, have mercy on us and on the whole world.

It is through the recitation of this chaplet that mercy will come to the world. Jesus told his humble instrument that sinners would find comfort and strength in it, and for those at the point of death, a means of obtaining salvation from God. This chaplet has fulfilled the desire of the pope for Catholics to pray for God's mercy to envelope the whole world; it being taken up by thousands, even millions of people in recent times as an expression of trust in the forgiveness of the Lord. Towards the end of the encyclical, the pope makes reference to the state of the world, implying that things are so grave that it deserves a chastisement rivaling the flood at Noah's time:

Like the prophets, let us appeal to that love which has maternal characteristics and which, like a mother, follows each of her children, each lost sheep, even if they should number millions, even if in the world evil should prevail over goodness, *even if contemporary humanity should deserve a new "flood" on account of its sins, as once the generation of Noah did.* Let us have recourse to that fatherly love revealed to us by Christ in His messianic mission, a love which reached its culmination in His cross, in His death and resurrection. Let us have recourse to God through Christ, mindful of the words of Mary's *Magnificat*, which proclaim mercy "from generation to generation." Let us implore God's mercy for the present generation. May the Church which, following the example of Mary, also seeks to be the spiritual mother of mankind, express in this prayer her maternal solicitude and at the same time her confident love, that love from which is born the most burning need for prayer. . . . The mystery of Christ, which reveals to us the great vocation of man and which led me to emphasize in the encyclical *Redemptor hominis* his incomparable dignity, also obliges me to proclaim mercy as God's merciful love, revealed in that same mystery of Christ. *It likewise obliges me to have recourse to that mercy and to beg for it at this difficult, critical phase of the history of the Church and of the world, as we approach the end of the second millennium.*[13]

13. Ibid., no. 15.

The very fact that Pope John Paul II devoted an encyclical, the highest form of teaching document, to the mercy of God shows the importance he attaches to it in the light of the times that humanity is passing through. When we bear in mind that he meditated upon all the messages contained in the diary of St. Faustina, including those that pertain to the end times, we can sense the urgency that he felt. It is not just in the encyclical that the Holy Father spoke on the subject: he proclaimed the message of Divine Mercy throughout the duration of his reign. One of the earliest expositions on the merciful love of God given by him came in 1981 at Collevalenza, Italy. Significantly, the pope related it to the scriptural passages concerning the Last Judgment:

> This Kingdom is the definitive gift of the Father, the Son, and the Holy Spirit. It is the gift prepared "from the foundation of the world" (Matt. 25:34), in the course of the whole history of salvation. . . . This Sunday's liturgy [Feast of Christ the King] makes us particularly aware that in the Kingdom revealed by the crucified and risen Christ the history of man and the world must be completed definitively: "But in fact Christ has been raised from the dead, the first fruits of all those who have fallen asleep" (1 Cor. 15:20). The Kingdom of Christ, which is the gift of Eternal Love, of Merciful Love, was prepared "from the foundation of the earth."

Later he added:

> How great is the power of Merciful Love, which we await until Christ has put all his enemies under his feet, completely overcoming sin and destroying death as his last enemy. *The Kingdom of Christ is moving towards the definitive victory of Merciful Love, towards the eschatological fullness of good and grace, of salvation and life.* . . . Here is the definitive fulfillment of Merciful Love: God: everything in everyone! All those in the world who daily repeat the words "Thy Kingdom come," pray, in a word, "that God may be everything in everyone."

The pope continued in words that seemed to flow straight from his heart:

Oh! What power of love modern man and the world need! What power of Merciful Love! In order that the Kingdom, which already exists in the world, may reduce to nothing the Kingdom of "rule and authority and power" which induce man's heart to sin, and spread over the world the horrible threat of destruction. Oh! What power of Merciful Love must be manifested in the cross and resurrection of Christ! *"He must reign".* . . . How much he desires to meet at the completion of the history of the world, those to whom he will say: "I was hungry and you gave me food, I was thirsty and you gave me drink" (Matt. 25:35).

The Holy Father ended his homily with this prayerful plea to Divine Mercy:

Merciful Love, we pray to you, do not fail! Merciful Love, be tireless! Be constantly greater than every evil, which is in man and in the world. Be greater than the evil which has increased in our century and our generation! Be more powerful with the power of the crucified King! *"Blessed be his Kingdom which is coming."*[14]

In 1997, the Holy Father visited the Shrine of Divine Mercy in Lagiewniki, where he thanked God for his role in spreading the devotion:

I give thanks to divine providence that I have been enabled to contribute personally to the fulfillment of Christ's will, through the institution of the Feast of Divine Mercy [at that time for Poland, not the universal Church]. Here, near the relics of Blessed Faustina Kowalska, I give thanks for the gift of her beatification. *I pray unceasingly that God will have "mercy on us and on the whole world"* (*Chaplet of Divine Mercy,* Diary, 476).[15]

The revelation that the pope prayed "unceasingly" for mercy from God is also an indication that he carried a tremendously heavy cross; no doubt feeling an immense duty to implore mercy from the Lord, and to obtain a "stay of execution" for our sinful humanity

---

14. John Paul II, "The Kingdom of God Already Exists: in the World, in Us!," *L'Osservatore Romano* English ed., November 30, 1981, 6–7.

15. Kosicki, *Pope John Paul II: The Great Mercy Pope,* 108.

while he remained the Vicar of Christ on earth. The last time he returned to his homeland, the Holy Father consecrated the new Basilica of Divine Mercy at Lagiewniki, near Krakow. He was more vigorous than ever in his proclamation of the message of Divine Mercy, and took the great step of entrusting the entire world to Divine Mercy at the same time. Is this not a sign that he sensed the day of justice looming ever larger on the horizon of history? The text of the homily delivered on August 17, 2002 seems to confirm this conviction:

> Like Saint Faustina, we wish to proclaim that apart from the mercy of God there is no other source of hope for mankind. We desire to repeat with faith: *Jesus, I trust in you!* This proclamation, this confession of trust in the all-powerful love of God, is especially needed in our own time, when mankind is experiencing bewilderment in the face of many manifestations of evil. *The invocation of God's mercy* needs to rise up from the depth of hearts filled with suffering, apprehension and uncertainty, and at the same time yearning for an infallible source of hope. That is why we have come here today, to this Shrine of Lagiewniki, in order to glimpse once more in Christ the face of the Father: "the Father of mercies and the God of all consolation" (2 Cor. 1:3). With the eyes of our soul, we long to look into the eyes of the merciful Jesus, in order to find deep within his gaze the reflection of his inner life, as well as the light of grace which we have already received so often, *and which God holds out to us anew each day and on the last day....* How greatly today's world needs God's mercy! In every continent, from the depth of human suffering, a cry for mercy seems to rise up.... Mercy is needed in order to ensure that every injustice in the world will come to an end in the splendor of truth. Today, therefore, in this Shine, I wish *solemnly to entrust the world to Divine Mercy.* I do so with the burning desire that the message of God's merciful love, proclaimed here through Saint Faustina, *may be made known to all the peoples of the earth* and fill their hearts with hope. May this message radiate from this place to our beloved homeland and throughout the world. *May the binding promise of the Lord Jesus be fulfilled: from here there must go forth "the spark which will prepare the world for his final coming"* (cf. Diary, 1732).

This spark needs to be lighted by the grace of God. This fire of mercy needs to be passed on to the world. *In the mercy of God the world will find peace and mankind will find happiness!* I entrust this task to you, dear Brothers and Sisters, to the Church in Krakow and Poland, and to all the votaries of Divine Mercy who will come here from Poland and from throughout the world. *May you be witnesses to mercy!*[16]

The following day, at a beatification ceremony in Blonie, Krakow, the theme of divine mercy was again taken up by the Holy Father, and once again, he explained the sense of urgency apparent in the messages:

From the beginning of her existence the Church, pointing to the mystery of the Cross and the Resurrection, has preached the mercy of God, a pledge of hope and a source of salvation for man. Nonetheless, it would appear that *we today have been particularly called* to proclaim this message before the world. We cannot neglect this mission, if God himself has called us to it through the testimony of Saint Faustina. God has chosen our own times for this purpose. Perhaps because the twentieth century, despite indisputable achievements in many areas, was marked in a particular way by the *"mystery of iniquity."* With this heritage both of good and of evil, we have entered the new millennium. New prospects of development are opening up before mankind, together with hitherto unheard-of dangers. Frequently man lives as if God did not exist, and even puts himself in God's place. He claims for himself the Creator's right to interfere in the mystery of human life. He wishes to determine human life through genetic manipulation and to establish the limit of death. Rejecting divine law and moral principles, he openly attacks the family. In a variety of ways he attempts to silence the voice of God in human hearts; he wishes to make God the "great absence" in the culture and the conscience of peoples. The "mystery of iniquity" continues to mark the reality of the world.

In experiencing this mystery, man lives in fear of the future, of emptiness, of suffering, of annihilation. Perhaps for this very rea-

---

16. John Paul II, Homily, "Dedication of the Shrine of Divine Mercy," August 17, 2002, http://www.vatican.va/.

son, it is as if Christ, using the testimony of a lowly Sister, entered our time in order to indicate clearly the source of relief and hope found in the eternal mercy of God. *The message of merciful love needs to resound forcefully anew.* The world needs this love. The hour has come to bring Christ's message to everyone: to rulers and the oppressed, to those whose humanity and dignity seem lost in the *mysterium iniquitatis. The hour has come when the message of Divine Mercy is able to fill hearts with hope and to become the spark of a new civilization: the civilization of love.*[17]

It is important that the pope speaks of the mystery of iniquity, because Sacred Scripture warns us that the Antichrist will be the last manifestation of this mystery before the Lord returns and destroys him with the "breath of his mouth and annihilates him with his glorious appearance at his coming" (cf. 2 Thess. 2:8). Furthermore, the pope says, "the hour has come when the message of Divine Mercy is able to become the spark of a new civilization." We know that the Holy Father is referring to the divine plan to gather redeemed humanity at the end of time into a civilization of love as explained in other magisterial documents.[18] We can conclude, therefore, that the Pontiff is suggesting the final hour has arrived; Divine Mercy will lead humanity through the last "hour" until the summer arrives (cf. Matt. 24:32).

The last great act of Pope John Paul, the witness and apostle of divine mercy, was his own ascent to Calvary at that unforgettable Easter of 2005. After bearing silent witness on Easter Sunday from

---

17. John Paul II, Homily, "Beatification Ceremony at Blonie, Krakow," August 18, 2002, http://www.vatican.va/.

18. John Paul II, *Vita Consecrata*: Throughout the Church's history, consecrated life has been a living presence of the Spirit's work, a kind of privileged milieu for absolute love of God and of neighbor, for witness to the divine plan of gathering all humanity into the civilization of love, the great family of the children of God. Available at http://www.vatican.va/.

[I]n a special way let us Christians welcome the prophet's appeal (Isaiah) and seek to lay the foundations of the civilization of love and peace in which there will be no more war, "and death will be no more, neither shall there be mourning, nor pain any more for the former things have passed away" (Apoc. 21:4). John Paul II, General Audience, September 4, 2002, http://www.vatican.va/.

his apartment window, he finally departed this world on the Feast of Divine Mercy itself, moments after the first Mass of Divine Mercy had been celebrated by his bedside. What was the Lord teaching us? If we look at the timing of the pope's death we see unfolding the whole message of salvation. Who could forget the image of the Holy Father clasping the Cross on Good Friday, or blessing us on Easter morning, knowing that soon his faith in the resurrection would be rewarded by the Risen Lord Himself? And finally, by departing for Heaven on the Feast of Divine Mercy, the Lord tells us that only by trusting in God's Mercy can we hope to reach salvation, and understand the Paschal mystery in its fullness. Divine Mercy has limited the power of sin and death, and Pope John Paul bore witness to that power through the Gospel of silent suffering, by uniting himself to the Cross of the Merciful Savior in order to participate in the task of renewing humanity.

This ultimately is where Divine Mercy leads us—to the liberation from slavery to evil. This explains why Jesus spoke often to St. Faustina about the second coming, because the work of Divine Mercy will only be complete when he returns to finally rid the world of corruption and all evil influences. The reservation of this devotion for these times is no coincidence; we may presume that Almighty God wants our understanding and appreciation of this attribute to shine forth in the epoch immediately preceding the Final Judgment.

Evidence suggests that Pope John Paul the Great was the "spark" sent by Jesus to prepare his final coming, and in the light of his unique contribution to the whole spirituality of mercy in the years since the message was given to St. Faustina, it does, I believe, point to this conclusion. It is worth remembering that the Lord was clear in telling his servant and "Secretary of Mercy" that she would "*prepare the world for His final coming*" (cf. Diary 429); therefore, the idea that this prophecy also refers to another individual is not beyond the realms of possibility. What the pope accomplished was to ensure the Divine Mercy devotion spread rapidly throughout the world. In this way he helped prepare the Church and the world for the day that would have no sunset—fulfilling all the wishes that the Lord entrusted to him. The reward for his faithfulness was to enter the Father's House on the first Saturday of the month, and on the

Vigil of the Feast of Divine Mercy—recalling in death the two great mystical occurrences associated with him: Fatima, where the first Saturday devotion[19] originated, and Divine Mercy, which the pope stated "forms the image of my Pontificate."[20]

19. On December 10, 1925, Our Lady appeared to Sr. Lucia explaining the first Saturday devotion in these terms: "See, My daughter, My heart surrounded by thorns which ungrateful men pierce at every moment by their blasphemies and ingratitude. . . . Say to all those who, for five months, on the first Saturday, confess, receive Holy Communion, recite the Rosary and keep Me company for 15 minutes while meditating on the fifteen mysteries of the Rosary, in a spirit of reparation, I promise to assist them at the hour of death with all the graces necessary for the salvation of their souls."

20. Kosicki, *Pope John Paul II: The Great Mercy Pope*, 108.

~8~

The Youth,
Watchmen of the Morning

*Watchman, how much longer the night? Watchman, how much
longer the night?*
  *Listen! Your sentinels raise a cry, together they shout for joy, for
they see directly, before their eyes, the Lord's return to Zion.*
                                                    (Is. 21:11, 52:8)

OUR JOURNEY through the eschatology of Pope John Paul II brings
us to a tremendously important area: the youth of the Church. The
title of this chapter might seem somewhat strange, but as the reader
will discover, the pope used this scriptural passage from Isaiah to
form the basis of a discussion with the youth of the Church, essentially entrusting to them the mission of preparing the world for the
second coming of the Lord through their joyful witness of hope.[1]
From the very beginning of his pontificate, John Paul II affirmed

---

1. Pope John Paul II explained the eschatological understanding of this scriptural passage in the General Audience of July 26, 2000: "The prophet Isaiah vividly
and forcefully describes this long wait [for night-time to pass in order to see the
light of dawn breaking on the horizon] by introducing a dialogue between two sentinels, which becomes a symbol for the right use of time: 'Watchman, how much
longer the night?' The watchman replies, 'Morning has come, and again night. If
you will ask, ask; come back again' (Is. 21:11–12).
  *"We must question ourselves, be converted and go to meet the Lord. Christ's three
appeals: 'Take heed, stay awake, watch!' limpidly sum up the Christian watchfulness
for meeting the Lord.* The waiting must be patient, as St. James urges us in his Letter:
'Be patient until the coming of the Lord. See how the farmer awaits the precious
yield of the soil. He looks forward to it patiently while the soil receives the winter
and the spring rains. You, too, be patient. Steady your hearts, because the coming of
the Lord is at hand'" (Jas. 5:7–8). Available at http://www.vatican.va/.

this aspect of his ministry by proclaiming them as the "hope of the Church."

In 1985, Pope John Paul addressed an apostolic letter to the youth of the world, exhorting them to "always be ready to give an explanation to anyone who asks you for a reason for your hope" (1 Pet. 3:15). Perhaps the pope's establishing of World Youth Day struck a chord most of all with the youth; literally millions of young people gathered together all over the globe, to pray with the pope and to listen to his inspiring message concerning the greatness of the Catholic faith and its implications for their future. It is apparent that one reason why huge crowds of young people loved the Holy Father and listened to him was the clarity of his message. He did not water down doctrines or patronize them in the hope of making the faith more appealing; on the contrary, he reminded them to follow *to the letter* the teachings of Jesus, and to be the Church's advocate, especially for those of their contemporaries living in a pagan culture.

The critical aspect lying at the heart of this chapter is the insistence of John Paul II that the youth be made aware of the seriousness of the situation, while recognizing the precise moment of history to which they belong. While reading this chapter, it is worth reflecting upon several questions: Why would the pope constantly encourage the youth to announce the return of Jesus if his coming were still far off in the distance? Would it not be better to avoid matters eschatological and concentrate instead on those sacramental?

Although reference will be made to messages given over the many years of Pope John Paul's reign, this passage from the World Youth Day held in the Great Jubilee of the Year 2000 at Tor Vergata, Italy, is a beneficial starting point to this discussion:

> In opening your Jubilee, dear young people, I would like to repeat the words with which I began my ministry as Bishop of Rome and Pastor of the universal Church; I would like them to guide your days in Rome: "Do not be afraid! Open, indeed, open wide the doors to Christ!" Open your hearts, your lives, your doubts, your difficulties, your joys and your affections to his saving power, and let him enter your hearts. Do not be afraid! Christ knows what is in man. He alone knows it." I said this on 22 October 1978. I repeat it with the same conviction, with the same force today, seeing the

hope of the Church and of the world shining in your eyes. *Yes, let Christ govern your young lives;* serve him with love. To serve Christ is freedom![2]

At the Vigil a few days later, he told the youth what he hoped and expected from them:

Dear friends, at the dawn of the Third Millennium I see in you the "morning watchmen" (cf. Is. 21:11–12). In the course of the century now past young people like you were summoned to huge gatherings to learn the ways of hatred; they were sent to fight against one another. The various godless messianic systems which tried to take the place of Christian hope have shown themselves to be truly horrendous. Today you have come together to declare that in the new century you will not let yourselves be made into tools of violence and destruction; you will defend peace, *paying the price in your person if need be.* You will not resign yourselves to a world where other human beings die of hunger, remain illiterate and have no work. You will defend life at every moment of its development; you will strive with all your strength to make this earth ever more liveable for all people. Dear young people of the century now beginning, in saying "yes" to Christ, you say "yes" to all your noblest ideals. *I pray that he will reign in your hearts and in all of humanity in the new century and the new millennium.* Have no fear of entrusting yourselves to him! He will guide you, he will grant you the strength to follow him every day and in every situation.[3]

Referring back to the apostolic letter of 1985 to the youth, the pope had then warned them of the dangers threatening the world as the third millennium drew closer:

We are all aware that the horizon of the lives of the billions of people who make up the human family at the close of the second millennium after Christ seems to portend the *possibility of calamities and catastrophes* on a truly apocalyptic scale. . . . On you depends the future, *on you depends also the end of this millennium and the*

2. John Paul II, "Address at Welcoming Ceremony for World Youth Day," St. John Lateran Square, August 15, 2000, http://www.vatican.va/.

3. John Paul II, "Address at Vigil of World Youth Day," Tor Vergata, August 19, 2000, http://www.vatican.va/.

beginning of the next. So do not be passive; take up your responsibilities—in all the fields open to you in our world.[4]

Evidently, we see that the Holy Father was not afraid to warn of apocalyptic dangers threatening the youth, in fact, as the years progressed; his message to them became ever clearer. On Palm Sunday, the day he published the apostolic Letter, he delivered a homily to the first ever gathering for a World Youth Day and gave this uplifting message about Jesus' return in glory: "He is the Lord of the coming age. In him the cause of man is filled with hope. Our 'hope in him is full of immortality!' (Wis. 3:4). Blessed, blessed is he who comes in the name of the Lord! Hosanna, Hosanna, Amen!"[5] It was at this weekend event in Rome that the Holy Father gave that wonderfully prophetic prayer, to which I referred at the end of the chapter concerning the New Advent: He stated: "*We believe that if the convulsions of our century are the death pangs of an old world, they are also the birth pangs of your new birth. We perceive that the hour of birth is approaching for the young mother of the new Advent.*"

In 1988, the pope visited Peru, and in prophetic terms, told a youth gathering that they would herald the dawn of a new era, a better world:

> You are the hope of the Church! *You will be the dawning of a new day,* if you are the bearers of the Life, which is Christ! This is both a challenge and a source of happiness: to receive the life which Christ has brought to us and to communicate it to others, with all the vitality and energy of your youth, with the innocence and dynamism that is part of your age. *Be the builders of a better world, starting today.*[6]

It is akin to a rallying cry, as the battle for the new world enters its final phase. Similar words are to be found in a speech that Pope John Paul II gave in Zagreb on September 11, 1994. Towards the end

---

4. John Paul II, Apostolic Letter *To the Youth of the World*, March 31, 1985, London, Catholic Truth Society, nos. 15, 16.

5. John Paul II, "Address to Youth," The Pope Teaches 1984/5, London, Catholic Truth Society, 106.

6. John Paul II, "Address to Youth of Peru," May 15, 1988, http://www.priestsfor-life.org/.

of the text, he turned to the Blessed Virgin for her help in bringing this hope to fruition:

> Holy Mary, the Mother of God of the Stone Gates, "Decus singulare Croatiae," stay by your sons who trust in you. You, "the Beginning of the better world," look upon them with merciful eye. May they respond to the Redeemer's call with your help. Make them more faithful messengers of your Son, the Prince of Peace. Renew their hearts and lives, make them stronger in the faith of the Apostles, *so that they may be joyful witnesses of the new times* and true peacemakers. Save them from danger and deliver them from all evils, O glorious and blessed Virgin. Amen![7]

The previous year had seen the pope make an apostolic voyage to the United States, where he met the youth in Denver. Once again he spoke frankly to them urging them to defend life and truth. Strikingly, he remarked: "*The world at the approach of a new millennium, for which the whole Church is preparing is like a field ready for the harvest.*"[8] Here Pope John Paul echoes the prophetic words found in Pope Paul VI's apostolic letter *Gaudete in Domino* as well as this passage from Sacred Scripture:

> Now in my vision I saw a white cloud and, sitting on it, one like a son of man with a gold crown on his head and a sharp sickle in his hand. Then another angel came out of the sanctuary, and shouted aloud to the one sitting on the cloud, "Put your sickle in and reap: harvest time has come and the harvest of the earth is ripe." Then the one sitting on the cloud set his sickle to work on the earth, and the earth's harvest was reaped. Another angel, who also carried a sharp sickle, came out of the temple in heaven and the angel in charge of the fire left the altar and shouted aloud to the one with the sharp sickle, "Put your sickle in and cut all the bunches off the vine of the earth; all its grapes are ripe." So the angel set his sickle to work on the earth and harvested the whole vintage of the earth and put it into a huge winepress, the winepress of God's anger. (Rev. 14:14–19)

---

7. John Paul II, "Angelus Address," September 11, 1994, http://www.vatican.va/.

8. John Paul II, "Homily for World Youth Day, Cherry Creek State Park," *L'Osservatore Romano* English ed., August 18, 1993.

What was the Holy Father suggesting here if not the separating of good and evil? He made further statements, which point towards the *Parousia*:[9]

> Maranatha! Here, from Cherry Creek State Park in Denver, from this gathering from all over the world, we cry out: Maranatha! Come Lord Jesus.... This pilgrimage must continue—it must continue in our lives; it must continue in the life of the Church as she looks forward to the Third Christian Millennium. *It must continue as a new advent, a moment of hope and expectation until the return of the Lord in glory.* Your celebration of this World Youth Day has been a pause along the journey, a moment of prayer and of refreshment, but a journey that must take us even further.[10]

The next World Youth Day was held in Manila in January 1995, calculated to be the largest ever gathering of people in history—about five million. The pope spoke of the need for the young to be lights shining in the darkness of our world, and to help prepare the temporal order for its renewal at the final coming of the Kingdom:

> "Jesus Christ is the same yesterday, today and forever" (Heb. 13:8). If you take up his cause and the mission which he gives you, then the whole human family and the church in every part of the world can look to the third millennium with hope and trust.... Dear people of God in the Philippines, go forth in the power of the Holy Spirit to renew the face of the earth—your own world first, your families, your communities and the nation to which you belong and which you love; and the wider world of Asia, toward which the church in the Philippines has a special responsibility before the Lord; and the world beyond, *working through faith for the renewal of God's whole creation. May God who began this work in you—400 years ago—bring it to completion in the day of our Lord Jesus Christ!* (cf. Phil. 1:6) Amen.[11]

Although this part of the book relates primarily to Blessed John

---

9. The *Parousia* is the theological definition of the final coming of the Lord for the Last Judgment.

10. John Paul II, "Vigil and Angelus Address for World Youth Day, Cherry Creek State Park," *L'Osservatore Romano* English ed., August 18, 1993.

11. John Paul II, "Homily for World Youth Day," Manila, January 15, 1995, http://www.ewtn.com/.

Paul II, it is important to stress that Pope Pius XII, in 1958 had also spoken prophetically, to the youth of Catholic Action. It is beneficial to offer it here as it displays once again continuity in papal teachings that are inspired by the Holy Spirit through the papal charism. It is the Spirit of love and truth who guides the popes to proclaim this message to the youth—that they will help prepare the world for the final events. Pius XII asked these questions to the youth on the Feast of St. Joseph, March 19, 1958:

> May we therefore remind you that the dark winter is behind you [World War II], but that before you there is a brilliant summer? May we urge you to live steadfastly the spring that God is about to grant to the world and the Church? But though you may have winter behind you, you have been promised a brilliant summer: *"Prope est aestas"* (Matt. 24:32): Summer is near.

He continued,

> But God, who permitted the dark winter and has prepared *a brilliant summer for the world*, obliges us all to live in a climate of reawakening, in a time of spring. In spring the earth reawakens, its lifeblood pulses, the buds open, and the leaves return to the trees. The hedges live once again, the meadows become green, and the fields rejoice with the trees in flower. The skies become clear. Days lengthen and the nights are shorter. There is more light than darkness.... The feast of nature becomes a feast of hearts because spring is the time of renewal, of confident waiting, of hope.... As in all springs, so in the one to come there will be storms and winds. *The Church has not finished her martyrdom....* Look around you, O youth, spring of humanity. Make our hope yours and tell everyone that *we are in a springtime of history.* May God grant that it will be one of the most beautiful springs man has experienced after one of the longest and bitterest winters, *a spring which precedes one of the most brilliant and rich summers.*[12]

In 1954, in a message to the Young Women's section of Italian Catholic Action, Pope Pius XII had already spoken of the "reawakening":

---

12. Pius XII, "The Springtime of History," Address to the Youth of Italian Catholic Action, March 19, 1958, *The Pope Speaks*, 427–430.

The Youth, Watchmen of the Morning

You know too our conviction that the moments through which we are now living are among the most crucial in history. . . . For this reason, with an awareness of present needs and possibilities, we have taken upon ourselves the duty of calling the whole Church to a great work, of shouting out that "cry of reawakening," which is now being echoed by pastors and faithful in many parts of Italy and of the world. It is our firm conviction that in less time than could be humanly foreseen, evil will be stopped in its tracks . . . Catholic Youth obeys without question: generously, quickly, because there is not a day, not a minute to lose in this hour which is one of action, of most urgent action.[13]

Therefore we discover in just a couple of examples that the prophetic nature of the role given to the youth of the Catholic Church has been recognized by more than just Pope John Paul, although the language he uses is obviously more urgent, hence the use of "Morning Watchmen," "Sentinels," and "Protagonists of the new times," to name but three used by the Polish Pontiff. From the end of the Great Jubilee, the pope talked often to the youth about their role, for instance in his message for World Youth Day 2002, he stated:

When the light fades or vanishes altogether, we no longer see things as they really are. In the heart of the night we can feel frightened and insecure, and we impatiently await the coming of the light of dawn. *Dear young people, it is up to you to be the watchmen of the morning* (cf. Is. 21:11–12) *who announce the coming of the sun who is the Risen Christ.*[14]

Similarly, when speaking to a group of participants of the twenty-first "Tendopolis" in August 2001 he said:

Dear young people! Christ is asking you to *be protagonists of a deep religious renewal in contemporary society that is focused on prayer, personal conversion and the constant search for ecclesial communion. . . . May your missionary activity make you ever more attentive to the "signs" and "challenges" of our time.* In this regard, I

13. Pius XII, "Message to Young Women's Section of Italian Catholic Action," December 8, 1954, *The Pope Speaks*, 65–68.

14. John Paul II, "Message to the Youth of the World on the Occasion of the Seventeenth World Youth Day," July 25, 2001.

remember what I asked the young people of the whole world at the unforgettable Prayer Vigil at Tor Vergata for World Youth Day during the Jubilee of the Year 2000. I said: "At the dawn of the third millennium I see in you the sentinels of the morning." I repeat this invitation to you, dear *"Tendopolis"* participants. To carry out this important task, faithfully follow the formation path of spiritual formality that requires you to be "pilgrims, sentinels and witnesses." Pilgrims in quest of God, *sentinels who keep watch, preparing for the glorious return of the risen Lord, undaunted and courageous witnesses of his message of salvation.*[15]

The message was constant wherever the Holy Spirit sent him; he asked the youth to be attentive to the signs of the times, sentinels who are always on the watch as the shepherds were in the fields of Bethlehem. They must be courageous and vigilant heralds of the Second Advent; encouraging others to stand firm in the faith until the universal renewal is complete. The following passages are more evidence of the trust our beloved pope had in the youth of the Church. To those from Ukraine while on pilgrimage there in June 2001 the Pontiff stated: "The Pope loves you and sees you as *the sentinels of a new dawn of hope.* He praises God for your generosity, while he prays for you with affection and with all his heart he blesses you."[16] To the Guanelli Youth Movement at the Vatican in April 2002 he said:

> On this important occasion, I would like to renew to you the appeal I made to all the young people at Tor Vergata: accept the commitment to be *morning watchmen at the dawn of the new millennium.* This is a primary commitment, which keeps its validity and urgency as we begin this century with unfortunate dark clouds of violence and fear gathering on the horizon. Today, *more than ever,* we need people who live holy lives, *watchmen who proclaim to the world a new dawn of hope, brotherhood and peace.*[17]

15. John Paul II, "Message to the Participants of the 21st 'Tendopolis,'" August 6, 2001, http://www.vatican.va/.

16. John Paul II, "Address to the Youth of Lviv, Ukraine," June 26, 2001, http://www.vatican.va/.

17. John Paul II, "Address to the Guanelli Youth Movement," April 20, 2002, http://www.vatican.va/.

During his pastoral visit to the Island of Ischia, the pope repeated the message: Your bishop introduced you as "sentinels of the dawn." Yes, dear young friends, *be faithful sentinels of the Gospel, who await and prepare for the coming of the new Day that is Christ the Lord.*[18]

In May 2003, the pope travelled to Spain and met the youth at the Air Base of Cuatro Vientos, Madrid. It was a very interesting address in which he called on them to enter the "*School of Mary*," as she would teach them true contemplation, which would enable them to build a new Europe based on the Gospel. He once more warned of the dangers threatening the world in the wake of the terrorist attacks of September 11, 2001:

> Beloved young people, you know well how concerned I am for peace in the world. The spiral of violence, terrorism and war still causes hatred and death, even in our day. Peace, as we know, is first of all *a gift from on High for which we must constantly ask* and which, furthermore, we must all build together by means of a profound inner conversion. Consequently, today I want to exhort you to *work to build peace and be artisans of peace.* Respond to blind violence and inhuman hatred with the fascinating power of love. *Overcome enmity with the force of forgiveness.* Keep far away from any form of exasperated nationalism, racism and intolerance.
>
> Witness with your life that *ideas are not imposed but proposed.* Never let yourselves be discouraged by evil! For this you will need the help of prayer and the consolation that is born from an intimate friendship with Christ. Only in this way, living the experience of God's love and radiating Gospel fellowship, will you be able to be the builders of a better world, genuine peaceful and peacemaking men and women.[19]

The Holy Father then gave his own personal witness, before making this intriguing statement: "It is worthwhile to give one's life for the Gospel and for one's brothers and sisters! *How many hours are there still to go until midnight? Three hours. Just three hours until*

18. John Paul II, "Pastoral Visit to the Island of Ischia," Address to Youth, May 5, 2001, http://www.vatican.va/.

19. John Paul II, "Address to Youth at Madrid Air Base," May 3, 2003, http://www.vatican.va/.

midnight and then comes morning."[20] What does this mean? It appears that he is paraphrasing two relevant scriptural passages: "the night is advanced, the day is at hand" (Rom. 13:12), and the question posed by Isaiah that forms the central fulcrum of this discussion: "Watchman, how much longer the night?" (Is. 21:11). If this really is the hidden meaning then it is a remarkable statement to make; all the more because the pope trusted the youth to understand the symbolism behind it. Adding weight to this interpretation, the Holy Father, immediately after that part of his address, implored the Blessed Virgin's help for the youth of Spain, while again referring to them as the *morning watchmen*:

> To conclude, I would like to call on Mary, *the shining star that announces the Sun* that is born from on High, Jesus Christ:
>
> Hail, Mary, full of grace!
> This evening I pray to you for the youth of Spain,
> *young people full of dreams and hopes.*
>
> They are the *dawn watchmen,*
> *the people of the beatitudes;*
> *they are the living hope of the Church and of the pope.*
>
> Holy Mary, Mother of the young,
> intercede so that they may be *witnesses* of the Risen Christ,
> humble and courageous *apostles* of the third millennium,
> generous *heralds* of the Gospel.
>
> Holy Mary, Immaculate Virgin,
> pray *with* us,
> pray *for* us. Amen.[21]

Evidently, there was an organic development in the way that Pope John Paul II spoke to the youth. In the early years he opened their minds and hearts to understand their role in contemporary society without being too explicit as to the unique generation in which they lived, but as these extracts show, the true vocation of the youth became more and more apparent: to be the "Sentinels," "Watch-

20. Ibid.
21. Ibid.

men," or "Heralds" of the new heaven and new earth. Whatever Catholics believe concerning the messages allegedly being given to visionaries and mystics concerning the approaching return of the Lord, there can be no denying that the Holy Father was inspired to proclaim the same message. This is the spectacular proclamation of hope that the Holy Spirit inspires in the Church: the message that can destroy the reign of mortal sin and despair if only we would listen to Christ's Vicar. We can put aside all the speculation about secrets and what the future may hold; the Holy Father has prophetically announced it with utter conviction. We can be sure that the new times are near if the pope indicates it. The following words from the arrival ceremony at Madrid Airport on May 3, 2003 sum up perfectly the feelings of Pope John Paul II:

> This afternoon I will meet *with the young people,* and I look forward with joy to that moment which will enable me to be in touch with those who are called to be *the protagonists of the new times.* I have total confidence in them, and I am certain that they do not want to disappoint God, the Church or the society from which they come.[22]

This is a time for action from the younger generation. Many are answering the call to be sentinels, through movements like *Communion and Liberation, Youth* 2000, *Catholic Action,* and *The Guanelli Youth Movement,* as well as ecclesiastical orders such as the *Franciscan Friars of the Renewal,* the *Priestly Fraternity of St. Peter* and the *Community of St. John.* There is no doubt that this is one of the remarkable fruits of the Second Vatican Council as confirmed by Pope Benedict XVI. While many young people throughout the world are being enticed into all kinds of immorality, there are many young Catholics who are remaining by the Cross of Jesus with their Holy Mother, as did St. John. They refuse to run away like the frightened apostles, but are resolute in their loyalty to the Crucified and Risen Christ; apostles of the last times, under the leadership of Mary. They know the weapons for this fight—the Rosary, regular

22. John Paul II, "Address at Arrival Ceremony," Madrid International Airport, May 3, 2003," http://www.vatican.va/.

reception of the Sacraments, Eucharistic adoration, and Consecration to the Immaculate Heart of Mary. For his part, the Holy Spirit will not fail them when the time comes for their final act of witness, just as he never failed the illustrious martyrs of earlier times. The Holy Father spoke openly to the youth about the possibility of martyrdom because he knew that this knowledge would not frighten them; on the contrary, it would spur them on to ever greater efforts in the struggle for Christ's Kingdom.

We have seen how various aspects of the *novissimis* were spoken about during the reign of Blessed John Paul II from his messages about the New Advent and the Morning Watchmen, to the mystical aspects of Fatima and Divine Mercy. I would now like to address the theme of the "Great Springtime of Christianity" which the Holy Father had prophesied on many occasions, and how it relates to the final coming of Jesus, and the installation of his eternal Kingdom when "God will be all in all" (Cor. 15:28).

9

A Great Springtime of Christianity: The Second Coming and the Eternal Kingdom of Christ

Then I saw a new heaven and a new earth. The former heaven and the former earth had passed away, and the sea was no more. I also saw the holy city, a new Jerusalem, coming down out of heaven from God, prepared as a bride adorned for her husband. I heard a loud voice from the throne saying, "Behold, God's dwelling is with the human race. He will dwell with them and they will be his people and God himself will always be with them as their God. He will wipe every tear from their eyes, and there shall be no more death or mourning, wailing or pain, for the old order has passed away." The one who sat on the throne said, "Behold, I make all things new." Then he said, "Write these words down, for they are trustworthy and true."

(Rev. 21:1–5)

IN THIS CHAPTER, we will examine the relevance of Pope John Paul's prophecy of a coming "great springtime of Christianity," and how it can be viewed as the final state of the Church after the second coming of Jesus. It will be possible to show how this explanation corresponds with the teachings of the Polish Pontiff. It will also be an opportunity to seek answers to certain questions, such as: "What signs are there that the end of time is dawning?" and "Do these signs represent an escalation of the eschatological tension inaugurated by the Resurrection of Christ?"

From the earliest days of John Paul's papacy, he actively encouraged the faithful to look towards the year 2000 as a focal point for renewal.[1] However, it was only approaching the mid-point of his reign that the great prophecy of a new springtime was first encountered. The encyclical *Redemptoris missio* on the Church's missionary activity, published in December 1990, is where we discover it for the first time. The pope stated: "God is preparing a great springtime for Christianity, and we can already see its first signs."[2] One may ask: what exactly is this springtime going to be and how will we know of its arrival? There could be a tendency to view it as a resurgence of Christianity in the new century and yes, that is a valid interpretation, but looking at the facts, we must ask ourselves if it is likely. The world is becoming more evil by the day; it proclaims the death of God. The pope had spoken of a "silent apostasy" while confirming that we are in *the* final battle, echoing words used by Pius XII.[3]

A decade or so before his election to the papacy, Pope Benedict XVI gave an interview in which he gave his assessment of the likelihood of any springtime in the near future: "Whether the vision is actually fulfilled is something we naturally have to leave entirely in God's hands. At the moment I do not yet see it approaching."[4] I believe the then-Cardinal Ratzinger was interpreting the pope's words in a non-eschatological light, which is why he was negative as to the prospects of a renewal in the near future. Who could see it approaching in the current climate of apostasy and heresy? And yet the pope is clear—we can already see its first signs. Therefore, we must ask ourselves what these first signs are. During an *ad Limina* address that the pope gave to the bishops of the Central African Republic in September 1999 he stated:

1. "In fact, preparing for the Year 2000 has become as it were a hermeneutical key of my Pontificate. It is certainly not a matter of indulging in a new millenarianism, as occurred in some quarters at the end of the first millennium; rather, it is aimed at an *increased* sensitivity to all that the Spirit is saying to the Church and to the Churches (cf. Rev 2:7)." John Paul, Apostolic Letter *Tertio Millennio Adveniente*, November 10, 1994, available at http://www.vatican.va/.

2. John Paul II, Encyclical Letter *Redemptoris Missio*, December 7, 1990, no. 86, http://www.vatican.va/.

3. Pius XII, *Acta Apostolicae Sedis* 1948, 248.

4. Ratzinger, *Salt of the Earth*, 238.

In contemplating the Incarnation of God's Son, may all the faithful of your Diocese see revealed the face of the merciful and compassionate Father! *By constantly listening to the Spirit, may they recognize the signs of the new times and wait ever more ardently for the Lord's return in glory."*[5]

It is significant that the Holy Father emphasizes the importance of being docile to the action of the Holy Spirit, as it is the Advocate's desire to reveal the signs of Jesus' return for those praying, Maranatha! Come Lord Jesus! John Paul II also wrote similar words in the Bull *Incarnationis Mysterium* of the Great Jubilee:

> It is the Spirit of Christ who is at work in the Church and in history: *we must listen to Him in order to recognize the signs of the new times* and to make the expectation of the glorified Lord's return ever more vibrant in the hearts of the faithful.[6]

Looking back over the past decades since the Second Vatican Council, we discover a deepening appreciation of the Holy Spirit's role in salvation history; a greater reflection from the magisterium and a growing awareness among the laity that sanctification comes from an interior life that is freely given to the Holy Spirit so that His love and wisdom can transform and renew.

In the same document, Pope John Paul continued with a prophetic message, linking the idea of divine mercy and repentance to the ultimate goal of everlasting liberation from original sin; in essence at the moment of absolution, the penitent prefigures the inhabitants of a new humanity:

> Let us therefore look to the future. The merciful Father takes no account of the sins for which we are truly sorry (Is. 38:17). *He is now doing something new,* and in the love that forgives he anticipates the new heavens and the new earth.[7]

It would seem strange for there to be signs pointing to a spring-

---

5. John Paul II, "ad Limina Address to Bishops of the Central African Republic," September 27, 1999, http://www.vatican.va/.

6. John Paul II, *Incarnationis Mysterium*, Papal Bull of the Great Jubilee of the Year 2000, no. 3, 11, http://www.vatican.va/.

7. Ibid.

time within salvation history as well as signs directing us towards the new times where, "He will wipe every tear from their eyes, and there shall be no more death or mourning, wailing or pain, for the old order has passed away" (Rev. 21:4). The following passage from the Holy Father's message for World Mission Sunday 1999 clarifies any possible misunderstanding:

> Let us thank the Lord for the immense good work that has been achieved by missionaries as, turning our eyes to the future, *we confidently await the dawn of a new Day.* Those who work on the outposts of the Church are like watchmen on the walls of God's city. We ask them: "Watchman, what of the night?" (Is. 21:11), and we hear the answer: "Hark, your watchmen lift up their voice, together they sing for joy: *for eye to eye they see the return of the Lord to Zion*" (Is. 52:8). Their generous witness in every corner of the earth proclaims: "As the third millennium of the Redemption draws near, God is preparing a great springtime for Christianity and we can already see its first signs." May Mary, the Morning Star, help us to say with ever new ardor our "yes" to the Father's plan for salvation that all nations and tongues may see his glory (cf. Is. 66:18).[8]

Can it be doubted that the Pontiff proclaims the new springtime as that time when the Lord will return with all his saints? The "new Day" spoken of at the beginning of the passage refers to the "Day of Christ," or the "Day of the Lord"; both hold the same meaning. The pope used this phrase or variations on the theme on many occasions. It is useful to offer several passages in order to give further weight to the discussion:

> *For centuries, tried in the crucible of suffering and persecution, you have been purified* for the "great springtime of Christianity" (*Redemptoris missio*, n.86) which the Lord is preparing for the Church as the Third Millennium draws near . . . pray that our Lady, the Morning Star heralding the coming Millennium of hope, will intercede for you.[9]

---

8. John Paul II, "Message for World Missions Sunday 1999," May 25, 1999, no. 9, http://www.vatican.va/.

9. John Paul II, "ad Limina Address to the bishops of Scotland," October 29, 1992, http://www.priestsforlife.org/.

The fact that the pope mentions the "crucible of suffering and persecution" over the centuries implies a great event that has been prepared, rather than a general but incomplete renewal that would be much the same as in earlier generations. Pope Benedict XVI teaches us how this eschatological springtime is in essence the "new creation" (2 Cor. 5:17) inaugurated by the first coming of Christ. In a beautiful passage extolling the greatness of the Blessed Virgin he explains:

> Indeed, she is the most beautiful flower to have unfolded since the Creation, the "rose" that appeared in the fullness of time when God, by sending his Son, gave the world a new springtime.[10]

The theological term, "fullness of time" (Gal. 4:4) is the key to understanding this new season for humanity. It describes the divine plan of salvation which takes humanity in an entirely new direction from the moment of God's definitive intervention in history through the Incarnation, until its full realization at the final coming of Jesus where the springtime blossoms for redeemed humanity:

> The risen Christ returns among us with the fullness of joy and with overflowing richness of life. Hope becomes certainty, because if he has conquered death, we too can hope to triumph one day in the fullness of time, in the period of the final contemplation of God.[11]

The following speech of Blessed John Paul was delivered to catechists in Malta. In it, he once more turns to the role of the Holy Spirit in the new times:

> As *catechists*, you are to provide sweet nourishment for all who hunger for God; you are to bring healing to those who are suffering for lack of light and love. If you do these things, you will truly be *a sign of the springtime which the Holy Spirit is now preparing for the Church.*[12]

---

10. Benedict XVI, "Regina Caeli," May 9, 2010, http://www.vatican.va/.

11. John Paul II, "Message for the IX and X World Youth Day," November 21, 1993, http://www.vatican.va/.

12. John Paul II, "Address to Members of the 'Societas Doctrinae Christianae,' 9 May 2001," http://www.vatican.va/.

Another prophetic announcement which sheds light on the new era, was given by Pope John Paul II in a letter to the Rogationist Fathers on the first centenary of the Congregation:

He [Saint Annibale Di Francia] saw in the "Rogate" the means God himself had provided to bring about *that "new and divine" holiness with which the Holy Spirit wishes to enrich Christians at the dawn of the third millennium, in order to make Christ the heart of the world.*[13]

What is this "new and divine holiness"? It would seem that a divine holiness can only come from a perfect relationship with God, one in which the stain of sin no longer disfigures the soul; and the fact that the pope says it will be a "new" holiness implies it is something which has not yet been experienced by humanity, with the exception of Adam and Eve before the fall, the Blessed Virgin Mary, and the Lord Jesus himself. The word "new" in biblical language means "final perfection," as the pope stated in his general audience of October 25, 2000.[14] The Holy Father continues by saying that this "holiness" will enable Christ to be the heart of the world, which is not the case at the moment. The Lord will only subject all creation to himself at the end of the world, not before (contrary to the belief of the millenarianists). The Catholic Catechism is clear on this. So we have one of the few occasions in which His Holiness spoke openly of what is to come, in detail, but the phrase "new and divine" is especially significant in interpreting the age to come.

We have seen in the chapter on the New Advent that the pope speaks to the Cardinals about the coming of Jesus and how they, above all, must watch and stay awake. In the consistory held in February 1998, he again took up the theme, and related it to the spring-

13. John Paul II, "Letter on the Centenary of the Rogationist Fathers," *L'Osservatore Romano*, English ed., July 9, 1997, 9.

14. Pope Benedict XVI explains how the term relates to the end of the world: "The hymn [Psalm 144 (143)] is defined as 'new,' a term which, in biblical language, evokes not so much the exterior novelty of the words, as the ultimate fullness that seals hope (cf. v. 9). It sings, therefore, *of the destination of history where the voice of evil, described by the Psalmist as 'lies' and 'perjury,' expressions which indicate idolatry (cf. v.11), will finally be silenced.*" General Audience, January 25, 2006, http://www.vatican.va/.

time to come, although here he expanded the concept to include the "summer" (Matt. 24:32), just as Pius XII had done in 1958 and John XXIII in 1962:

> With a heart trustfully open to this vision of hope, I implore from the Lord an abundance of the Spirit's gifts for the whole Church, so that the "springtime" of the Second Vatican Council can find in the new millennium its "summertime," that is to say its full development.[15]

What we discover here once again is the prophetic nature of the Council, in that it was oriented towards something much greater than itself. We know that spring leads into summer, and so when the Holy Father talks of the Church's "full development," he can only mean its passage from its present initial stage, to its final state as the Kingdom of God on earth. Further weight is added to this interpretation when we consider that the general audience of September 23, 1998 was concerned with the signs of the times in relation to the eschaton, and at the end of his address, the Pontiff quoted the above passage from the consistory. Furthermore, in a homily delivered in Santa Cruz, Bolivia, providentially on May 13, 1988, the Fatima anniversary, Pope John Paul proclaimed:

> Jesus Christ, who in his Sermon on the Mount gives us the message of the Beatitudes, leads man to the Kingdom. The Kingdom of God is this "new earth where justice will abide and whose blessedness will answer and surpass all the longings for peace which spring up in the human heart." (*Gaudium et Spes*, 39). *This is the teaching of the last Council.* In this perspective one can accomplish in a definitive way what the psalm speaks of in today's liturgy: "Mercy and truth have met, justice and peace have embraced" (Ps. 85 [84]:11).[16]

The same point was emphasized in the *ad Limina* address given to the bishops of Ghana in 1999; the Holy Father prophesied the imminent coming of the Kingdom:

15. John Paul II, "Address at the Ordinary Public Consistory," *L'Osservatore Romano* English ed. February 25, 1998, 2.

16. John Paul II. "Homily at Mass at Santa Cruz, Bolivia," May 13, 1988, http://www.vatican.va/.

The more faithfully and devotedly the religious in your Dioceses live out their commitment to Christ in chastity, poverty and obedience, the more clearly will the men and women of Ghana see that "the kingdom of God is at hand" (Mk 1:15).[17]

At this point let us look at the true meaning of spring. Pope Pius XII, in his speech to Italian Catholic Action on March 19, 1958, gave a precise answer to this question: "In spring the earth reawakens, its lifeblood pulses, the buds open and the leaves return to the trees."[18] Therefore a kind of renewal takes place; new life appears, even a kind of resurrection in nature. But of course what relates to the season of spring in nature also relates to the season of the Church. The springtime of the Church will be the resurrection after its crucifixion, in exact imitation of its Master. The following passage from Pope John Paul's message to the sick present at Fatima on May 13, 2000 gives reason to believe that the spring season for humanity is none other than its definitive state of glory:

If someone or something makes you think that you have reached the end of the line, do not believe it! If you know the eternal Love who created you, you also know that there is an immortal soul within you. *There are various seasons in life; if by chance you feel winter approaching, I want you to know that it is not the last season, because the last one will be spring: the springtime of the Resurrection.* Your whole life extends infinitely beyond its earthly limits: heaven awaits you. Dear sick people! Know that "the sufferings of this present time are not worth comparing with the glory that is to be revealed to us" (Rom. 8:18). Take courage! He comes to you with the promise: "Behold, I make all things new" (Rev. 21:5). Have trust! Abandon yourselves to his provident hands, as did the little shepherds Francisco and Jacinta.[19]

Why should this analogy be any different for the Church? The first resurrection for all believers occurs at the moment of baptism,

17. John Paul, "ad Limina address to the bishops of Ghana," February 20, 1999, http://www.vatican.va/.

18. Pius XII, "The Springtime of History," Address to the Youth of Italian Catholic Action, March 19, 1958, *The Pope Speaks*, 429.

19. John Paul II, "Message to the Sick," Fatima, May 13, 2000, http://www.vatican.va/.

when they enter into the tomb with the Lord only to be reborn into the life of grace and spiritual resurrection. This could in a sense be called the first spring. The second spring will only occur for the Church and every one of the redeemed at the last judgment—when the Kingdom is installed in its fullness (Matt. 25:34). The pope also spoke of a second spring in these terms: "At this beginning of the millennium, I hope for all a time of grace that signals a second spring of Christian life and allows everyone to respond boldly to the call of the Spirit."[20] Once more it is worth recalling the remarks made to the bishops of the Central African Republic, in which His Holiness asked them to listen to the Spirit proclaiming the signs of the new times. The Holy Spirit, in the pope's mind, is the leading protagonist in preparing this springtime, and alongside his purifying, sanctifying work, is his spouse the Blessed Virgin Mary, often invoked by Pope John Paul II as the "dawn of the new times." The new Pentecost prophesied by the popes of the Vatican II era will come about when the Holy Spirit descends in a universal manner, as opposed to his first coming in the Upper Room. The Holy Father implored us to help make this renewal of the face of the earth a reality by constantly invoking his coming:

> In our time that is so hungry for hope, make *the Holy Spirit* known and loved. Help bring to life that *"culture of Pentecost,"* that alone can make fruitful the civilization of love and friendly coexistence among peoples. With fervent insistence, never tire of praying, "Come Holy Spirit! Come! Come!"[21]

The awareness of Mary's role in preparing the Church for the second coming had been a constant theme for the pope; in her he saw the Moon rising, before the full splendor of the Sun shines over the world:

> In preparing ourselves to celebrate the Jubilee of the Year 2000 and to begin the third Millennium of the Christian Faith with the hope

---

20. John Paul II, "ad Limina Address to Brazilian Bishops," September 5, 2002, http://www.vatican.va/.

21. John Paul II, "Address to Members of the Renewal in the Holy Spirit Movement," March 14, 2002, http://www.vatican.va/.

and the dedication of a *new Advent* the Church proposes to renew and to increase her missionary effort, so that the proclamation of the Gospel may be brought with greater efficacy to those peoples who have not yet received or accepted it. *To Mary, who prepared the first coming of the Lord, I entrust this hope: through her maternal mediation, may she obtain, for all the People of God an ever more vivid and active consciousness of their own responsibility for the coming of the Kingdom of God* through missionary evangelization.[22]

To the bishops of Yugoslavia on their *ad Limina* visit to Rome in February 2001 the Pontiff proclaimed: "*May Mary, the dawn of the new times*, obtain for you the gift of fidelity to the mission you have received, the courage to continue zealously proclaiming the Gospel and the joy of bearing witness to Christ."[23]

Our Lady's power in heaven is such that she alone is capable of obtaining from the Lord a lessening of the trial. In the Apostolic Letter *Rosarium Virginis Mariae*, the Holy Father spoke of the divine intervention that is now needed in order to bring an end to all forms of evil. This intervention will be won for us by Mary, the Co-redemptrix, Mediatrix, and Advocate:

> The grave challenges confronting the world at the start of this new Millennium lead us to think that only *an intervention from on high*, capable of guiding the hearts of those living in situations of conflict and those governing the destinies of nations, can give reason to hope for a brighter future.[24]

One aspect of Mary's influence in these times is her ability to teach the faithful to strive for true inner conversion, to become poor and humble, charitable and merciful. She desires the Lord to have a positive response to his own question, as recounted in St. Luke's Gospel when he asks: "When the Son of man comes, will he find faith on earth?" (Lk. 18:8). The Holy Trinity has willed that Our Blessed Mother lead the army of faithful Christians through

22. John Paul II, "Message for World Missions Sunday 1988," available at http://www.fides.org/.

23. John Paul II, "ad Limina Address to Yugoslav Bishops," *L'Osservatore Romano* English ed. March 7, 2001, 5.

24. John Paul II, Apostolic Letter *Rosarium Virginis Mariae*, October 16, 2002, no. 40, http://www.vatican.va/.

the last battle before Satan is finally chained up in Hell for all eternity. We know this is the case because Sacred Scripture assures us that it is so. The Church at the end must be pure and chaste; it must resemble St. John the Baptist who ate only locusts and honey in the wilderness. It must be stripped of its political power, pomp, and regalia. In fact, with the loss of the Papal States at the end of the nineteenth century—an event prophesied in detail by St. Hildegard of Bingen as belonging to a stage of history shortly before the great apostasy and coming of the Antichrist,[25] the political power has disappeared; and the papal tiara is no more, leaving the last popes to concentrate on readying the Church for the storm of the last night through its overwhelming spiritual power. However, just as Mary, the bright Morning Star, has appeared over our era, so too has her adversary in all his terrible power. We know of the massive increase in demonic possessions in recent years, thanks to the testimony of the exorcist priests: Father Gabriel Amorth, Father Candido Amantini, and Father Peter Rookey to name but three. The increase in witchcraft under the guise of the "new age," and satanic culture in particular are influencing large numbers of the younger generations. All this has come to pass as a sign of the return of the Lord of history. It appears now that we have almost exhausted ourselves with evil. The present day murder of the innocents through abortion can and should be recognized as comparable to the genocide committed by the Nazis, while the corruption of conscience has contributed greatly to the disregarding of the natural law—that internal presence of God that is the guide for the soul. These are certainly some of the signs that show the increasingly violent struggle between the forces of good and evil, of faith and rationalism.

Another prophetic sign that must be fulfilled before the end of the world is the preaching of the Gospel to all the nations.[26] The

25. Hildegard of Bingen, *Liber divinorum operum*, "Vision 10," *Book of Divine Works* (Santa Fe: Bear & Company, 1987), 250.

26. Pope John XXIII recalled in his radio address of September 11, 1962 the importance that the Council would place on the advancement of this prophecy: "True joy for the universal Church of Christ is what the ecumenical council intends to be. Its reason for existence is the continuation, or better still the most *energetic revival*, of the response of the entire world, of the modern world, to the testament

Holy Father had confirmed the completion of this universal dimension in at least two speeches.[27] In the already cited passage at the end of the World Mission Sunday Message for 1999, he said in reference to missionaries: "Their generous response in *every corner of the earth* proclaims" that they see the return of the Lord to Zion. Why does the pope say that missionaries are the ones to see the Lord coming? It is because they, above all, have fulfilled the sign that all the nations must hear the Gospel before the end of the world. Another reference to this fulfillment came during the homily for the new cardinals in February 2001:

> You come from twenty-seven countries on four continents and speak various languages. Is this not a sign of the Church's ability, *now that she has spread to every corner of the globe,* to understand peoples with different traditions and languages, in order to bring to all the message of Christ?[28]

Pope Paul VI, even as far back as 1967 had spoken in a similar way to that of Pope John Paul, while acknowledging the obstacles that stand in the way of re-evangelizing certain areas:

> Now that the Gospel message has reached the ends of the earth, is missionary work, properly so called at an end? Isn't it more difficult today than it was yesterday to preach in nations that are no longer primitive but self-conscious of their own culture?... These are real and forceful difficulties. But they cannot and should not

---

of the Lord, formulated in those words which He pronounced with divine solemnity and with hands stretched out toward the farthest ends of the world: 'Go, therefore, and make disciples of all nations, baptizing them in the name of the Father, and of the Son, and of the Holy Spirit, teaching them to observe all that I have commanded you' (cf. Matt. 28:19–20)." John XXIII, "Nuntius Radiophonicus: Universis catholici orbis christifidelibus, mense ante quam Oecumenicum Concilium sumeret initium," *AAS* 54 (1962): 678–685.

27. It is important to note that the prophecy cannot be defined on purely geographical grounds. As the world's population continues to grow, the missionary effort in a sense is continually beginning again; added to that is the issue of previously evangelized regions that are in need of renewal once again. We can therefore state that it is unlikely that a point can be reached whereby missionary activity is said to be completely finished.

28. John Paul II, "Address at the Ordinary Public Consistory," February 21, 2001, http://www.vatican.va/.

weaken missionary enthusiasm because the plan of salvation conceived by God is always that of belief in Christ—the only plan, *the necessary plan.*[29]

Although the Lord Jesus never proclaimed that every single human would hear the Gospel preached, only that it would spread to a universal level: "throughout the world as a witness to all nations" (Matt. 24:14), the Church, however, does have a duty to press on with its missionary mandate until the last day dawns for mankind. This is the reason for the new evangelization. In fact, Pope John Paul was explicit in its eschatological significance, stating to Spanish bishops:

> May the Virgin, Mother of the Church, Our Lady of Hope and Advent, give us the grace to accomplish the task of a new evangelization *to prepare hearts for the coming of the Lord.*[30]

It is therefore a great missionary effort to catch as many souls as possible in the time of grace remaining. In April 2001, the Holy Father gave a speech in preparation for World Youth Day in which he talked about the struggle for missionary success in difficult and dangerous regions; he told the youth that they must be prepared to haul in a miraculous catch. This confirms the reason why the pope's main phrase after the Great Jubilee year was "set out into the deep" (*duc in altum!*) (Lk. 5:4). There is therefore no conflict or contradiction between evangelization and a growing hostility to the faith, only the facts which show much of the world is far away from God and in desperate need for the message of salvation.

The statements of various popes from the last century clearly show that nations and kingdoms have fought each other in such ferocity as to fulfill the prophecy of Matthew 24:6–7. The figure of roughly eighty-seven million dead from wars alone in the last century bears testimony to that. Wars and rumors of war have lurked in the psyche of humanity for many decades and so continue at the present moment. Earthquakes and famine, storms, tsunamis and other natural disasters have multiplied in recent times. Who could

---

29. Paul VI, "Message for World Mission Sunday," October 22, 1967, *The Pope Speaks*, Vol. 12, 362, no. 4.

30. John Paul II, "ad Limina Address to Spanish Bishops," December 19, 1986, http://www.vatican.va/.

ever forget the terrible suffering of countless millions during the famines of the 1980's in Ethiopia and Sudan? Floods have devastated many countries including India, Bangladesh, and Venezuela, while earthquakes have killed thousands in Turkey, Armenia, Japan, and Italy, to name but a few. Australia, Canada, and the United Sates have all suffered huge forest fires. Might this point to the signs of nature reacting to the abuse that it has received; groaning and gradually giving birth to the new earth?

A further event which must come in the last days concerns the final persecution of the Church under the regime of the Antichrist; therefore, we may ask: what of the appearance of this "Son of perdition"? Where is he if many of the other signs are evident? To answer this question, it is necessary to reread the biblical text from St. Paul's Second Letter to the Thessalonians:

> And you know, too, what is holding him back from appearing before his appointed time. Rebellion is at its work already, but in secret, and the one who is holding it back has first to be removed before the rebel appears openly. (2 Thess. 2:6–7)

It would seem that the figure of the pope is the one holding the Antichrist back, since he is the principle enemy of the apostates and the "foundation of unity of both the bishops and of the faithful" (*Lumen Gentium*, 23). We know that Jesus gave the keys of the Kingdom to Peter and his successors, and promised that the gates of the underworld would not prevail against the Catholic Church. What the Lord did not confirm was that there would be a pope alive at the time of his return. The Church survives for several weeks—and at times in its history, even years—without a pope every time a new conclave has to be convened; therefore, we may ponder whether at the time of the death of the last pope, the Antichrist will appear and take his place in the Holy Temple of God.

Although the Holy Father did not speak of the specific timing of the coming of the Antichrist, he did, however, hint at the lateness of the hour during a sobering homily at the *Te Deum* of thanksgiving in Rome's St. Ignatius Church on New Year's Eve 1993. The text that he based his homily on was 1 John 2:18: "*It is the last hour*":

Dear brothers and sisters, while the Apostle tells us that "this is the last hour," he adds immediately: *"just as you heard that the antichrist was coming,* so now many antichrists have appeared. Thus we know this is the last hour" (1 Jn. 2:18). Perhaps these words seem a little strange in the context of the solemn "Te Deum." They are not far, however from human experience. The Apostle recalls that the world "is under the power of the evil one" (1 Jn. 5:19). It is good for *this evil one* present in the world *to be called by name. . . .* Indeed, we cannot close our eyes to what is about us. We cannot fail to see that Christ and his Gospel are and remain a "sign of contradiction" (Lk. 2:34). We cannot fail to notice that, together with the civilization of love, the civilization of truth and life, another civilization is spreading: *this is precisely what St. John is speaking of in the context of the "last hour."* The Apostle writes: "Many antichrists have appeared." And he adds: "They went out from us, but they were not really of our number" (1 Jn. 2:19). It is as if he were repeating in other words *the parable of the wheat and the tares* (cf. Matt. 13:24–30), in recounting which Christ invited us to be patient until harvest time.[31]

The pope reminds us that the civilization of the antichrist, in its cycle of terror and death, is spreading, and that we must be prepared to confront it. Complacency in the spiritual life is the greatest danger, allowing this apocalyptic menace to spread throughout the world. Therefore, the Holy Father urges us to stay awake so that we are not influenced by those "who are not really of our number" (cf. 1 Jn. 2:19). For Pope John Paul II, St. John's words concerning the last hour are coming to fruition in our time. It is noticeable that he ends this passage by reminding us to be patient until "harvest time"; the parable of the wheat and the tares tells us that good and evil will only be separated at the Last Judgment. The pope recalled in prophetic fashion this teaching during the Mass for the Assumption of Mary during the 1993 World Youth Day in Denver: "The world at the approach of a new millennium, for which the whole Church is preparing, is like a field ready for the harvest."[32]

---

31. John Paul II, "Homily at Te Deum Mass of Thanksgiving, Gospel Still a Sign of Contradiction," *L'Osservatore Romano* English ed. January 12, 1994, 5.
32. John Paul II, "Homily for World Youth Day," August 15, 1993, Denver, http/www.vatican.va/.

Even before his election to the papacy, John Paul II had spoken prophetically about the events leading to the reign of the Antichrist. In 1976, he was invited by Pope Paul VI to preach the Lenten spiritual retreat for the Roman Curia. His observations were startling. In one meditation entitled *The Ways of Denial*, he explained how Satan's temptation to Adam and Eve in chapter three of Genesis to "make themselves like God" has gradually wound its devious way throughout history to the extreme form that it takes today, where man rejects the very notion of God. Cardinal Wojtyla stated:

> We could even say that in the first stage of human history this temptation not only was not accepted but had not been formulated. *But the time has now come; this aspect of the Devil's temptation has found the historical context that suits it.* Perhaps we are experiencing the highest level of tension between the Word and the anti-Word in the whole of human history.[33]

Then, again in the presence of Paul VI, he spoke these ominous words:

> We may now be wondering if this is the *last* lap along that way of denial which started out from around the tree of the knowledge of good and evil. To us, who know the whole Bible from Genesis to Revelation, no stretch of that route can come as a surprise. *We accept with trepidation but also with hope the inspired words of the Apostle Paul, "Let no man deceive you in any way, because first it is necessary for the rebellion to come, and for the man of sin, the son of perdition to reveal himself"* (2 Thess. 2–3).[34]

In the view of Blessed John Paul II, laicist anthropocentrism and its quest to rid humanity of God and Satan, good and evil, is the culmination of all temptation and one which is daily constructing the civilization of the antichrist. The temptation from the third chapter of Genesis is now finding its fullest expression in the signs of our times. The pope knew that the Antichrist himself would be the perfection of the "evil of denial," placing himself in the position of God.

---

33. Karol Wojtyla, *Sign of Contradiction* (London: Hodder And Stoughton, 1980), 34.
34. Ibid., 35.

The great theologian, Hans Urs von Balthasar pointed to the spreading of the antichristian civilization in these terms:

> The intention is that mankind will be incorporated in the new and ultimate principle through the sacramental mediation of the "body" of Christ, the Church. The individual can freely allow this to happen, but he can also freely refuse; and since, as a result of Christ's victory, the antichristian powers have become really alert and ready for combat, his victory ushers in the most decidedly dramatic period of world history. As the history of man's theological liberation marches forward, the pendulum swings more and more freely, both for each individual and for mankind as a whole, between Yes and No. The Apocalypse that concludes the word of God shows in the clearest manner that there can be no question of one-dimensional progress in history: the nearer the end approaches, the more fierce becomes the battle.[35]

This view of the increase of evil was explained by the Holy Father in a general audience in 1986:

> As the end of the struggle gradually draws nearer, it becomes in *a certain sense ever more violent*, as Revelation, the last book of the New Testament, shows in a special emphasis (cf. Rev. 12:7–9). But it is precisely this book that emphasizes the certainty that is given to us by all of divine Revelation that the struggle *will finish* with the definitive *victory of the good*.[36]

At least one cardinal has discussed the possibility that the Antichrist may be alive at this moment. He is the retired Archbishop of Bologna, Italy, Cardinal Giacomo Biffi. He is a great admirer of the brilliant Russian Orthodox mystic and philosopher, Vladimir Soloviev. Although Soloviev is not very well known in the western world, he is a much-admired figure in the Church, having been cited favorably by John Paul II and Benedict XVI; von Balthasar even set him on a level with St. Thomas Aquinas and regarded his work as "the most universal speculative reaction to the modern

---

35. Hans Urs von Balthasar, *Theo-Drama, Vol.* 3, *The Dramatis Personae: The Person of Christ* (San Francisco: Ignatius Press, 1992), 37–38.

36. John Paul II, "General Audience, Christ's Victory Conquers Evil," *L'Osservatore Romano* English ed., August 28, 1986.

period."[37] Soloviev himself was tremendously ecumenical; he wanted the Russian Orthodox Church to return to the flock under the leadership of the pope, he accepted Peter's primacy above all others and was himself eventually received into the Byzantine-Russian Catholic Church. But why is he important to this discussion? The answer to this question comes from various lectures given by Cardinal Biffi in recent years in which he states the remarkable accuracy of Soloviev's prophecies for the twentieth century:

> As early as 1882, in his "Second Discourse on Dostoevsky," Soloviev foresaw—and condemned—the sterility and cruelty of the collective tyranny which a few years later would oppress Russia and mankind. "The world must not be saved by recourse to force," Soloviev said. "One could imagine men toiling together toward some great end to which they would submit all of their own individual activity; but if this end is imposed on them, if it represents for them something hated and oppressive . . . then, even if this unity were to embrace all of mankind, universal brotherhood would not be the result, but only a giant anthill." This "anthill" was later constructed through the obtuse and cruel ideology of Lenin and Stalin. In his final work, *The Three Dialogues and the Story of the Antichrist* (finished on Easter Sunday 1900), one is struck by how clearly Soloviev foresaw that the twentieth century would be "the epoch of great wars, civil strife, and revolutions." All this, he said would prepare the way for the disappearance of "the old structure of separate nations" and "almost everywhere the remains of the ancient monarchical institutions would disappear." This would pave the way for a "united states of Europe."

The accuracy of Soloviev's vision of the great crisis that would strike Christianity is astonishing. He represents this crisis using the figure of the Antichrist. This fascinating figure will succeed in influencing and persuading almost everyone. It is not difficult to see in this figure of Soloviev the reflection, almost the incarnation of the confused and ambiguous religiosity of our time. The Antichrist will be a "convinced spiritualist," Soloviev says, an admirable philanthropist, a committed, active pacifist. . . . He will also be among other things an expert exegete. His knowledge of the Bible will lead the theology faculty of Tubingen to award him an

---

37. Hans Urs von Balthasar, *Gloria III*, 263.

honorary doctorate. Above all he will be a superb ecumenist, able to engage dialogue "with words full of sweetness, wisdom, and eloquence." He will not be hostile "in principle" to Christ's teaching. Indeed he will appreciate Christ's teaching. But he will reject the teaching that Christ is unique, and will deny that Christ is risen and alive today. One sees here described—and condemned—a Christianity of "values," of "openings," of "dialogue," a Christianity where it seems there is little room left for the person of the Son of God crucified for us and risen, little room for the actual event of salvation.[38]

Interestingly, Pope Benedict XVI turned to Cardinal Biffi in March 2007 to deliver the Lenten Spiritual Exercises for the Vatican Curia, and again His Eminence used Soloviev's thesis on the Antichrist as the basis for his presentation. In the pope's address thanking the Cardinal, he all but confirmed the seriousness of the hour of history we face: "I would also like to say "thank you" because you have given us a very *acute and precise diagnosis of our situation today.*"[39]

We must remember that what Soloviev wrote were not private revelations that he had received, but his own prophetic insights, no doubt inspired by the Holy Spirit. What Cardinal Biffi agrees with is the idea put forward by Soloviev that after a century of terrible wars and revolutions when sovereign nations would disappear, the Antichrist could reign somewhere near the beginning of the twenty-first century. All the churches would unite under the leadership of the pope, bringing unity back to the flock of Christ while they waited, in the midst of the Antichrist's persecutions, for the return of Jesus in glory. Soloviev has been the subject of much criticism in the Orthodox Church because of his leanings toward the Catholic Church and his loyalty to the papacy, but it may be that the Lord is still using him to bridge the gap between the two sister churches in the hope that, to use the expression of Pope John Paul II, "The Church may breath with both lungs."

38. "Vladimir Soloviev: A Prophet Unheeded," March 4, 2000, *Inside The Vatican*, June/July 2000.

39. Benedict XVI, "Address at the conclusion of the Lenten Spiritual Exercises," March 3, 2007, http://www.vatican.va/.

Before leaving the subject of the Antichrist, we might gain an insight into what life may be like during his reign. That the Mass will be abolished for three and a half years has been confirmed by the prophet Daniel, the early Church Fathers, notably Cyril of Jerusalem, as well as Doctors of the Church such as St. Robert Bellarmine. It is also the teaching of the magisterium that the Catholic Church will face the most terrible persecution that it has ever known; a persecution that will be on a universal level. We know that many will be enticed by his charming words at first; in fact for many they will never perceive the true identity of this man who would usurp the throne of God. Only those who are absolutely loyal to the true and unchanging teachings of the Catholic Church will be aware of the real identity of the "rebel."

The following little anecdote offers some food for thought concerning the deception to be sprung upon all humanity: In the January 2002 issue of the "Voice of Padre Pio" magazine, which is published by the Capuchin Friars in San Giovanni Rotondo, Italy, an article appeared about Fr. Joseph Pius Martin, an American priest who for many years until his death in 2000 lived in San Giovanni. He had helped look after St. Pio in his final years. One striking passage that stood out when reading the article was a revelation in which Padre Pio stated, "*One day they will doubt I ever existed.*" Fr. Pius suggested that in the time of the Antichrist, this prophecy would be fulfilled;[40] for the "son of perdition," a figure like St. Pio, who for so many was and would continue to be a type of "holy door" through which to pass to heaven,[41] would have to be erased from the memory of all, firmly and forever. On a more universal level, the Antichrist would attempt to erase from our collective memory any trace of the great spiritual happenings of the time of grace currently being experienced, denying the appearances of the Blessed Virgin throughout the world. No doubt, in time, he will claim that the whole of salvation history is just an illusion, an attempt by certain people (including Jesus) to mask the reality that

---

40. *Voice of Padre Pio, No. 1*, 2002, San Giovanni Rotondo, 23–24.

41. In the sense of conversion through St. Pio's promotion of Confession, regular Mass attendance, and devotion to the Mother of God.

death has the final word within history. He will forcefully attempt to wear down the faith of believers, to induce despair, confusion, and anxiety.

Certainly, this will be a test for all who live through it. For just as Jesus was abandoned by the Father in the Garden of Gethsemane, with only his angel to comfort him, perhaps a similar experience will await the remnant few. These sobering thoughts remind us that to neglect the great graces that are being offered to us now could have catastrophic implications for us in the near future, because a time will come when the sacraments will be banned and churches destroyed. When that day comes, we will need to be spiritually "fit," like an athlete at the peak of his powers. It will be no different for the Christians of the final hour.[42]

One last event of huge significance that must come before the end of the world, is the conversion of the Jews to the Catholic faith. Obviously there is no sign of this at present, but if what mystics say is true concerning extraordinary warnings to be given to the entire world, then it would seem inconceivable that these events would not bring about their conversion. If they do come to pass, then no one open to the action of the Holy Spirit would ignore the fact that the Mother of Jesus has come to warn them of the imminence of the end. It does seem logical that only some divine intervention can bring about the conversion of the chosen people; the irony being that the first to be chosen would be the last to accept the message of salvation. Saint Bernard of Clairvaux (1090–1153), in his famous text *De Consideratione* which was written as advice for Pope Eugene III

---

42. Fr. Gabriele Amorth recently recounted an extraordinary dialogue he had with the devil during an exorcism in Italy. The girl in question was being forced to consume pounds of bread and pizza at incredible speed each day, yet she remained extremely underweight—a sight the Priest described as "terrible, terrible." After the devil had proclaimed himself "God," Father Amorth retorted, "Shut up liar. God is the Lord of heaven and earth and you must remain subject to him." The devil responded, "You know nothing, priest. Look around you. It is full of my disciples. Who am I to them? I am God! . . . The world is mine and will be mine forever. . . . *Soon my son will be loved by all. . . . They will call him God*" The allusion here is to the Antichrist. Padre Gabriel Amorth & Paolo Rodari, *L'ultimo Esorcista*, Edizioni Piemme (Milan, 2012), 255.

states: "Granted, with regard to the Jews, time excuses you; for them a determined point in time has been fixed, which cannot be anticipated. The full number of Gentiles must come in first" (*De Consideratione* III/1, 2). Therefore, while the time of the Church relates to bringing conversion to the rest of humanity, the time for the Jews is still a mystery which as we are told by St. Paul, will bring about the resurrection of the dead (cf. Rom. 11:15). We may also recall that many of the Fathers of the early Church taught that God would send Enoch and Elijah to convert the Jews, and their preaching would deflect the terrible assault of the Antichrist in the last days. We must, however, leave the exact way in which these events will come to pass in the providential hands of the Lord.

Now that we have explored the signs of the end in relation to what the Church teaches, let us look forward to the second coming and the instillation of the second earthly paradise. The pope spoke on many occasions, as we have already seen, about certain aspects of the return of the Lord. He talked of a new humanity, the civilization of love and a new era. This is what he told bishops from the Czech Republic when visiting the country in 1997:

> I allow myself to ask you, at the culmination of the celebrations commemorating St. Adalbert: Custos, quid de nocte? Custos, quid de nocte? "Watchman, what of the night? Watchman, what of the night?" (Is. 21:11). The day must dawn. *The new dawn of the Sun of justice* must come (cf. Mal. 3:20): Jesus Christ, God from God, Light from Light, without whom, the civilization of love cannot be built. *Be sentinels then, pointing out to the flock that better times are coming.* Through the harmonious efforts of all who are sincerely concerned for the good of man, I express my hope for the coming of that peace of Christ, which is indispensable for the creation of an order of justice, peace and progress.[43]

Pope John Paul also related the great jubilee year to the second coming, as an opportunity to look ahead to our eventual full salvation; in essence, that magnificent event was a foreshadowing of the splendor of the new heavens and the new earth and explains why

---

43. John Paul II, "Address to Bishops of the Czech Republic," April 25, 1997, http://www.vatican.va/.

the Holy Father suggested in *Tertio Millennio Adveniente* that the year was the "hermeneutical key" to his pontificate:

> The challenge is to see to it that the world is properly informed of the true meaning of the Year 2000, the anniversary of the birth of Jesus Christ. The Jubilee cannot be a mere remembrance of a past event, however extraordinary. It is to be the celebration of a Living Presence, *and an invitation to look towards the Second Coming of our Savior, when he will establish once and for all his kingdom of justice, love, and peace.*[44]

Exactly one month later, on Good Friday at the end of his meditations for the Stations of the Cross, the pope again joyfully looked forward to the second coming:

> As the shades of night envelop us, an eloquent image of the mystery which surrounds our existence, we cry to You, Cross of our salvation, our faith! O Lord, a ray of light shines from your Cross. In your Death our death is conquered, and we are offered the hope of resurrection. Clinging to your Cross, *we wait in joyful hope for your return, Lord Jesus, our Redeemer!* "Dying you destroyed our death, rising you restored our life. Lord Jesus, come in glory." Amen.[45]

The new era will consist of a recapitulation of all things in Christ; all things in heaven and on earth (Eph. 1:10). St. Irenaeus, the great second-century Church Father, spoke of this recapitulation, explaining that our Savior, Jesus Christ in his incarnation sums up the whole of salvation history, he is the "new Jerusalem": "He, as the eternal King, recapitulates all things in himself."[46] It is Jesus who is the center of history; it is through him that all things must pass; every evil is destroyed by him. As he took on human flesh, so he bridged the gap between the heavenly and the earthly; the spiritual and the corporeal. Most importantly of all, his death and resurrection gave birth to the new creation, he is the "first fruits of those who have fallen asleep" (1 Cor. 15:20). Christ is the new Adam, who

---

44. John Paul II, "Address to the Plenary Assembly of the Pontifical Commission for Social Communications," February 28, 1997, http://www.vatican.va/.
45. John Paul II, "Address at the Conclusion of the Stations of the Cross," March 25, 1997, http://www.vatican.va/.
46. Irenaeus of Lyons, *Adversus Haereses III*, 21, 9.

faithfully carries out perfectly the Father's will; however, only at the end of time will this be the case for the redeemed. Finally the new earth will be the restoration of the Kingdom prepared since the foundation of the world, except unlike Adam and Eve, the saints will never suffer temptations anymore; the former things will have passed away. Satan will be bound forever in hell with his demonic legions. Christ, at that moment having brought about the recapitulation of all humanity will reign supreme as the King of the universe: "The beatific vision, in which God opens Himself in an inexhaustible way to the elect, will be the ever-flowing well-spring of happiness, peace, and mutual communion" (*Catechism of the Catholic Church*, n. 1045). The Holy Father spoke, in December 1998, of the universal renewal which will see the New Jerusalem come down from heaven (cf. Rev 21:2):

> Dear brothers and sisters, let us prepare to meet Christ! Let us prepare the way for him in our hearts and in our communities. The figure of the Baptist, who is simply clad and lives on locusts and wild honey, is a powerful call to be watchful and to look for the Savior's coming. . . . We too need to renew this trusting expectation of the Lord. Let us listen to the prophet's words. They invite us to look with hope to the definitive foundation of the kingdom of God, which he describes with highly poetic images that can shed light on the triumph of justice and peace to be brought about by the Messiah. "*The wolf shall dwell with the lamb . . . the calf and the lion and the fatling together, and a little child shall lead them*" (Is. 11:6). These are symbolic expressions which anticipate the reality of universal reconciliation. We are all called to collaborate in this work of cosmic renewal, sustained by the certainty that one day all creation will be completely subject to the universal lordship of Christ.[47]

The Catholic Catechism teaches that "the visible universe, then, is itself destined to be transformed, 'so that the world itself, restored to its original state, facing no further obstacles, should be at the service of the just,' sharing their glorification in the risen Christ" (CCC, n. 1047; cf. St. Irenaeus, *Adversus Haereses* 5, 32, 1). There is much debate as to whether these times are the prelude to an inter-

47. John Paul II, "Homily for the Second Sunday of Advent," St. Peter's Basilica, December 6, 1998, http://www.vatican.va/.

mediate "spiritual" coming of Christ, but this interpretation is not to be found in any papal teaching; it is also a distortion of the teaching of St. Bernard concerning the *adventus medius*, and the Letters of St. Paul. Therefore when Jesus returns, he will reign in his glorified body on earth with the elect, but only after the universal restoration has taken place (cf. Acts 3:20–21).[48] We know from the last pages of Sacred Scripture that the heavenly city comes down from heaven onto the earth. In reality the Most Holy Trinity is "heaven" because our primary enjoyment after death will be the beatific vision, or understanding of God. All other pleasures, for example, seeing our families or the beauty of the restored nature, will be secondary to that overwhelming joy. The pope gave a prophetic speech to the bishops of Latin America in which he proclaimed the coming of a new humanity:

> Jesus Christ, the faithful Witness, the Pastor of pastors, is in our midst.... With us is the Spirit of the Lord which guides the Church to the fullness of truth and renews her with the revealed word in a new Pentecost.... Be faithful to your baptism ... give new life to the great gift you have received, turn your hearts and gaze at the center and origin, to him who is the basis of all happiness, the fullness of everything! *Be open to Christ, welcome the Spirit, so that a new Pentecost may take place in every community! A new humanity, a joyful one, will arise in your midst; you will experience again the saving power of the Lord* and "what was spoken to you by the Lord" will be fulfilled. What "was spoken to you," is his love for you, his love for each one, for all your families and peoples ... today the Lord is passing by. He is calling you. In this moment of grace, he is once again calling you by name and renewing his covenant with you.[49]

There can be no doubt that Pope John Paul II helped to prepare the Church and the entire world for the second coming of our Savior, Jesus Christ through his many extraordinary writings and speeches. He also complied with two great wishes from Heaven, namely the consecration to the Immaculate Heart of Mary, and the

---

48. A greater analysis of this theological position can be found in chapter 10.

49. John Paul II, "Address to the Bishops of Latin America," *L'Osservatore Romano* English ed. October 21, 1992, 7.

institution of the Feast of Divine Mercy on the second Sunday of Easter. The many statements are often prophetic and joyful, proclaiming that our liberation is near. This therefore is not a time of anguish or fear, but of hope: hope that the Holy Spirit will descend again and renew the face of the earth; hope that Jesus will soon liberate humanity from its bondage to sin. This old world is passing away, and a new world is dawning. The Lord is at the gates of this generation pleading with us to wake up before it is too late. Our beloved pope, Blessed John Paul II, proclaimed to the whole Church, "Watch," so that we may be ready to greet Him when he descends on the clouds of heaven with all the saints. In the midst of all the sufferings of the body, may we look forward to the day when our mortal nature will be clothed with immortality. In that moment our bodies will be obedient to our spirit; living in complete conformity with the divine will. We will see Jesus face to face and all the mysteries of salvation history will be uncovered. In the meantime we must face the final trial with the knowledge that the Lord is granting great graces for us now, so that we may be properly prepared.

This is a time of grace, truly the *"Kairos,"* as the Holy Father said, and it is up to us to recognize its benefits now. It is not for us to know specific times, but the signs are there, and have been there for the best part of a century now, as the previous pontiffs recognized. This tells us that if time was short at the beginning of the twentieth century, then now it is only "three hours to midnight," to borrow the phrase of John Paul II.

I would like to end this chapter with a small but prophetic message from the Holy Father, delivered to the crowds gathered in Edmonton, Canada, on September 17, 1984 which summarizes, in a simple way, the hour of history in which we find ourselves: "The Judgment spoken of in today's Gospel (Matt. 25:31–46) is constantly being prepared. . . . May justice and peace embrace at the end of the second millennium which prepares us for the coming of Christ in glory."[50]

50. John Paul II, "Homily for Mass at Edmonton Airport," Canada, September 17, 1984, http://www.vatican.va/.

PART III

Epilogue

Pope Benedict XVI
Excita, Domine, potentiam tuam, et veni

The Spirit and the bride say, "Come." Let the hearer say, "Come." Let the one who thirsts come forward, and the one who wants it receive the gift of life-giving water. The one who gives this testimony says, "Yes, I am coming soon." Amen! Come, Lord Jesus! (Rev. 22:17, 20)

THE PONTIFICATE of Pope Benedict XVI began on April 19, 2005 amid great rejoicing among the faithful, who saw the election of Joseph Ratzinger as a continuation of the legacy of his great friend, Blessed John Paul II. Cardinal Ratzinger had worked since 1981 as Prefect for the Congregation for the Doctrine of the Faith, overseeing various important projects and documents, such as the *Catechism of the Catholic Church*, *Dominus Iesus*, concerning the salvific universality of Jesus Christ and the Church, and the *Message of Fatima*. The twenty-four years that he spent as Prefect allowed him to gain first-hand knowledge of the growing threats to the Church, both internal and external.

The internal threats related to teachings that did not conform to the Catholic faith—mainly from priests, sadly, as the document archives from the CDF testify. The other great threat was liberation theology from South America which bore a close resemblance to Marxist ideology in that it placed too great an emphasis on political solutions for the poor at the expense of the Christian message of salvation—in essence a modern form of millenarianism. External threats came from moral relativism, atheism, and rationalism, which in time began to seep its way even into the Church like an oil spill. Those years of service in the Roman Curia would prove to be decisive, as the cardinals turned to Joseph Ratzinger to steer the bark of Peter closer to the safe harbor that is Jesus Christ. They saw in this humble servant of the Gospel a brilliant theologian, a pastor of souls, and a man of prayer who could deepen the faith of his flock through the clarity of his teaching. In this chapter, it is my intention to shed light on the eschatological dimension of Pope Benedict's magisterium: a dimension which includes the theology of transformation; of humanity and all creation.

The title of this chapter: *Excita, Domine, potentiam tuam, et veni—Rouse up your might, Lord, and come,* was a phrase taken from the Advent liturgy, which Pope Benedict used frequently as a reference point in a particularly somber pre-Christmas address to the cardinals of the Roman Curia in 2010. He said: "Amid the great tribulations to which we have been exposed during the past year, this Advent prayer has frequently been in my mind and on my lips."[1] Of course he was referring primarily to the priest abuse scandals which had exploded in the very same year as the "Year for Priests," but that is not the entire reason why it had been on his mind. In the same address he compares the state of the declining Roman Empire with the situation in the world today:

> The sun was setting over an entire world [the Roman Empire]. Frequent natural disasters further increased this sense of insecurity. There was no power in sight that could put a stop to this decline. All the more insistent, then, was the invocation of the power of God: the plea that he might come and protect his people from all these threats. . . . Today too, we have many reasons to associate ourselves with this Advent prayer of the Church. For all its new hopes and possibilities, our world is at the same time troubled by the sense that moral consensus is collapsing.[2]

The pope then turned to the grave crisis of the Church and used a vision of St. Hildegard of Bingen to portray the terrible situation unfolding.

> In the vision of Saint Hildegard, the face of the Church is stained with dust, and this is how we have seen it. Her garment is torn—by the sins of priests. The way she saw and expressed it is the way we have experienced it this year.[3]

---

1. Benedict XVI, "Address to the Roman Curia," December 20, 2010, http://www.vatican.va/.
2. Ibid.
3. Ibid.

Excita, Domine, potentiam tuam, et veni

This passage recalls the damning words contained in Cardinal Ratzinger's Stations of the Cross (written at the invitation of Pope John Paul II) weeks before his election to the papacy:

We can also think, in more recent times, of how a Christianity which has grown weary of faith has abandoned the Lord.... Should we not also think of how much Christ suffers in his own Church? How often is the holy Sacrament of his Presence abused, how often must he enter empty and evil hearts! How often do we celebrate only ourselves, without even realizing that he is there! How often is his Word twisted and misused! What little faith is present behind so many theories, so many empty words! How much filth there is in the Church, and even among those who, in the priesthood, ought to belong entirely to him! How much pride, how much self-complacency! What little respect we pay to the Sacrament of Reconciliation, where he waits for us, ready to raise us up whenever we fall! All this is present in his Passion. *His betrayal by his disciples, their unworthy reception of his Body and Blood, is certainly the greatest suffering endured by the Redeemer; it pierces his heart.* We can only call to him from the depths of our hearts: *Kyrie eleison*—Lord, save us (cf. Matt. 8:25).

Lord, your Church often seems like a boat about to sink, a boat taking in water on every side. In your field we see more weeds than wheat. The soiled garments and face of your Church throw us into confusion. Yet it is we ourselves who have soiled them! It is we who betray you time and time again, after all our lofty words and grand gestures. Have mercy on your Church; within her too, Adam continues to fall. When we fall, we drag you down to earth, and Satan laughs, for he hopes that you will not be able to rise from that fall; he hopes that being dragged down in the fall of your Church, you will remain prostrate and overpowered. But you will rise again. You stood up, you arose and you can also raise us up. Save and sanctify your Church. Save and sanctify us all.[4]

The gravity and emotion contained in these words reveal the depth of the pope's knowledge concerning the great apostasy which scourges the Church of our day. He is not interested in covering up

4. Joseph Ratzinger, "Meditations on the Way of the Cross," Good Friday, 2005, http://www.vatican.va/.

the shame in order to protect the image of the Church because he believes conversion can only come from an interior transformation, instigated by sincere repentance and a willingness to speak the truth no matter how painful it is. This takes us back to the centrality of the Fatima message—one of repentance, conversion, and penance as the remedy for the ills of the Church. Those ills, explains Pope Benedict, form a central part of Fatima's third secret and give a glimpse of the eschatological reality concerning the falling away of the faith in the last times.

The Holy Father made his first comments about the famous secret in 1984, in an interview with the Italian journalist Vittorio Messori. He linked its contents to "the absolute importance of history; *the dangers threatening the faith and life of the Christian, and therefore the world. And then the importance of the 'novissimi.'"*[5] The *novissimi,* as explained by Cardinal Wojtyla, the future John Paul II, concern not only the last things (death, judgment, heaven, and hell) but also, critically, in the role that the Second Vatican Council played in preparing for the Lord's return, the eschatology of mankind. He states that the council enlarged the understanding of the term: "There is more to this subject than is covered by our traditional tracts *De novissimis . . .* the conciliar eschatology of the Church and the world is *dominated* by the truth of the "making new" of all things in Christ (cf. Eph. 1:10), of the new heaven and new earth."[6] This clarification is extremely important because it gives further evidence that the council was prophetic and viewed eschatology as a central theme that needed to be understood by the faithful in a more profound way. In view of this, we can understand Cardinal Ratzinger's use of "*novissimis*" as pertaining to the end of the world.[7]

At this point, it is useful to question the assumption held by

---

5. Socci, *The Fourth Secret of Fatima,* 90.
6. Wojtyla, *Sign of Contradiction,* 153.
7. Cardinal Wojtyla's clarification concerning the *novissimis* is especially relevant because until the Second Vatican Council, the assumption among Catholics was that the world would actually end completely after the Final Judgment. Thus heaven was never associated with any future age on earth. A probable reason for this was that pre-Vatican II catechism manuals tended not to refer to the eschatological truth that the world would be renewed after the final coming of Jesus. The

many that the Fatima prophecies yet to be realized relate not to the end of the world but to the end of an era leading to a triumph which brings forth some sort of temporal reign of Jesus Christ. The truth, however, is somewhat different as is shown by the explanations of three popes of the past century, Pius XII, John Paul II, and Benedict XVI. In order to answer satisfactorily this important point we have a precious document in the form of correspondence between Bishop Pavel Hnilica and Cardinal Ratzinger from the year 2000. The background to the exchange relates to the interpretation given by the Cardinal at the June 26, 2000 revelation of the third secret and how it seemed only to relate to the assassination attempt of John Paul II and the martyrdoms of the twentieth century. Bishop Hnilica meditated on this interpretation all through the summer and decided to write to Cardinal Ratzinger asking him for clarification; most importantly, whether the prophecy could be extended into the future. The Cardinal's reply is certainly more enlightening than what was officially released in June. He states: "We see in the 'secret of Fatima' the martyrs of the last century, in which, however, is *also* reflected the *persecution until the end of the world*."[8]

He would return to this same interpretation as pope whilst on pilgrimage to Fatima in May 2010. During the flight to Portugal, he was asked by journalists how the secret related to us today. He gave this revelatory answer:

> I would say that, here too, beyond this great vision of the suffering of the Pope, which we can in the first place refer to Pope John Paul II, an indication is given of *realities involving the future of the Church, which are gradually taking shape and becoming evident.* So it is true that, in addition to the moment indicated in the vision, there is mention of, there is seen, *the need for a passion of the Church,* which naturally is reflected in the person of the Pope, yet the Pope stands for the Church and thus it is sufferings of the

deepening theological reflection from the Council and the papal magisterium on the new heaven and new earth could be seen as one of the great developments of the last fifty years, although unfortunately it has gone relatively unnoticed.

8. This correspondence was published in the review *Pro Deo et Fratribus* November/December, n.36–37/2000. Available at http://www.alleanzacattolica.org/temi/fatima/fatima_hnilica_ratzinger.htm.

Church that are announced. *The Lord told us that the Church would constantly be suffering, in different ways, until the end of the world.*[9]

So we may ask: if the vision of the martyrdom of the pope and the Church refers to the final persecution, which is stated clearly by Benedict, what does the prophecy "In the end my Immaculate Heart will triumph" mean? Surely it must consequently refer to the final victory of Jesus Christ in his second coming. For confirmation of this assumption, we have a recent statement from the pope contained in the book interview *Light of the World* in which he states that praying to hasten the triumph of the Immaculate Heart *"is equivalent in meaning to our praying for the coming of God's Kingdom."*[10] The pope prayed this stunning prayer at the Mass in Fatima on May 13, 2010: "May the seven years which separate us from the centenary of the apparitions hasten the fulfillment of the prophecy of the triumph of the Immaculate Heart of Mary, to the glory of the Most Holy Trinity."[11]

Pius XII had also spoken in similar fashion recalling:

The hope that our wishes will be favourably received by the Immaculate Heart of Mary, and will hasten the hour of Her triumph and the triumph of the Kingdom of God.[12]

And on another occasion:

Continue then untiringly your work of a most exquisite Christian charity; do not forget however that today the great "patient" is the world itself. Unceasingly request for it the miraculous intervention of the most high Queen of the World, so that the hopes for an era of true peace are fulfilled as soon as possible, and that the

---

9. Benedict XVI, "Meeting with Journalists aboard the plane to Portugal," May 11, 2010, http://www.vatican.va/.

10. Benedict XVI, *Light of the World*, 166.

11. Benedict XVI, "Homily for Mass at Fatima Shrine," May 13, 2010, http://www.vatican.va/.

12. Michel de la Sainte Trinite, *The Whole Truth about Fatima, Volume III, The Third Secret* (Buffalo: Immaculate Heart Publications, 1990), http://www.catholicvoice.co.uk/fatima3/.

triumph of the Immaculate Heart of Mary ushers in more quickly the triumph of the Heart of Jesus in the Kingdom of God.[13]

Pius XII recalls here St. Louis de Montfort's teaching:

When our loving Jesus comes in glory once again to reign upon earth—as he certainly will—he will choose no other way than the Blessed Virgin, by whom he came so surely and so perfectly the first time. The difference between his first and his second coming is that the first was secret and hidden, but the second will be glorious and resplendent. Both are perfect because both are through Mary.[14]

Pope John Paul II on several occasions also identified the Fatima revelations as heralding the coming of the Kingdom; for instance in the first general audience upon returning from his pilgrimage to the Shrine in May 1991 he stated:

Mary's message at Fatima can be summed up in these early and clear words of Christ: "The Kingdom of God is at hand: repent and believe in the Gospel" (Mk. 1:15).[15]

What we have seen in recent years from Pope Benedict is a deepening of the *future* prophetic reality of Fatima and how it relates to the Church and the *novissimis*. He sheds light on the bitter trial of the Church and most importantly his insistence that the greatest threats come from within:

As for the new things which we can find in this message [the third secret] today, there is also the fact that attacks on the Pope and the Church come not only from without, but the sufferings of the Church come precisely from within the Church, from the sin existing within the Church. This too is something that we have always known, *but today we are seeing it in a really terrifying way*: that the greatest persecution of the Church comes not from her enemies without, but arises from sin within the Church.[16]

13. Ibid.

14. Louis de Montfort, *God Alone: The Collected Writings of St. Louis Marie de Montfort* (Bayshore, NY: Montfort Publications, 1987), 339.

15. John Paul II, "General audience," May 15, 1991.

16. Benedict XVI, "Meeting with journalists aboard the plane to Portugal," May 11, 2010, http://www.vatican.va/.

In his homily during Mass on May 13, 2010, at Fatima he stated:

Who keeps watch, in the night of doubt and uncertainty, with a heart vigilant in prayer? Who *awaits the dawn of the new day*, fanning the flame of faith? Faith in God opens before us the horizon of a sure hope, one which does not disappoint. . . . We would be mistaken to think that Fatima's prophetic mission is complete.[17]

Pope Benedict returned to this same theme barely six weeks later on the Feast of Ss. Peter and Paul:

If we think of the two millenniums of the Church's history, we may note as the Lord Jesus had foretold (cf. Matt. 10:16–33) that trials for Christians have never been lacking and in certain periods and places have assumed the character of true and proper persecution. Yet, despite the suffering they cause, they do not constitute the gravest danger for the Church. Indeed she is subjected to the greatest danger by what pollutes the faith and Christian life of her members and communities, corroding the integrity of the Mystical Body, weakening her capacity for prophecy and witness, and marring the beauty of her face. The Pauline Letters already testified to this reality. The First Letter to the Corinthians, for example, responds precisely to certain problems of division, inconsistence, and infidelity to the Gospel that seriously threaten the Church. However, the Second Letter to Timothy a passage to which we listened also speaks of the perils of the "last days," identifying them with negative attitudes that belong to the world and can contaminate the Christian community: selfishness, vanity, pride, the attachment to money, etc. (cf. 2 Tm. 3:1–5).[18]

It is worth recalling here St. John's First Letter: "Many antichrists have appeared." And he adds: "They went out from us, but they were not really of our number" (1 Jn. 2:19). It seems that there is a clear link between what the pope warns us about; the greatest threat being an internal one, and the biblical precedence of "antichrists" as described by St. John. Surely the conclusion we can draw

17. Benedict XVI, "Homily for Mass at Fatima Shrine," May 13, 2010, http://www.vatican.va/.

18. Benedict XVI, "Homily on the Feast of St. Peter & St. Paul," June 29, 2010, http://www.vatican.va/.

from these various threads is that the pope indirectly warns us of the coming of the Antichrist. The evidence found in his own words confirms this. The Fatima third secret concerns the persecution of the the Church until the end of the world, evolving as it does from the *greatest* threat to the Church, "antichrists" within its own ranks.

At this point it is beneficial to return to that extraordinary figure of the Middle Ages, St. Hildegard of Bingen, who significantly has been granted the rare distinction of being named a Doctor of the Church.[19] Pope Benedict had devoted two general audiences to her in 2010; certainly with the intention of revealing to the faithful her remarkable sanctity. She was born in 1098, probably at Bermersheim, Rhineland, and died in 1179 at the age of 81, in spite of having always been in poor health. Hildegard belonged to a large noble family and her parents dedicated her to God from birth for his service. She was blessed with a rich mystical life and during the years when she was superior of the Monastery of St. Disibodenberg, Hildegard began to dictate the visions that she had been receiving for some time to the monk Volmar, her spiritual director. In order to confirm that her visions were not the product of illusions, Hildegard turned to St. Bernard of Clairvaux for guidance and he, seeing their divine origin, comforted and encouraged her. In 1147, official approval for these revelations came from Pope Eugene III who authorized the mystic to speak of them publicly. Her most famous visions are contained in *Scivias*, that is, "You know the ways"; twenty-six visions containing the events of the history of salvation from the creation of the world to the end of time. Pope Benedict, without doubt devoted to this *true* feminist icon sees in her a "great woman, this 'prophetess' who also speaks with great timeliness to us today, with her courageous ability to discern the signs of the times."[20]

The way in which Hildegard speaks to us today, especially in the context of this discussion, relates to the vision of the last days

---

19. Pope Benedict XVI named St. Hildegard of Bingen and St. John of Avila as Doctors of the Church during the opening Mass for the Synod of Bishops for the New Evangelization on October 7, 2012.

20. Benedict XVI, "General Audience on St. Hildegard of Bingen," September 1, 2010, http://www.vatican.va/.

(*Scivias* 3.11),[21] more precisely the figure of a Woman, who represents Holy Mother Church and the beast to which she gives birth. The seer describes it thus:

> And from her waist to the place that denotes the female, she had various scaly blemishes; and in that latter place was a black and monstrous head. It had fiery eyes, and ears like an ass', and nostrils and mouth like a lion's; it opened wide its jowls and terribly clashed its horrible iron-coloured teeth. And from this head down to her knees, the figure was white and red as if bruised by many beatings; and from her knees to her tendons where they joined her heels, which appeared white, she was covered with blood.[22]

The blood on the legs signifies cruel sufferings inflicted on the Woman by the beast, while the white feet refer to ultimate victory and purity of the Woman. But who is this beast? The answer comes from the next scene:

> And behold! That monstrous head moved from its place with such a great shock that the figure of the woman was shaken through all her limbs. And a great mass of excrement adhered to the head; and it raised itself up upon a mountain and tried to ascend the height of Heaven.[23]

According to apocalyptic tradition, it is the Antichrist who attempts to imitate Christ's Ascension in one final parody of the life of Jesus. Confirmation of his identity comes from the heavenly explanation granted to Hildegard:

> For God's power will manifest itself and destroy the son of perdition, striking him with such jealousy that he will fall violently from the height of his presumption, in all the pride with which he stood against God.[24]

In envisioning the Antichrist in the form of a demonic head integrated with the body of the Church, Hildegard is clearly stressing the fact that he is born from the sin of the Church. The sexual abuse of its priests, the apostasy of its children, and conformity to the

---

21. Hildegard of Bingen, *Scivias* (Mahwah, NJ: Paulist Press, 1990), 493.
22. Ibid.
23. Ibid.
24. Ibid., 507.

world are fertile ground for the rise of this particularly wicked tree. It is the seed of evil planted in the womb of the Church by its own, that allows us to understand that the *greatest* threat comes from within, from its own unfaithfulness. The attitude of those who betray the Church is to turn away from the Truth and repeat the defiance of Satan: *"Non serviam!"* In this way the embryo of pure evil is allowed to develop gradually over time leading to the shocking scene described by this great mystic. Apostasy is the oxygen that gives life to the Antichrist because without it he cannot enter and deceive the faithful. Previous generations, although at times suffering from certain evils within the Church, still had enough knowledge and belief in God to have rendered his efforts futile. Now, however, that is no longer the case. Satan's war on the Church has left it exposed to this final assault, paving the way for the man of sin to place himself in the Holy Temple of God. It is in this context that we can understand better the *Via Crucis* meditations of the Holy Father from 2005. They articulate perfectly the internal rebellion of those who prefer their own gods to those of the true God, and above all, they could be seen to provide a prophetic commentary to the vision as described by St. Hildegard. It would seem that in recent years, Pope Benedict has decided to enlighten the Church in its understanding of the "mystery of iniquity" present within. By proclaiming the greatness of this prophetess, and the importance of her visions—together with those of Fatima—we are presented with a clear message: "If you do not repent you shall all perish" (Lk. 13:3).

The obvious extension to this apocalyptic scenario is one of judgment: judgment for the Church and for the world. Jesus warns many times in the Gospels that true justice will come, and in a sense that judgment is constantly in progress as humanity passes across the sea of history. The centrality of this doctrine has guided Christians throughout the ages as a compass for their conscience and as a sure hope for justice especially in times of persecution. Pope Benedict linked apostasy and judgment in a homily at the opening of the eleventh synod of Bishops in October 2005:

> In the Old and New Testaments, the Lord proclaims judgment on the unfaithful vineyard. The judgment that Isaiah foresaw is

brought about in the great wars and exiles for which the Assyrians and Babylonians were responsible. The judgment announced by the Lord Jesus refers above all to the destruction of Jerusalem in the year 70. *Yet the threat of judgment also concerns us*, the Church in Europe, Europe and the West in general. With this Gospel, the Lord is also crying out to our ears the words that in the Book of Revelation he addresses to the Church of Ephesus: "If you do not repent I will come to you and remove your lampstand from its place" (Rev. 2:5). Light can also be taken away from us and we do well to let this warning ring out with its full seriousness in our hearts, while crying to the Lord: Help us to repent! Give all of us the grace of true renewal! Do not allow your light in our midst to blow out! Strengthen our faith, our hope and our love, so that we can bear good fruit![25]

In his encyclical letter *Spe Salvi* (on the virtue of Hope), the Holy Father speaks at length about the Last Judgment and he explains that it is only through the existence of God that true justice can come, that sufferings endured throughout history can be undone: "a reparation that sets things aright."[26] He continues:

The image of the Last Judgment is not primarily an image of terror, but an image of hope; for us it may even be the decisive image of hope. Is it not also a frightening image? I would say: it is an image that evokes responsibility, an image, therefore, of that fear of which Saint Hilary spoke when he said that all our fear has its place in love. God is justice and creates justice. This is our consolation and our hope.[27]

In the midst of great tribulations, the Holy Father reminds us that hope and faith are central components for any believer who longs for an end to the first heaven and earth and the dawning of the new. He places before the Church of the third millennium a renewed focus on the fact that judgment will come for each of us:

---

25. Benedict XVI, "Homily at the Opening of 11th Ordinary General Assembly of the Synod of Bishops," October 2, 2005, http://www.vatican.va/.

26. Benedict XVI, Encyclical letter *Spe Salvi*, November 30, 2007, http://www.vatican.va/.

27. Ibid., no. 44.

The judgment of God is hope, both because it is justice and because it is grace. If it were merely grace, making all earthly things cease to matter, God would still owe us an answer to the question about justice—the crucial question that we ask of history and of God. If it were merely justice, in the end it could bring only fear to us all. The incarnation of God in Christ has so closely linked the two together—judgment and grace—that justice is firmly established: we all work out our salvation "with fear and trembling" (Phil. 2:12). Nevertheless grace allows us all to hope, and to go trustfully to meet the Judge whom we know as our "advocate," or *parakletos* (cf. 1 Jn. 2:1).[28]

The pope's teaching on eschatology contains what I would describe as the *theology of transformation*. It is intimately linked to the miracle of the Holy Eucharist in which bread and wine are transformed into the Body and Blood of the Lord Jesus. The Holy Sacrifice of the Mass is eschatological in that it points us towards the ultimate encounter with the risen Lord at His second coming. The fact that He comes to meet us in the Eucharistic banquet, in a sense anticipates that final encounter and allows us to prepare for that by being drawn ever closer into the life of the Lord, so we may begin to live heaven on earth even now.

Another aspect of eschatological transformation concerns the original celebration of Mass, during which the priest would face the east, looking towards the returning Lord, symbolized by the rising sun. The Holy Father has celebrated Mass *ad orientem* on several occasions in recent years, seemingly encouraging priests to follow suit. It is absolutely certain that he sees authentic renewal in the liturgy as a central tool in the fight for the soul of the Church, and as a means to focus our attention on the eschatological reality of the faithful. Renewal and transformation are two sides of the same coin; without renewal no transformation can take place, but genuine renewal can only come from the Church stripping itself of innovation and improvisatory gestures and returning to what the Lord directs us to: the heavenly liturgy which the saints celebrate perfectly. That is where the grandeur of the Church's mission is seen

28. Ibid., no. 47.

because in the beauty of the liturgy, the soul of the faithful is lifted high towards the cosmic Christ.

Pope Benedict linked several strands of the theology of transformation in his homily during the Mass of the Lord's Supper in 2009:

> The nourishment that man needs in his deepest self is communion with God himself. Giving thanks and praise, Jesus transforms the bread; he no longer gives earthly bread, but communion with himself. This transformation, though, seeks to be the start of the transformation of the world—*into a world of resurrection, a world of God.* Yes, it is about transformation—of the new man and the new world that find their origin in the bread that is consecrated, transformed, transubstantiated.[29]

We see here how transformation is eschatological because it involves leaving behind the old and putting on the new—in fact it recalls the whole history of salvation from Genesis to Revelation. It also sheds light on the salvific journey from the Garden of Eden where death entered history, to the Garden of Gethsemane where Jesus' suffering began to transform humanity, and finally, to the Garden of the Resurrection where the transformation was completed. The symbolism here reflects the role of Jesus Christ the Divine Gardener, he who comes to till, not only the soil of our soul ready for the harvest of the end of the world, but also the soil of the earth, ready for its definitive renewal.

The most detailed exposition of this theological point came during the 2005 World Youth Day held in Benedict's native Germany. Once again the pope took as his starting point the transforming self-sacrifice of the Savior:

> By making the bread into his Body and the wine into his Blood, he anticipates his death, he accepts it in his heart, and he transforms it into an action of love. What on the outside is simply brutal violence—the Crucifixion—from within becomes an act of total self-giving love. This is the substantial transformation which was accomplished at the Last Supper and was destined to set in motion a *series of transformations leading ultimately to the transformation*

29. Benedict XVI, "Homily at the Mass of the Lord's Supper," April 9, 2009, http://www.vatican.va/.

of the world when God will be all in all (cf. 1 Cor. 15:28). In their hearts, people always and everywhere have somehow expected a change, a transformation of the world. Here now is the central act of transformation that alone can truly renew the world: violence is transformed into love, and death into life. Since this act transmutes death into love, death as such is already conquered from within, the Resurrection is already present in it. Death is, so to speak, mortally wounded, so that it can no longer have the last word. To use an image well known to us today, this is like inducing nuclear fission in the very heart of being—the victory of love over hatred, the victory of love over death. Only this intimate explosion of good conquering evil can then trigger off the series of transformations that little by little will change the world. All other changes remain superficial and cannot save. For this reason we speak of redemption: what had to happen at the most intimate level has indeed happened, and we can enter into its dynamic. Jesus can distribute his Body, because he truly gives himself. This first fundamental transformation of violence into love, of death into life, brings other changes in its wake. Bread and wine become his Body and Blood. But it must not stop there; on the contrary, the process of transformation must now gather momentum. The Body and Blood of Christ are given to us so that we ourselves will be transformed in our turn. We are to become the Body of Christ, his own Flesh and Blood.[30]

The significance of transformation and renewal in eschatological terms cannot be underestimated because at its heart is the expectation that evil does not have the last word in history and that by partaking in the great communion of faithful Christians, a new world—a civilization of love—can prevail. The Holy Father draws our attention to it in order to increase our hope for the future and to spur us on to greater efforts of interior conversion. In terms of liturgical matters, we can better understand why it is essential that a proper solemn celebration of Mass is offered; it is the only way that the mystery of transformation can be truly grasped. Novelties and abuses distort the true message of the Holy Sacrifice; reducing the

30. Benedict XVI, "Homily at Mass for the 20th World Youth Day," Cologne, August 21, 2005, http://vatican.va/.

clarity of the eschatological realism present and detracting from the magnificence of the Eucharistic wonder. In renewal and transformation, we are able to show forth our true Catholic identity in a world where the flame of faith is dying out and atheism is rampant. Pope Benedict teaches us that this is the path to holiness in this life and the next.

This path, in fact, becomes a pilgrimage throughout life, oriented towards sainthood; we may recall the Lords words: "Amen, I say to you, among those born of women there has been none greater than John the Baptist; yet the least in the kingdom of heaven is greater than he" (Matt. 11:11). In these words a veil is lifted on the greatness of the company of heaven. It is the destiny for all the redeemed, one of perfect charity. Benedict XVI's insistent message of transformation leading to this state of perfection is also linked to his prophetic understanding of these times:

> We have been told with regard to Christ's definitive return in the Parousia that he will not come alone but with all his saints. *Thus, every saint who enters history already constitutes a tiny portion of Christ's second Coming*, his new entry into time which shows us his image in a new dimension and assures us of his presence. Jesus Christ does not belong to the past, nor is he confined to a distant future whose coming we do not even have the courage to seek. He arrives with a great procession of saints. *Together with his saints he is already on his way towards us, towards our present.*[31]

While drawing attention to this future reality, he also explains the significance of relics, which as we know from the incorruptible saints are also a prophetic witness to the resurrection of the dead:

> By inviting us to venerate the mortal remains of the martyrs and saints, the Church does not forget that, in the end, these are indeed just human bones, but they are bones that belonged to individuals touched by the living power of God. The relics of the saints are traces of that invisible but real presence which sheds light upon the shadows of the world and reveals the Kingdom of

---

31. Benedict XVI, "Address to the Roman Curia," December 21, 2007, http://www.vatican.va/.

Heaven in our midst. They cry out with us and for us: "Maranatha!"—"Come, Lord Jesus!"[32]

The unity of eschatological thought evident throughout the papacies of the twentieth century continues as a beacon of light in the magisterium of Pope Benedict; it is in the "school of Mary" that sanctity is taught, and the message to the youth of the Church is consistent:

> O Immaculate Mother, who are a sign of certain hope and comfort to everyone, help us to let ourselves be attracted by your immaculate purity. Your beauty, *Tota Pulchra*, as we sing today, assures us that the victory of love is possible; indeed, that it is certain. It assures us that grace is stronger than sin, and that redemption from any form of slavery is therefore possible. . . . May you be a loving mother for our young people, so that they may have the courage to be "*watchmen of the dawn*," and give this virtue to all Christians so that they may be the heart of the world in this difficult period of history. Virgin Immaculate, Mother of God and our Mother, *Salus Populi Romani*, pray for us![33]

One of the main characteristics of this papacy has been Benedict's expositions on the Book of Revelation. Many times in speeches, homilies, and general audiences, he has explained various passages, giving greater depth to the understanding of the symbolic language, and revealing their true message. It is as if he says to us "Who is wise enough to understand these things? Who is intelligent enough to know them?" (Hos. 14:10). During his pilgrimage to Africa in 2009, he spoke at length to the youth revealing once more the prophetic aspect of his office:

> My young friends, you hold within yourselves the power to shape the future. I encourage you to look to that future through the eyes of the Apostle John. Saint John tells us: "I saw a new Heaven and a new earth . . . and I saw the holy city, the new Jerusalem, coming down out of Heaven, from God, prepared as a bride adorned for

32. Benedict XVI, "Address to Young People, Cologne-Poller Weisen," August 18, 2005, http://www.vatican.va/.

33. Benedict XVI, "Homage to the Immaculate Virgin," December 8, 2008, http://www.vatican.va/.

her husband; and I heard a loud voice from the throne saying, 'Behold the dwelling of God is with men'" (Rev. 21:1–3). . . . Yes, my friends! God makes all the difference . . . and more! God changes us; he makes us new! This is what he has promised: "Behold, I make all things new" (Rev. 21:5). It is true! The Apostle Paul tells us: "If anyone is in Christ, he is a new creation; the old has passed away, behold the new has come. All this is from God, who through Christ reconciled himself to us" (2 Cor. 5:17–18). In ascending to Heaven and entering eternity, Jesus Christ has become the Lord of all ages. So he can walk with us as a friend in the present, carrying in his hand the book of our days. In his hand he also holds the past, the foundation and source of our life. *He also carefully holds the future, allowing us to catch a glimpse of the most beautiful dawn we will ever see: the dawn that radiates from him, the dawn of the Resurrection.* God is the future of a new humanity, which is anticipated in his Church. When you have a chance, take time to read the Church's history. You will find that the Church does not grow old with the passing of the years. Rather, she grows younger, for she is journeying towards her Lord, day by day drawing nearer to the one true fountain overflowing with youthfulness, rebirth, the power of life. Dear young people, the future is God. As we have just heard, "he will wipe away every tear from their eyes, and death shall be no more; neither shall there be mourning, nor crying nor pain any more, for the former things have passed away" (Rev. 21:4). . . . Young people of Angola, unleash the power of the Holy Spirit within you, the power from on high! Trusting in this power, like Jesus, risk taking a leap and making a definitive decision. Give life a chance! In this way islands, oases and great stretches of Christian culture will spring up in your midst, and bring to light that "holy city coming down out of Heaven, from God, prepared as a bride adorned for her husband." This is the life worthy of being lived, and I commend it to you from my heart.[34]

Another unifying feature of Pope Benedict and his recent predecessors concerns the eschatological element of Vatican II. When Joseph Ratzinger was elected Supreme Pontiff, many traditionalists wondered if he would perhaps leave the council "on the shelf" so to

34. Benedict XVI, "Meeting with Youth at Dos Coqueiros Stadium," Luanda, March 21, 2009, http://www.vatican.va/.

speak. However this has definitely not been the case; rather, he has dismantled the notion that the council was a "rupture" and reinterpreted it in the light of living Tradition: "There is the 'hermeneutic of reform,' of renewal in the continuity of the one subject-Church which the Lord has given to us. She is a subject which increases in time and develops, yet always remains the same, the one subject of the journeying People of God."[35] The then-Cardinal Ratzinger back in 1984 had spoken of the council in these terms: "Today, in fact we are discovering its 'prophetic' function: some texts of Vatican II at the moment of their proclamation seemed really to be ahead of the times."[36] In answer to whether the clock could be turned back to the pre-conciliar Church he went on to state: "If by 'restoration' is meant a turning back, no restoration of such kind is possible. The Church moves forward toward the consummation of history, *she looks ahead to the Lord who is coming*."[37] More recently as pope he has returned to the eschatological dimension:

> Ours is a time which calls for the best of our efforts, prophetic courage. . . . *The Council laid the foundation for an authentic Catholic renewal and for a new civilization—"the civilization of love"—* as an evangelical service to man and society. Dear friends, the Church considers that her most important mission in today's culture is to keep alive the search for truth, and consequently for God; *to bring people to look beyond penultimate realities and to seek those that are ultimate.*[38]

It has become absolutely clear in recent times that the Holy Spirit has instilled a greater sense of urgency in the prayer life of the Church. The active participation of the faithful which is without doubt a fruit of Vatican II, is a participation in the Church's mission to fulfill the prophecy that the Gospel will be spread throughout the

---

35. Benedict XVI, "Address to the Roman Curia," December 22, 2005, http://www.vatican.va/.

36. Joseph Ratzinger with Vittorio Messori, *The Ratzinger Report* (San Francisco: Ignatius Press, 1985), 34.

37. Ibid., 37.

38. Benedict XVI, "Address for the Meeting with the World of Culture," May 12, 2010, http://www.vatican.va/.

world (cf. Mk. 16:15). It concerns the truth that sanctity is not just for religious, but for the laity as well. Yes, it is true that a false understanding has led some to blur the distinction between the baptismal priesthood shared by all the faithful and the ministerial priesthood, however, it cannot be denied that under the guidance of the Blessed Virgin, a counter offensive has been launched against the evil one, comprised in part by a number of the faithful. Into this prayer of supplication for the coming of the Kingdom we see the urgency of the pope's prayer; in fact we are granted a privileged window into the soul of him who carries the burden of the world on his shoulders. It is striking that in the Christmas Midnight Mass of 2010, the Holy Father prayed this prophetic prayer:

> Lord, make your promise come fully true. Break the rods of the oppressors. Burn the tramping boots. Let the time of the garments rolled in blood come to an end. *Fulfill the prophecy that "of peace there will be no end"* (Is. 9:7). We thank you for your goodness, but we also ask you to show forth your power. *Establish the dominion of your truth and your love in the world—the "kingdom of righteousness, love and peace."*[39]

The following year he returned in almost identical fashion:

> At this hour, when the world is continually threatened by violence in so many places and in so many different ways, when over and over again there are oppressors' rods and blood-stained cloaks, we cry out to the Lord: O mighty God, you have appeared as a child and you have revealed yourself to us as the One who loves us, the One through whom love will triumph. And you have shown us that we must be peacemakers with you. We love your childish estate, your powerlessness, but we suffer from the continuing presence of violence in the world, and so we also ask you: manifest your power, O God. *In this time of ours, in this world of ours, cause the oppressors' rods, the cloaks rolled in blood and the footgear of battle to be burned, so that your peace may triumph in this world of ours.*[40]

---

39. Benedict XVI, "Homily at Christmas Midnight Mass," December 24, 2010, http://www.vatican.va/.

40. Benedict XVI, "Homily at Christmas Midnight Mass," December 24, 2011, http://www.vatican.va/.

During the homily for Corpus Christi 2011, Benedict evoked the image of night falling over the world in a similar way to that of Blessed John Paul in addressing the youth of Madrid, and Pius XII in his Urbi et Orbi of Easter 1957:

> We know that God prepares for all men and women new heavens and a new earth, in which peace and justice reign—and in faith we perceive the new world which is our true homeland. This evening too, let us start out: while the sun is setting on our beloved city of Rome: Jesus in the Eucharist is with us, the Risen One who said: "I am with you always, to the close of the age" (Matt. 28:20). Thank you, Lord Jesus! Thank you for your faithfulness which sustains our hope. Stay with us because night is falling.[41]

This powerful vision of the darkness of night, symbolizing the last days of the world, as described by Isaiah's question (cf. Is. 21:11), not only strongly influenced Blessed John Paul, but Pope Benedict as well. On several occasions he has made reference to the "watchmen" and their essential role, while also giving expression to a message of supreme importance and hope: "In her prophetic role, whenever peoples cry out to her: "Watchman, what of the night?" (Is. 21:11), the Church wants to be ready to give a reason for the hope she bears within her (cf. 1 Pet. 3:15), *because a new dawn is breaking on the horizon*" (cf. Rev. 22:5).[42]

During the 2009 pilgrimage to the Holy Land, while visiting Mount Nebo where Moses contemplated the Promised Land, the Holy Father directed his thoughts once more to the fulfillment of the promise of universal peace and harmony that would set a Christian seal on human history:

> Dear friends, gathered in this holy place, let us now raise our eyes and our hearts to the Father. As we prepare to pray the prayer which Jesus taught us, let us beg him to hasten the coming of his Kingdom so that *we may see the fulfillment of his saving plan*, and experience, with Saint Francis and all those pilgrims who have

---

41. Benedict XVI, "Homily for Corpus Christi," June 23, 2011, http://www.vatican.va/.

42. Benedict XVI, Apostolic Exhortation *Africae Munus*, November 19, 2011, http://www.vatican.va/.

gone before us marked with the sign of faith, the gift of untold peace—*pax et bonum*—which awaits us in the heavenly Jerusalem.[43]

Can we not see in these prayers the sense of urgency that the pope feels? Do we not perceive in this present magisterium a continuous call to stay awake for the coming of the Lord? For all the so-called rationalistic approach of Joseph Ratzinger as opposed to the mysticism of Blessed John Paul, the facts actually point to a deepening of eschatological thought throughout this pontificate. Most recently, in his post synodal Apostolic Exhortation *Ecclesia in Medio Oriente* we are presented with more evidence of the pope's concerns for the fate of humanity:

> The urgency of the present hour and the injustice of so many tragic situations invite us to reread the First Letter of Peter and to join in bearing witness to Christ who died and rose again. This "togetherness", this communion willed by our Lord and God, is needed now more than ever. Let us put aside all that could be cause for discontent, however justifiable, in order to concentrate unanimously on the one thing necessary: *the goal of uniting the whole of humanity and the entire universe in God's only Son* (cf. Rom. 8:29; Eph. 1:5, 10).[44]

Furthermore, we read:

> Him alone, Christ, the Son of God, do we proclaim! *Let us repent, then, and be converted, "that sins may be blotted out, that times of refreshing may come from the presence of the Lord"* (Acts 3:19–20).[45]

Looking closer at these two extracts, the scriptural passages to which Pope Benedict refers are full of references to the end of the world. The invitation to reread the First Letter of St. Peter in the light of the "urgency of the present hour" is startling because of its deep eschatological undercurrent. For instance, 1 Pet. 4:7 states:

---

43. Benedict XVI, "Address at the Ancient Basilica of the Memorial of Moses," May 9, 2009, http://www.vatican.va/.
44. Benedict XVI, Apostolic Exhortation *Ecclesia in Medio Oriente*, September 14, 2012, http://www.vatican.va/.
45. Ibid.

"The end of all things is at hand. Therefore, be serious and sober for prayers," while 1 Pet. 4:17 refers to the judgment of the Church—a theme dwelt upon at length during this pontificate: "For it is time for the judgment to begin with the household of God; if it begins with us, how will it end for those who fail to obey the gospel of God?" The passage from Acts chapter three refers to the universal restoration to come with the second coming of Jesus (verse 21), while Ephesians 1:10 is similarly direct: "as a plan for the fullness of times, to sum up all things in Christ, in heaven and on earth."

The major theme of eschatological transformation is a central teaching, because, on the one hand, it directs us to see with the eyes of faith the ultimate physical manifestation of universal renewal to come, and on the other hand, directs us to an interior *metanoia* that in itself prepares us for our meeting with the Just One. In the dark night of tribulation we are presented with beautiful teachings on hope and love, we are granted great theological insights into Sacred Scripture which bring to life the path of salvation history, and we are told to look towards the future, knowing that Jesus is always with us:

> My message today is intended for everyone, and, as a *prophetic proclamation*, it is intended especially for peoples and communities who are undergoing a time of suffering, that the Risen Christ may open up for them the path of freedom, justice and peace. . . . Dear brothers and sisters! The risen Christ is journeying ahead of us towards the new heavens and the new earth (cf. Rev. 21:1), in which we shall all finally live as one family, as sons of the same Father. He is with us until the end of time. Let us walk behind him, in this wounded world, singing Alleluia. In our hearts there is joy and sorrow, on our faces there are smiles and tears. Such is our earthly reality. But Christ is risen, he is alive and he walks with us. For this reason we sing and we walk, faithfully carrying out our task in this world with our gaze fixed on heaven.[46]

A similar message was given to bishops from Taiwan on their *ad Limina* visit:

---

46. Benedict XVI, "Urbi et Orbi Easter Message," April 24, 2011, http://www.vatican.va/.

May the words of the prophet Isaiah never fail to enliven your hearts: "Fear not! Here is your God!" (Is. 40:9). The Lord indeed dwells among us! He continues to teach us by his word and feed us with his Body and Blood. The expectation of his return stirs us to voice the cry raised by Isaiah and echoed by John the Baptist: "Prepare the way of the Lord!" (cf. Is. 40:3). *I am confident that your faithful celebration of the Holy Sacrifice will prepare you and your people to meet the Lord when he comes again.*[47]

It is certain that while we still live in a time of grace and mercy, a time of judgment is approaching; a time of sifting the wheat and weeds, a time of passing sentence on the world. We have been the beneficiaries of two prophetic streams in recent times, one from heaven in the form of private revelation, and another from the teaching authority of the Vicar of Christ on earth. Together, they have warned us of the approaching storm, but more importantly, of the victory, that final triumph of God himself which will see earth become heaven. The entire history of salvation is culminating in our days. That power of divine love which gave life to the universe at the dawn of time will bring to completion the work of sanctification for all creation. It is in this hope that our prayer must be persistent and faith filled, so that when the Lord knocks, we are eager to open the door to Him. Now is the time to stay awake, watching like the shepherds on Bethlehem night with joy in our hearts waiting for the final fulfillment of that angelic song of joy: "Glory to God in the highest and on earth peace to those on whom his favor rests" (Lk. 2:14).

I hope that what I have shown in this book gives a clear understanding of the eschatological reality that confronts us today. There is much confusion concerning apocalypticism, from the rapture and millenarianism, to the idea of a temporal, spiritual kingdom of Christ within history, which would lack a physical coming of Jesus. However the picture painted by the popes in their ordinary magisterium—and importantly their interpretation of the eschatological revelations such as Fatima and Divine Mercy—do not point us

---

47. Benedict XVI, "ad Limina Address to the Bishops of Taiwan," December 12, 2008, http://www.vatican.va/.

in any of those directions. They clearly direct us to the definitive coming of Jesus. Their words are completely in conformity with the sequence of events as contained in the Catechism of the Catholic Church:

> Before Christ's second coming the Church must pass through *a final trial* that will shake the faith of many believers. The persecution that accompanies her pilgrimage on earth will unveil the "mystery of iniquity" in the form of a religious deception offering men an apparent solution to their problems at the price of apostasy from the truth. The supreme religious deception is that of the Antichrist, a pseudo-messianism by which man glorifies himself in place of God and of his Messiah come in the flesh. The Church will enter the glory of the kingdom only through this final Passover, when she will follow her Lord in his death and Resurrection. The kingdom will be fulfilled, then, not by a historic triumph of the Church through a progressive ascendancy, but only by God's victory over the final unleashing of evil, which will cause his Bride to come down from heaven. God's triumph over the revolt of evil will take the form of the Last Judgment after the final cosmic upheaval of this passing world.[48]

It cannot be denied that the prevailing opinion among Marian devotees tends toward the theory of the temporal kingdom within history; although this is not a view expressed by most theologians outside Marian apparition circles or within the Magisterium. One assumption usually made is that St. Louis de Montfort was referring to a time prior to the temporal kingdom throughout *True Devotion to Mary*; a time that would lead into a symbolic thousand year reign of Christ (cf. Rev. 20:1–6) after the defeat of the Antichrist. However, Pope John Paul corrected this misinterpretation in a Letter to the Montfort Religious Family in the most stringent of terms:

> The Holy Spirit invites Mary to reproduce her own virtues in the elect, extending in them the roots of her "invincible faith" and "firm hope" (cf. Treatise on True Devotion, n.34). The Second Vatican Council recalled this: "The Mother of Jesus in the glory

---

48. *Catechism of the Catholic Church*, no. 675, 677, http://www.vatican.va/.

which she possesses in body and soul in heaven is the image and beginning of the Church as it is to be perfected in the world to come. Likewise, she shines forth on earth until the day of the Lord shall come, a sign of certain hope and comfort to the pilgrim People of God" (Dogmatic Constitution *Lumen Gentium*, n.68). This eschatological dimension is contemplated by St. Louis Marie especially when he speaks of the "apostles of the latter times" formed by the Blessed Virgin to bring to the Church Christ's victory over the forces of evil (cf. Treatise on True Devotion, nn. 49–59). *This is in no way a form of "millenarianism,"* but a deep sense of the eschatological character of the Church linked to the oneness and saving universality of Jesus Christ. *The Church awaits the glorious coming of Jesus at the end of time.* Like Mary and with Mary, the saints are in the Church and for the Church to make her holiness shine out and to extend to the very ends of the earth and the end of time the work of Christ, the one Savior.[49]

Significantly, the passage cited by the Holy Father in the complete text of *Lumen Gentium* contains a reference to the Second Letter of St. Peter which concerns the end of the world: "But the day of the Lord will come like a thief, and then the heavens will pass away with a mighty roar and the elements will be dissolved by fire, and the earth and everything done on it will be found out" (2 Pet. 3:10).

In his theological masterpiece, *Eschatology: Death and Eternal Life*, Cardinal Ratzinger delves deeper into the reasons why millennial theories do not find a place in the teachings of the magisterium:

> The Christian hope knows no idea of an inner fulfillment of history. On the contrary, it affirms the impossibility of an inner fulfillment of the world. This is, indeed, the common consent shared by the various fragmentary pictures of the end of the world offered us by Scripture. The biblical representation of the End rejects the expectation of a definitive state of salvation within history. This position is also rationally correct, since the idea of a definitive intra-historical fulfillment fails to take into account the permanent openness of history and of human freedom, for which

---

49. John Paul II, "Letter to the Montfortian Religious Family," January 13, 2004, http://www.vatican.va/.

failure is always a possibility. . . .[50] Faith in Christ's return is faith that, in the end, truth will judge and love will conquer. *Naturally, this victory is won only when we take a step beyond history as we know it, a step further for which history itself yearns. The historical process can only be perfected beyond itself.*[51]

In the understanding of history being open to freedom of will and failure, we see why theories of the millennium on earth are contradictory to the message of Jesus. For instance, in what way could history continue freely if in this temporal era, the world was inhabited by those martyrs sharing in a first resurrection, living alongside people still battling against the effects of original sin? In essence, a conflict of time and eternity would be apparent upon a physical earth awaiting its own transcendence. A further question arises concerning the eschatological sequence of events in the theory of a temporal reign. That supposition is based upon the idea that the Antichrist comes not at the end of the world, but before the temporal kingdom, suggesting that there is some kind of final coming of Satan before the end—but in what sense? And furthermore that is in direct contradiction with the Catechism, which affirms it is the Antichrist himself who forms the final conflict before the Last Judgment.

In addition to *Eschatology: Death and Eternal Life*, written in 1977, Cardinal Ratzinger also wrote an article entitled "Eschatology and Utopia" in the same year; a further study of millennial errors well worth reflecting on by those who try to separate the end times from the end of the world:

The most striking attempt to synthesize eschatology with action is the experiment which history labels *chiliasm*. The name is derived from Revelation, Chapter 20, where it is announced that Christ and the saints will reign on earth for a thousand years before the

---

50. A similar clarification is found in the radio address of Pope John XXIII from September 11, 1962: Good and evil are with us still and will remain with us in the future. This is because the free will of man will always have the freedom to express itself and the possibility of going astray. But the *final and eternal victory* will be with Christ and His Church in every chosen soul and in the chosen souls of every people. *Acta Apostolicae Sedis*, 1962, 678–685.

51. Joseph Ratzinger, *Eschatology: Death and Eternal Life* (Washington, DC: The Catholic University of America Press, 1988), 213–214.

end of the world. The term refers to a conception which is indeed based in eschatology, that is, the expectation of a new world of God's making, but is not satisfied with the eschaton beyond time and beyond the end of the world. *Instead, it virtually duplicates eschatology by expecting God to achieve his purpose with man and history in this world as well as in the next, so that even within history there must be an end time* in which everything will be as it should have been all along. This entails a confusion of the intra-historical and the meta-historical categories. Chiliasts are waiting for something in history, but in forms which per se do not belong to historical thought; the meta-historical becomes miraculous by being expected in an historical form. *Such a schizoid expectation has its roots in the plurality of meanings and the plurality of forms taken by the Old Testament and Jewish hope of salvation.*[52]

A theory that has also been disseminated within the idea of a "spiritual millennium" concerns the concept of two instances of Judgment: the first leading into the beginning of the temporal Kingdom, and the second ushering in the end of the world. The first instance of judgment would have an "apparition" (not in his glorious Body) of Jesus;[53] thus avoiding the heresy of millenarianism. The Scriptural basis of this would supposedly in part, stem from St. Paul's two letters to the Thessalonians. However, Pope Benedict has stated that passages supposedly relating to the first instance of judgment (1 Thess. 4:15, 2 Thess. 2:1–13) do in fact refer to the definitive return of Jesus at the end of the world:

Very likely it was in the year 52 that St. Paul wrote the first of his Letters, the First Letter to the Thessalonians, in which he speaks of this return of Jesus, called *parousia* or advent, his new, *definitive and manifest presence* (cf. 4:13–18). The Apostle wrote these words

---

52. Cardinal Joseph Ratzinger, *Joseph Ratzinger in Communio: Volume 1: The Unity of the Church*, (Grand Rapids, Michigan: Eerdmans Publishing Co., 2010), 13.

53. The term "coming of the Lord in glory" has been applied erroneously to this theory especially in recent years. However, the *Compendium of the Catechism of the Catholic Church*, approved by Pope Benedict XVI, gave a definitive answer to this question in no.134: "How will the coming of the Lord in glory happen? *After the final cosmic upheaval of this passing world* the glorious coming of Christ will take place. *Then will come the definitive triumph of God in the Parousia and the Last Judgment.* Thus the Kingdom of God will be realized." Available at http://www.vatican.va/.

to the Thessalonians who were beset by doubts and problems: "For if we believe that Jesus died and rose, God will bring forth with him from the dead those who have fallen asleep" (4:14). And Paul continues: "Those who have died in Christ will rise first. Then we, the living, the survivors, will be caught up with them in the clouds to meet the Lord in the air. Thenceforth we shall be with the Lord unceasingly" (4:16–17). Paul describes Christ's *parousia* in especially vivid tones and with symbolic imagery which, however, conveys a simple and profound message: we shall ultimately be with the Lord for ever.

In his Second Letter to the Thessalonians, Paul changes his perspective. He speaks of the negative incidents that must precede the *final and conclusive event*. We must not let ourselves be deceived, he says, to think that, according to chronological calculations, the day of the Lord is truly imminent: "On the question of the coming of our Lord Jesus Christ and our being gathered to him, we beg you, brothers, not to be so easily agitated or terrified, whether by an oracular utterance, or rumor, or a letter alleged to be ours, into believing that the day of the Lord is here. "Let no one seduce you, no matter how" (2:1–3). The continuation of this text announces that before the Lord's arrival there will be apostasy, and one well described as the "man of lawlessness", "the son of perdition" (2:3) must be revealed, who tradition would come to call the Antichrist.[54]

In 1995, the Congregation for the Doctrine of the Faith issued a doctrinal notification concerning the alleged revelations to Vassula Ryden. One of the reasons for this was the erroneous eschatology contained within the "messages"—the exact interpretation of which is accepted by so many today:

These alleged revelations predict an imminent period when the Antichrist will prevail in the Church. *In millenarian style*, it is prophesied that God is going to make a *final, glorious intervention which will initiate on earth, even before Christ's definitive coming, an era of peace and universal prosperity.*[55]

54. Benedict XVI, "General audience," November 12, 2008, http://www.vatican.va/.

55. Congregation for the Doctrine of the Faith, "Notification on the writings and activities of Mrs. Vassula Ryden," October 6, 1995, http://www.vatican.va/.

Thus we are given a clear and unambiguous clarification, in an official document that the idea of an era of peace, a "spiritual millennium" before the end of the world, is millenarian in essence, as is the suggestion that the Antichrist is not the *last* supreme manifestation of all evil.[56] Pope John Paul reaffirmed the truth that history would continue with the destructive power of sin until the very end of the world during an *ad Limina* address to Brazilian Bishops in 1996:

> Since the beginning of my Pontificate, I have invited the universal Church to turn her gaze to the advent of the third millennium. . . . I also had the opportunity to point out that this is not "to indulge in a new millenarianism" (*Tertio millennio adveniente*, n.23), with the temptation to predict *substantial changes in it in the life of society as a whole* and of every individual. *Human life will continue, people will continue to learn about successes and failures, moments of glory and stages of decay,* and Christ our Lord always will, until the end of time, be the only source of salvation.[57]

It is appropriate to end this book with a prophetic message from Pope Benedict which summarizes the reasons for writing it; not to speculate upon dates, but simply to state in the words of St. Paul: "For our salvation is nearer now than when we first believed; the night is advanced, the day is at hand" (Rom. 13:11–12).

> Hope marks humanity's journey but for Christians it is enlivened by a certainty: the Lord is present in the passage of our lives, he accompanies us and will one day also dry our tears. *One day, not far off, everything will find its fulfillment in the Kingdom of God, a Kingdom of justice and peace.*[58]

---

56. Interestingly, in Cardinal Ratzinger's *Eschatology and Utopia*, he refers to St. Irenaeus's supposed millennial tendencies, but stresses that the notion of a Kingdom of Christ on earth "is really only a postulate of his [Irenaeus's] Christology and concept of God." Ratzinger also quotes Hans Von Balthasar who says that Irenaeus was reflecting his belief in the coming of a new earth, as well as Old Testament prophecies that the just would finally and irrevocably possess the land (*Joseph Ratzinger in Communio Volume* 1, 17).

57. John Paul II, "ad Limina address to Brazilian Bishops," January 29, 1996, http://www.vatican.va/.

58. Benedict XVI, "Homily for 1st Vespers of Advent," November 28, 2009, http://www.vatican.va/.

Appendix I

St. Hildegard of Bingen
—Doctor of the Church
The Five Ferocious Epochs

THE GREAT prophetic visions of St. Hildegard known as *Scivias*, a work cited several times recently by Pope Benedict XVI and approved by Pope Eugene III in 1147, presents us with a tableau of five epochs from the time of St. Hildegard until the end of the world. These eras of history are described in detail in vision eleven of *Scivias* and are explained by the "Voice from Heaven," that is God the Father. Each epoch has the symbolic name of an animal, and is written in such a way as to recall the visions found in the Books of Daniel and Ezekiel.

In chronological order they are:

The fiery dog:

One is like a dog, fiery but not burning; for that era will produce people with a biting temperament, who seem fiery in their own estimation, but do not burn with the justice of God.

The yellow lion:

Another is like a yellow lion; for this era will endure martial people, who instigate many wars but do not think of the righteousness of God in them; for those kingdoms will begin to weaken and tire, as the yellow color shows.

The pale horse:

Another is like a pale horse; for those times will produce people who drown themselves in sin, and in their licentious and swift-moving pleasures neglect all virtuous activities. And then these kingdoms will lose their ruddy strength and grow pale with the fear of ruin, and their hearts will be broken.

The black pig:

And another is like a black pig; for this epoch will have leaders who blacken themselves with misery and wallow in the mud of impurity. They will infringe the divine law by fornication and other like evils, and will plot to diverge from the holiness of God's commands.

The gray wolf:

And the last is like a gray wolf. For those times will have people who plunder each other, robbing the powerful and the fortunate; and in these conflicts they will show themselves to be neither black nor white, but gray in their cunning. And they will divide and conquer the rulers of those realms; and then the time will come when many will be ensnared, and the error of errors will rise from Hell to Heaven. And the children of light will be pressed in the winepress of martyrdom; and they will not deny the Son of God, but reject the son of perdition who tries to do his will with the Devil's arts.[1]

The manner in which these epochs are described is reminiscent of the theological position that the battle of good and evil is renewed periodically, in ever more violent ways throughout history. In the context of the Book of Revelation, Hans Urs von Balthasar explains thus:

> The concluding visions there are not to be viewed as an encoded description of the future of world history but rather are a depiction of the ever-new intersection of the drama now taking place between heaven and earth.[2]

What we discover in St. Hildegard's mystical visions of these five ages is the ebb and flow of two civilizations that develop across the centuries: the Christian and the Anti-Christian. At times, the pendulum swings further in one direction, and then in the other. However, the undercurrent that pervades the passage of time is one of a gradual rebellion both within the Church and without. It is this eschatological tension that dominates Hildegard's prophetic

---

1. Hildegard of Bingen, *Scivias* (Mahwah, NJ: Paulist Press, 1990), 494–495.
2. Hans Urs von Balthasar, *Explorations in Theology IV: Spirit and Institution* (San Francisco: Ignatius Press, 1995), 466.

charism and explains her central message of renewal and reform of ecclesial life; notably similar to that of Pope Benedict XVI.

Twenty years after *Scivias* was completed, the great mystic from the Rhineland further elaborated on the five epochs in the book of prophetic revelations entitled *Liber divinorum operum*, imparting a greater understanding of the travails contained within each of them. In fact, we are able to decipher from certain details in a general sense the times to which they refer.

The *Liber divinorum operum*, also known as *De operatione Dei*, embellishes the explanation of the epoch of the fiery dog by presenting a vision of corrupt clergy and injustice:

> And people will say to each other, "How long must we suffer and endure these predatory wolves? They should be physicians but are not." But because they have the power to bind and loose, they bind us as if we were the most savage of wolves. Their wantonness attacks us, and the whole Church is diminished as a result. For they no longer announce what is just, and they undermine the Law just as wolves devour sheep. They are voracious in their carousing and often commit adultery.[3]

Furthermore we read:

> How can it be suitable for those who wear the tonsure as well as stoles and cassocks to have more soldiers than we do? Is it fitting that a clergyman should be a soldier, and that a soldier should be a clergyman?[4]

It appears that this epoch relates to the high Middle Ages (c. 1000 –1300) in which St. Hildegard herself was at the center of the battle for reform in the wake of the Gregorian Reforms of Pope Gregory VII (1073–85). The principle aims of which were to eradicate the sin of simony and reinforce the ideal of clerical celibacy, while at the same time enhancing papal supremacy over secular rulers; as shown in the so-called "Investiture Controversy."

The epoch of the yellow lion is described as one of terrible and cruel wars causing the deaths of countless men and women and the

---

3. Hildegard of Bingen, *Book of Divine Works* (Santa Fe: Bear & Company, 1987), 240.

4. Ibid., 241.

destruction of many cities, permitted by God as a punishment for sin. However, in the *Liber divinorum operum* another aspect of this epoch is expounded upon—that of an authentic renewal of the spiritual life:

> And just as clouds let down a mild rain suitable for the germination of seeds, the Holy Spirit will pour forth the dew of grace, along with wisdom, prophecy and holiness, upon people so that, just as if turned around, they will lead different and good lives. . . . The true angels will then cling to human beings in trust, for they will see in them a new and holy transformation.[5]

In discerning the presence of this second element, we may recall the birth of great new forms of spirituality: the monastic Carthusians and Cistercians, and the five great mendicant orders—Franciscans, Dominicans, Servites, Carmelites, and Augustinians. From these orders came a succession of great theologians: St. Thomas Aquinas, St. Bonaventure, Blessed Duns Scotus, and St. Albert the Great. The pre-eminent figure of St. Francis of Assisi, however, is the luminous center of this transformation of the corrupt worldly Church to one modeled on the heavenly:

> It has been said that Francis represents an *alter Christus*, that he was truly a living icon of Christ. He has also been called "the brother of Jesus." Indeed, this was his ideal: to be like Jesus, to contemplate Christ in the Gospel, to love him intensely and to imitate his virtues. In particular, he wished to ascribe interior and exterior poverty with a fundamental value, which he also taught to his spiritual sons.[6]

The other great reforming figure at this time was Dominic de Guzman, founder of the Dominicans and a legendary preacher. Together with the development of the Mendicant Orders, both these giants of evangelical Catholicism read the signs of the times and sought to restore the purity of the faith seen in the earliest centuries after Christ.

---

5. Ibid., 244.
6. Benedict XVI, "General Audience on St. Francis of Assisi," January 27, 2010, http://www.vatican.va/.

On the other hand, this same stretch of history (c.1200–1600) is pervaded by a whole series of bloody conflicts: the Hundred Years' War (1337–1453), the Burgundy wars, countless civil conflicts, as well as great confrontations between the Christian West and the Islamic Ottoman Empire in the sixteenth century. Added to that, the explosive ruptures that led to the Protestant Reformation throughout northern Europe, and we discover a dichotomy of enormous proportions within Western Christianity itself, as well as between the religious and secular.

The third epoch of the pale horse seems to foresee a time of absolute moral degradation as explained in the *Liber divinorum operum*:

> It is a time of decadence and clerical ostentation, of bold pleasures and vanities that always spring up when we humans doze away in a kind of lazy peace and are smothered by too many possessions. . . . A time will come when unbelievers and dreadful people will break everywhere into the property and possessions of the Church and strive to destroy them, just as vultures and hawks slaughter whatever lies beneath their pinions and talons.[7]

The Age of Enlightenment (c.1650–1800) and its offshoots of baroque culture and the French *Grand Siecle* seem to apply to the beginning of this era when excess and luxury were the hallmarks of a new age. But alongside these lavish traits was a growing hostility to the faith and we see echoes in Hildegard's *Liber* of the terrible persecutions of the French Revolution (1789–1799), when churches were destroyed on a massive scale and the blood of martyrs sanctified the streets across the country.

We are given two further precious indications in the *Liber* as to the specific times to which they refer: the fall of the Holy Roman Empire, and the loss of the temporal power of the popes. In Vision Ten: 25, we read:

> In those days the emperors, despite their Roman solemnity, will experience a decline in the power by which they once held the Roman Empire. They will lose their glory and the empire in their hands will little by little crumble away and fall into pieces. . . . And

---

7. Bingen, *Book of Divine Works*, 246, 248.

so kings and leaders of countless peoples once subject to the Roman Empire will grow independent and no longer submissive. *Thus the Roman Empire will be doomed and broken up.*[8]

The Roman Empire to which St. Hildegard refers lasted from 962 until 1806, and the term Holy Roman Empire was only introduced from 1254. What we can say is that the prophetic element was absolutely accurate in that from the Thirty Years War (1618–48) until its complete demise, the empire gradually disintegrated as individual territories became more autonomous; the Peace of Westphalia in 1648 being one example of that process. In the eighteenth century, a series of wars of succession and the German Mediatization (annexing the lands of one sovereign monarchy) caused the dissolution to become almost inevitable. The Empire was formally dissolved on August 6, 1806 when the last Holy Roman Emperor, Francis II, abdicated, following a military defeat by the French under Napoleon.

Concerning the loss of the Papal States and the diminishing of papal temporal power the great prophetess continues:

> Since princes and other secular or spiritual leaders will find it hard to find anything religious in the apostolic name, they will form a low opinion of both that office and that name. They will prefer teachers and bishops with other names and from different regions. As a result, the Apostolic See will find that the territory over which it has authority will be diminished. Only Rome and a few nearby regions will remain under papal control. *This will come about partly as a result of warlike invasions and partly as a result of agreements and decisions made by spiritual and secular leaders.*[9]

This remarkable prophecy found its fulfillment in various ways in the eighteenth, nineteenth and twentieth centuries; the French Revolution can certainly be seen as the beginning of their demise. In 1791 the enclave of *Comtat Venaissin* was annexed by France and two years later the Papal States as a whole were invaded by French forces, who declared a Roman Republic. Pope Pius VI was to die an exile in Valence (France) in 1799. Although the states were restored to papal control on several occasions in the early decades of the

8. Ibid., 249.
9. Bingen, *Book of Divine Works*, 250.

nineteenth century, the turning point came in 1860 when Bologna, Ferrara, Umbria, the Marches, Benevento, and Pontecorvo were all formally annexed. Ten years later, in September 1870, the Italian armed forces finally took control of Rome after Napoleon III had ordered his forces to withdraw because of the onset of the Franco-Prussian War in July of that year. Pope Pius IX was now a prisoner in the Vatican; the Papal States no more.[10]

The culmination of this prophecy came during the reign of Pope Pius XI in 1929 when he renounced the bulk of the Papal States, and signed the Lateran Treaty (or Concordat) with Italy, creating the Vatican City State and thus forming the sovereign territory of the Holy See. With this political agreement we see the pinpoint accuracy of St. Hildegard's startling revelations come to fruition, and it allows us to place the epoch of the pale horse firmly in the latter centuries of the second millennium.

The fourth epoch, that of the black pig, is the era in which we appear to find ourselves today, although for how much longer is a mystery hidden in the secrets of the Most Holy Trinity. In the *Liber Divinorum operum* we discover a return to the two opposing civilizations that grow in the field of humanity (cf. Matt. 13:24–30). Vision Ten: 26 presents what seems to be a veiled reference to the great mystical happenings in the Marian Era:

> In those days there will be many wise sayings and many sages: The riddles of the prophets and the writings of the sages will be completely explained in this way. Their sons and daughters will prophesy, as it was foretold long ago. And all these things will take place in such purity and truthfulness that the spirits of the air will no

---

10. On May 15, 1871, Pope Pius IX issued the encyclical *Ubi Nos*, on the Pontifical States in which he seemingly discerns the gravity of what has occurred: "When We were defeated by Our enemies *in accordance with the mysterious design of God*, We observed the severely bitter fortunes of Our City and the downfall of the civil rule of the Apostolic See in the face of military invasion. . . . We are compelled to repeat the words of St. Bernard: 'This is the beginning of the evils; we fear worse evil' [Epistle 243]. For wickedness advances on its path and promotes its designs. No longer does it take pains to conceal its worst deeds since they cannot remain hidden, but it is eager to carry off the last spoils from the overthrow of justice, honor, and religion." Available at http://www.papalencyclicals.net/.

longer be able to ridicule the sons and daughters. They will prophesy, as the prophets of old announced God's mysteries and as the apostles proclaimed their teaching, which exceeded all human understanding.[11]

We may recall here the great mystics of our recent history who would have fulfilled this prophecy: Sr. Lucia of Fatima, Blessed Elena Aiello, St. Faustina Kowalska, Maria Esperanza, St. Pio of Pietrelcina, Marthe Robin, Natuzza Evolo, Blessed Alexandrina da Costa, and so many more faithful souls full of zeal for the glory of God. In a more general sense, the post-Vatican II movements could also be seen as prophetic voices contributing to this fulfillment. However, *immediately* after Hildegard proclaims this seemingly wondrous state of peace and holiness she adds:

> At this same time, however, so many false teachings and false deeds will arise along with other misdeeds—*as a sign of the imminent arrival of the Antichrist*—that people in these days will claim that never before have there been such crimes or such iniquities as then. . . . The time of crisis has arrived, for purity and tranquillity of faith will disappear and believers will fall away on a massive scale.[12]

As has been documented throughout this book, our age displays the essential features of this epoch of the black pig, both good and evil. The colossal decline in practicing Catholics in the last century is something that has greatly troubled the popes, and has caused Pope Benedict XVI to form a new Vatican curial department in order to re-evangelize the lost sheep of Western Christianity. Returning to the description of this era from the *Scivias* revelations, we read how leaders will "*plot to diverge from the holiness of God's commands.*" A brief observation of secular leadership over the past fifty years in various parts of the world shows a complete disregard for the commandments of the Lord. We may consider the pro-abortion laws, the desire to redefine marriage as something open to homosexuals, and the approval for scientists to manipulate life in its most fragile, defenceless forms.

11. Bingen, *Book of Divine Works*, 251.
12. Ibid.

One disconcerting aspect of the *Liber* is the comprehensive depiction of the Antichrist, from the abject immorality of his mother (the complete antithesis of the purity of the Blessed Virgin), to his birth, development in the evil arts, and eventual savage persecution of the Mystical Body of Christ. In terms of the epoch of his reign, it is that of the gray wolf. However, it is not clear where his birth falls; in fact, St. Hildegard describes those circumstances in Vision Ten: 28, immediately after the passage concerning the massive falling away of the faithful. It could certainly be seen to fall within the epoch of the black pig, although what *is* certain, is that the last era is one of short duration, essentially encompassing his diabolical reign of terror. The epoch of the gray wolf ends with the death of the Antichrist:

> For he dared to ascend into heaven, and the Lord and Savior of the nations, the Son of God, will kill him. The Son will accomplish this with the power by which he, who is the Word of the Father will judge the whole globe in a just judgment.... Therefore rejoice, O you who have your dwelling place in heaven as well as on Earth. After the fall of the Antichrist the glory of the Son of God will be seen to its full extent [Vision Ten: 37].[13]

In terms of the eschatological sequence of events, both *Scivias* and the *Liber divinorum operum* allow for no era of peace within history after the Antichrist's reign and before the end of the world. The death of the son of perdition leads to the Last Judgment, and the glorious splendor of the Church Triumphant is seen in the new heaven and new earth as the definitive conclusion of salvation history.[14]

---

13. Ibid., 262, 264.

14. It should be noted that in certain books concerning Catholic prophecy, elements of St. Hildegard's prophetic writings have been taken out of context thus distorting their original meaning. For example, the "temporal era of peace" quoted in reference to the end times actually refers, in Hildegard's original writings, to the Age of the Lion—which we have seen alludes to the spiritual renewal brought about, in part, by the Mendicants nearly eight hundred years ago. These errors stem from Hildegard's works not being known in their original form for many centuries, but instead through the writings of the Cistercian Prior Gebeno von Eberbach who, in his *Speculum futurorum temporum* or *Pentachronon* (c.1220), hand-picked various prophetic excerpts from two of Hildegard's three large visionary volumes, *Scivias* and the *Liber divinorum operum*, as well as her own private correspondence.

Appendix II

Urbi et Orbi Easter Allocution of Pope Pius XII, 1957[1]

ERROR, in well-nigh countless forms, has made slaves of the intellects of men, for all their great gifts, and evil habits in every form have reached such degrees of precocity, impudence, and universality as to arouse serious misgivings in those who have at heart the destinies of the world. The human race seems like a body, infected and wounded, in which the blood circulates with great difficulty, since individuals, classes, and peoples persist in remaining divided and consequently without social intercourse; and when they are not ignorant of each other they are hating each other; they plot against, struggle with and destroy one another. *But even this night in the world shows clear signs of a dawn that will come, of a new day receiving the kiss of a new and more resplendent sun.* Meanwhile, under Providence, methods are about to be multiplied in the world for the fuller and freer development of life. While the discoveries of science broaden the horizon of human possibilities, technical development and organization render such conquests effective by putting them at the immediate service of man. Nuclear energy has, in fact, already opened up a new age. Houses are already lighted by the use of energy flowing from the application of nuclear fission, and the days seem not far distant when cities will be lit and machines driven by synthetic processes similar to those by which the sun and the planets have been giving heat for many millions of years. Electronics and mechanics are in process of changing the world of production and labor through automation. Man becomes thus ever more the master of his works, and sees his labor endowed with an improved quality and skill. Means of transport link one point of the earth from another in a single network, and the earth can be encircled at a speed

---

1. Extracts taken from *The Tablet*, April 27, 1957.

greater than the apparent movement of the sun. Missiles cleave a path through the depths of the skies, and artificial satellites are about to startle space with their presence. Agriculture, by means of nuclear chemistry, multiplies the possibilities of feeding a human race much more numerous than that of today, while biological research daily wins ground in the battle against the most terrible diseases.

And yet, all this is still night; night, indeed, full of hope, but night; night which could also, even unexpectedly, become engulfed in storm, if occasional flashes of lightening should appear and the crack of thunder be heard. Is it not perhaps true that science, technology, and organization have often been the sources of terror to men? They are, therefore, not more certain now than in the past. They see clearly that no progress, taken by itself alone, can make the world come to birth again. Many are already beginning to perceive—and admit it—that this night of the world has come about because Christ has been arrested; because they wished to exclude him from family, cultural, and social life; because the people have risen up against Him; because He has been crucified and rendered voiceless and motionless. And there is a greater number of souls, courageous and eager, aware that such a death and burial of Christ was possible only because among His friends was found one who denied and betrayed Him and there were many who fled in confusion before the threats of His enemies. These souls are aware that timely, harmonious, and organized action will change the face of the earth, bringing it to renewal and improvement. It is essential to remove the stone from the tomb in which men desire to bury truth and goodness. A new resurrection of Jesus is necessary: a true resurrection, which admits no more lordship of death. *Surrexit Dominus vere* (Lk. 24:34): *Mors illi ultra non dominabitur* (Rom. 6:9). In individuals, Christ must destroy the night of mortal sin with the dawn of grace regained. In families, the night of indifference and coolness must give way to the sun of love. In factories, in cities, in nations, in lands of misunderstanding and hatred the night must grow bright as the day, *nox sicut dies illuminabitur,* and strife will cease and there will be peace.

Come Lord Jesus. The human race has not the strength to move the stone which it has itself fashioned seeking to impede Thy return. Send thy angel, O Lord and make our night grow as bright as the day. How many hearts, O Lord, await Thee! How many souls are longing for the hastening of the day in which Thou alone wilt live and reign in their hearts! Come, Lord Jesus. There are numerous signs that Thy return is not far off. O Mary, who hast seen Him risen: from whom the first appearance of Jesus took away the unspeakable anguish produced by the night of the Passion; Mary, we offer the first fruits of this day to thee; to thee, spouse of the Divine Spirit, we offer our heart and our hope. Amen.

Select Bibliography

Amorth, Gabriel. *An Exorcist Tells His Story*. San Francisco: Ignatius Press, 1994.

Augustine. *The City of God.*, translated by Marcus Dods. Peabody, MA: Hendrickson Publishers, Inc., 2009.

Balthasar, Hans Urs von. *Theo-Drama: The Dramatis Personae. The Person of Christ*, vol. 3. San Francisco: Ignatius Press, 1992.

_____. *Explorations in Theology IV: Spirit and Institution*. San Francisco: Ignatius Press, 1995.

Benedict XVI. *Jesus of Nazareth: Holy Week: From the Entrance into Jerusalem to the Resurrection*. San Francisco: Ignatius Press, 2011.

_____. *Light of the World*. London: Catholic Truth Society, 2010.

Bingen, Hildegard of. *Book of Divine Works*. Santa Fe: Bear & Company, 1987.

_____. *Scivias*. Mahwah, NJ: Paulist Press, 1990.

Brown, Michael H. *The Final Hour*. Milford, OH: Faith Publishing Company, 1992.

D'Herbingy, Michel. *Vladimir Soloviev: A Russian Newman*. Ghent, NY: Sophia Perennis, 2007.

Duffy, Eamon. *Saints and Sinners: A History of the Popes*. New Haven and London: Yale University Press, 1997.

Gobbi, Stefano. *To the Priests: Our Lady's Beloved Sons*. St. Francis, ME: Marian Movement of Priests, 1998.

Guardini, Romano. *The Last Things*. New York: Pantheon, 1954.

_____. *The Lord*. London: Longmans, 1956.

Guitton, Jean. *The Pope Speaks: Dialogues with Paul VI*. New York: Meredith Press, 1968.

Ilibagiza, Immaculee. *Our Lady of Kibeho: Mary Speaks to the World from the Heart of Africa*. New York: Hay House, 2008.

Irenaeus. *Against Heresies, vol. 5*. Whitefish, MT: Kessinger Publishing, 2004.

John Paul II. *Crossing the Threshold of Hope*. London: Jonathan Cape, 1994.

_____. *Rise Let Us be on Our Way*. London: Jonathan Cape, 2004.

Kelly, Anthony. *Eschatology and Hope*. New York: Orbis Books, 2006.

Kosicki, George. *Pope John Paul II: The Great Mercy Pope*. Stockbridge:

John Paul II Institute of Divine Mercy, 2001.

Kowalska, Faustina. *Divine Mercy in my Soul.* Stockbridge: Marians of the Immaculate Conception, 1987.

Lucia, Mary. *Fatima in Lucia's Own Words:* Fatima, Postulation Center, 1989.

Martin, Ralph. *Is Jesus Coming Soon?* San Francisco: Ignatius Press, 1997.

———. *The Catholic Church at the End of an Age.* San Francisco: Ignatius Press, 1994.

Miceli, Vincent P. *The Antichrist.* Harrison, NY: Roman Catholic Books, 1981.

Michel de la Sainte Trinite. *The Whole Truth About Fatima, Volume II, The Secret and the Church.* Buffalo: Immaculate Heart Publications, 1990.

———. *The Whole Truth About Fatima, Volume III, The Third Secret.* Buffalo: Immaculate Heart Publications, 1990, republished in 2001.

Mondin, Battista. *The Popes of the Modern Ages.* Vatican City: Urbaniana University Press, 2004.

Montfort, Louis de. *True Devotion to Mary.* Rockford, IL: Tan, 1941.

O'Callaghan, Paul. *Christ our Hope: An Introduction to Eschatology.* Washington, DC: The Catholic University of America Press, 2011.

Ratzinger, Joseph. *Dogmatic Theology: Eschatology Death and Eternal Life,* vol. 9. Washington, DC: The Catholic University of America Press, 1988.

———. *The Ratzinger Report.* San Francisco: Ignatius Press, 1985.

———. *Salt of the Earth.* San Francisco: Ignatius Press, 1997.

Socci, Antonio. *The Fourth Secret of Fatima.* Fitzwilliam, NH: Loreto Publications, 2009.

Weigel, George. *Witness to Hope.* New York: Harper Collins, 1999.

Wojtyla, Karol. *Sign of Contradiction.* London: Hodder and Stoughton, 1980.

INDEX

Adalbert, Saint, 172
Adam 82, 181
  Christ as the New Adam, 173
  Adam and Eve, 156, 166, 174
Adrian VI, Pope, 95
Age of Enlightenment, 213
Aiello, Blessed Elena, 216
Albert the Great, Saint, 212
Amantini, Fr. Candido, 161
Amorth, Fr. Gabriel, 34, 161, 171, 221
Antichrist, 23–29, 33, 36, 39, 80, 104, 119, 121, 135, 161, 164–172, 187–189, 203, 205, 208, 216–217, 222
Apocalypse, 66, 167
Aquinas, Saint Thomas, 167, 212
Augustine, Saint, 1, 20, 25, 68, 82, 221
Augustinians, 212

Balthasar, Fr. Hans Urs von, 167–168, 208, 210, 221
Baouardy, Blessed Mariam, 91
Bellarmine, Saint Robert, 170
Benedict XV, Pope, 30, 41–44
  Ad Beatissimi Apostolorum, 41–43
  Letter to Cardinal Gasparri, 43
Benedict XVI, Pope, 4, 10–11, 30, 67–68, 90, 111, 121, 125, 149, 152, 155–156, 167, 169, 179, 180, 182–212 passim, 216, 221
  Africae Munus, 199

Coming of the kingdom of God, 198–199
  Ecclesia in Medio Oriente, 200
  Fatima Third Secret, 111, 182–187 passim
  Last Judgment, 190, 206
  Light of the World, 125, 184, 221
  ad Orientem, 191
  Prophetic Prayer, 198–202
  on Saint Hildegard of Bingen, 4, 180, 187, 189, 209
  Spe Salvi, 190
  Transformation and Renewal, 180, 182, 191–194, 201
Benelli, Cardinal Giovanni, 95
Bernard of Clairvaux, Saint, 20, 51, 69, 172, 175, 187, 215
Bertone, Cardinal Tarcisio, 29
Biffi, Cardinal Giacomo, 167–169
Blue Army of Fatima, 23
Bonaventure, Saint, 212
Book of Revelation, 13, 66, 77, 190, 195, 210
  Rev. 3: 13, 100, 104
  Rev. 12: 11, 112, 114, 119, 167
  Rev. 13: 111
  Rev. 14: 77, 142
  Rev. 20: 203
  Rev. 21: 58, 66, 114, 128, 129, 151, 154, 158, 174, 195–196, 201
  Rev. 22: 70, 72, 77, 105–106, 109, 121, 179, 199
Bridget, Saint, 20
Brzezinski, Zbigniew, 8

Carmelites, 212
Carthusians, 212
Catechism of the Catholic Church, 1, 33, 156, 174, 179, 203, 206
Catherine of Siena, Saint, 91
Chiliasm, 205
Cistercians, 212
Civilization of Love, 3, 15, 135, 159, 165, 172, 193, 197
Colin, Fr. Jean Claude, 19
Communism, 8, 43–48, 115, 117
Congregation of the Most Holy Redeemer, 19
Council of Trent, 17
Courveille, Fr. Jean Claude, 19
Cupertino, Saint Joseph, 17

da Costa, Blessed Alexandrina, 2, 216
Daniel (Prophet), 27, 170, 209
de Guzman, Saint Dominic, 212
de Montfort, Saint Louis, 19, 21–24, 29, 31, 51, 120, 185, 203, 222
True Devotion to Mary, 22, 120, 203, 222
de Porres, Saint Martin, 17
Di Francia, Saint Annibale, 156
Divine Mercy, 4, 87, 122–137, 150, 153, 176, 202, 222
Chaplet, 129, 130, 132
Dives in Misericordia, 125–130
Divine Mercy Sunday, 125
Entrustment of the World to Divine Mercy, 133
Image of Divine Mercy, 123
Second Coming, 124–136 passim
Dominicans, 212
Duns Scotus, Blessed, 212

Eberbach, Gebano von, 217
Elijah (Prophet), 172
Enoch, 172
Esperanza, Maria, 216
Eugene III, Pope, 171, 187, 209
Evolo, Natuzza, 216

Fatima, 2–4, 13, 30, 32, 40–51 passim, 56, 64, 73–74, 89–90, 111–122, 125, 137, 150, 157–158, 179, 182–186, 189, 202, 216, 222
Consecration to the Immaculate Heart of Mary, 56, 119–120, 175
Miracle of the Sun, 57, 112
in relation to the Novissimis, 116, 182, 185
Third Secret, 51, 64, 111–113, 121, 182–186, 222
Triumph of the Immaculate Heart, 121, 184
First Vatican Council, 33
Francis of Assisi, Saint, 199, 212
Francis Xavier, Saint, 19
Francisco of Fatima, Blessed, 56, 74, 119–120, 158
Francis II, Holy Roman Emperor, 214
Franciscans, 212
French Revolution, 21, 51, 213–214
Fuentes, Fr. Augustin, 56, 73–74

Gaudium et Spes, 71–72, 157
God,
Marian era willed by, 19, 29, 74
Judgment, 32, 36, 48, 75, 99, 101, 131, 136, 143, 159, 176, 189, 200–206, 210–211, 217
The Great Springtime, 59, 144, 150–155, 158
Beatific Vision, 174–175

Index

Gonzaga, Saint Aloysius, 17
Gregory VII, Pope, 211

Hildegard of Bingen, Saint, 4,
  161, 180, 187–189, 209–217
  Five Ferocious Epochs, 209–217
    passim
Hitler, Adolph, 48
Hnilica, Bishop Pavel, 125, 183
Holy Spirit, 1, 3, 7, 10, 12, 22–23,
  25, 29, 33, 35–37, 43, 50, 58–62,
  68–71, 77, 83, 86–89, 97, 98,
  100–101, 105–109, 113, 115, 121,
  131, 143–159 passim, 169, 171,
  176, 196–197, 203, 212
  Assisting the Popes, 88, 108
  Dominum et Vivificantem, 11–
    12, 105
  Missionary Activity, 69, 86, 146
  *Preparing for the Second
    Coming*, 3, 22, 25, 29, 37, 58–
    59, 61, 70, 88, 105–107, 153,
    155, 156, 159, 203

Ibarra, Dr., 18
Irenaeus, Saint, 1, 30, 173–174,
  208, 221
Isaiah (Prophet), 128, 135, 138,
  148, 189, 202
Islamic Ottoman Empire, 213

Jacinta of Fatima, Blessed, 56, 74,
  119–120, 158
Jansen, Cornelius, 19
Jansenism, 19, 21
Jesus Christ,
  Adventus medius, 69, 175
  Divine Mercy Image, 123
  Divine Mercy Sunday, 125
  *Eschatological discourse in
    Matthew ch.* 24: 41, 46, 59

Eucharist, 11, 19, 39, 69, 97–98,
  107, 191, 199
  *Passion of Jesus and the
    Church*, 69, 79, 91, 100, 116,
    129, 181, 183, 220
  Prophecy for Poland, 124–125,
    133–134
  Recapitulation of all Things,
    173–174
  Sacred Heart, 17, 36–37, 45–48,
    73, 123
  Second Coming, 1–2, 15, 22, 32,
    58, 64, 73, 88, 91, 96, 99, 102,
    108, 114, 120, 124, 133–138,
    143, 151, 154, 159, 161, 172–175,
    184–185, 191, 194, 201–203,
    219–220
  Vision given to St. Pio, 40–41
(St.) John, Apostle, 7, 79, 149,
  165, 186
John of Avila, Saint, 187
John of the Cross, Saint, 17
John Paul I, Pope, 89–91, 95
  *Urbi et Orbi Address, 27 August
    1978*, 90
John Paul II, Blessed, Pope, 2, 4,
  7, 10–15, 24, 28, 31, 35, 37, 51, 54,
  64, 67, 73–75, 88, 91, 95–176
  passim, 179, 181–183, 185, 204,
  208, 221
  *Act of Entrustment to Divine
    Mercy*, 133–134
  Antichrist, 164–166, 203
  Civilization of Love, 15, 135, 159,
    165, 172
  *Consecration of the World to
    the Immaculate Heart of
    Mary*, 116–121, 175
  Crossing the Threshold of Hope,
    7, 100, 121, 221
  Dives in Misericordia, 125–130

225

Dominum et Vivificantem, 11, 105

Ecclesia in Europa, 13, 28, 103

Great Springtime of Christianity, 150–151, 154, 157–158

Incarnationis Mysterium, 153

ad Limina visits, 106, 107, 152–154, 157–160, 163, 208

Marian Year 1987–88, 109

Millenarianism, 105, 152, 204, 208

a New and Divine Holiness, 156

New Evangelization, 15, 74, 163

Redemptor Hominis, 97, 107, 127, 130

Redemptoris Mater, 73, 100–101, 109

Redemptoris Missio, 152, 154

Rosarium Virginis Mariae, 160

Second Coming, 14, 96, 98, 102, 105–106, 108, 121, 124–125, 131–133, 136, 138–139, 141, 143, 145–156, 158, 163, 172–174, 176

Tertio millennio adveniente, 67, 105

Veritatis Splendor, 12

Vita Consecrata, 135

World Youth Day, 11, 12, 108–109, 139, 140–143, 145–146, 155, 163, 165

John XXIII, Blessed, Pope, 3, 60–68, 75, 77, 157, 161, 205

Address for the opening of the Second Vatican Council, 11 October 1962, 67–68

Aeterna Dei Sapientia, 65

Apostolic letter: The Rosary, 65

Grata Recordatio, 64

Radio Address, 11 September 1962, 63–64, 161, 205

Sacrae Laudis, 67–68

Urbi et Orbi Address Easter 1962, 64

Juan Diego, Saint, 18

Kolbe, Saint Maximilian, 74–75

Konig, Cardinal Franz, 95

Kowalska, Saint Faustina, 4, 91, 122–136 passim, 216, 222

Krol, Cardinal John, 95

Laboure, Saint Catherine, 24

Legion of Mary, 23

(St.) Leo the Great, Pope, 50, 65

Leo XIII, Pope, 33–38, 43–44, 86

Annum Sacrum, 36

Augustissimae Virginis Mariae, 35

Consecration of the World to the Sacred Heart of Jesus, 36–37

Depuis Le Jour, 35

Divinum Illud Munus, 36, 86

Inscrutabili Dei, 33

Quod Apostolici Muneris, 44

Liber divinorum operum, 161, 211–217 passim

Liguori, Saint Alphonsus, 19–21, 31

Lucia of Fatima, Sr., 13, 44, 48, 56, 73–74, 90, 112–113, 117, 137, 216, 222

Luciani, Cardinal Albino, 89–91

Luigi Marie Monti, Blessed, 31

Lumen Gentium, 72–73, 121, 164, 204

Margaret Mary, Saint, 17, 46, 123

Marian era, 19, 24, 29–33, 37, 43, 48, 51, 53, 59, 63, 74, 89–90, 215

Marian Movement of Priests, 23, 32, 221

Martin, Fr. Joseph Pius, 170
Mary, Blessed Virgin, 2–3, 18, 21,
29–33, 43, 48–59 passim, 70,
74–75, 80, 86, 89, 100–124
passim, 142, 148, 155–156, 159,
163, 170, 185, 195, 198, 204, 217
Advocate, 23, 80, 160
Assumption into Heaven, 53–
54, 57, 109, 165
Co-redemptrix, 53, 101, 160
Eschatological mission, 29, 54,
100–102
Imitation of her virtues, 22, 75,
203
Mediatrix, 20, 23, 29, 30, 73, 75,
80, 102, 160
Spouse of the Holy Spirit, 70,
108–109, 159, 220
*in the Teaching of St. Louis de
Montfort*, 22–24, 29, 31, 51, 120,
185, 203
Third Secret of Fatima, 111–113,
121
Menendez, Sr. Josefa, 91
Mengele, Joseph, 10
Messori, Vittorio, 182, 197
Miceli, Fr. Vincent, 39, 222
(St.) Michael, Archangel, 34–35
Michael of the Saints, Saint, 91
Miligno, Emmanuel, 9
Millenarianism, 105, 152, 179, 202,
204, 206, 208

Napoleon III, 215
Nazism, 8, 48
New Age Movement, 9, 13, 161
New Evangelization, 15, 70, 74,
163, 187
Newman, Blessed John Henry,
25–28, 33
Novissimis, 3, 116, 150, 182, 185

Obando, Cardinal Miguel, 8
Our Lady of Guadalupe, 18
Our Lady of Kibeho, 30, 221
Our Lady of La Salette, 2, 25, 30,
90
Our Lady of Laus, 21
Our Lady of Lourdes, 3, 25, 30, 51,
56, 90

Paul, Saint, 28, 36, 82–83, 172, 175,
206–208
Paul VI, Pope, 10, 75–78, 80–88,
91, 97, 112, 162–163, 166, 221
Christi Matri, 80
Evangelii Nuntiandi, 85–86
Gaudete in Domino, 77–78, 142
*General Audience on the Activ-
ity of Satan*, 81–84
Humanae Vitae, 10, 84–85
Signs of the End Times, 87–88
Philippe, Fr. Marie Dominique,
79, 103
Pio of Pietrelcina, Saint, 40–41,
170, 216
Pius VI, Pope, 214
Pius IX, Blessed, Pope, 24–25, 31–
33, 38, 43, 48, 75, 215
*Dogma of the Immaculate Con-
ception*, 30–32
Syllabus of Errors, 31
Ubi Nos, 32, 215
Ubi Primum, 31–32
(St.) Pius X, Pope, 3, 18, 37–41
E Supremi, 38–39
Letter to French Bishops, 40
Pius XI, Pope, 44–48, 50, 52, 123,
215
Divini Redemptoris, 45, 47
Lateran Treaty, 215
Miserentissimus Redemptor,
45–46, 50

Pius XII, Pope, 2, 11, 37, 48–60,
    64, 117, 144–145, 152, 157–158,
    183–184, 199, 218–220
  *Consecration of Russia to the
    Immaculate Heart of Mary*,
    49, 53
  Christmas Radio Message 1944,
    53
  Divino Afflante Spiritu, 49
  Doctor Melliflus, 51
  *Dogma of the Assumption of
    Our Lady*, 53–54, 57
  Evangelii Praecones, 55
  Le Pelerinage de Lourdes, 51
  Mystici Corporis Christi, 49–50
  *Proclamation of the Queenship
    of Mary*, 53
  Second Coming of Jesus Christ,
    2, 57–59, 64, 219–220
  *Triumph of the Immaculate
    Heart of Mary*, 184–185
  Urbi et Orbi Easter 1957, 2, 64,
    218–220
Puyavnik, Fr. Ivan, 32

Ratzinger, Cardinal Joseph, 10,
    69, 111, 121, 152, 179, 181–183,
    196–197, 200, 204–208, 222
  Chiliasm, 205
  Fatima, 111, 182–184
  On Millennial Theories, 204–
    206, 222
  Stations of the Cross, 181
Rencurel, Benoite, 21
Robin, Marthe, 216
Roman Empire, 27, 180, 213–214
Rookey, Fr. Peter, 161
Rue de bac, Apparitions of Our
    Lady, 24, 30

Satan, 2, 10, 14, 22, 34, 74, 80–84,
    119, 161, 166, 174, 181, 189, 205
Scivias, 187, 209–217 passim
Second Special Assembly for
    Africa: Instrumentum
    Laboris, 9
Second Vatican Council, 1, 3, 33,
    35, 41, 58, 60, 66–68, 70–75, 79,
    97, 100, 105, 127, 149, 153, 157,
    182, 204
  Gaudium et Spes, 71–72, 157
  *In the thought of Fr. Marie
    Dominique Philippe*, 79
  Lumen Gentium, 1, 72–73, 121,
    164, 203–204
  *Preparation for the Lord's
    Return*, 63–79 passim, 105
Servites, 212
Siri, Cardinal Giuseppe, 95
Society of Mary [Marists], 19, 23
Soloviev, Vladimir, 167–168,
    221
Soubirous, Saint Bernadette, 25

Theresa of Avila, Saint, 17
Tisserant, Cardinal Eugene, 56
Tornielli, Andrea, 90

Vincent de Paul, Saint, 17

Winning, Cardinal Thomas, 10
Wojtyla, Cardinal Karol, 95–97,
    101, 122, 126, 166, 182, 222
  Antichrist, 166
  Co-redemptrix, 101
  Novissimis, 182
Wyszynski, Cardinal Stefan, 57,
    100

Printed by BoD™in Norderstedt, Germany